D0722000

Turn of the Tortoise

Turn of the Tortoise

The Challenge and Promise of India's Future

T N NINAN

OXFORD
UNIVERSITY PRESS

OXFORD
UNIVERSITY PRESS

Oxford University Press is a department of the University of Oxford. It furthers the University's objective of excellence in research, scholarship, and education by publishing worldwide. Oxford is a registered trade mark of Oxford University Press in the UK and certain other countries.

Published in the United States of America by Oxford University Press
198 Madison Avenue, New York, NY 10016, United States of America.

Published in India in 2015 by Penguin Books India.

Library of Congress Cataloging-in-Publication Data
Names: Ninan, T N, author.
Title: Turn of the tortoise : the challenge and promise of India's future /
T N Ninan.
Description: New York, NY : Oxford University Press, [2017] |
Originally published by Allen Lane, New Delhi, in 2015. | Includes index.
Identifiers: LCCN 2016017261 | ISBN 9780190603014 (hardcover) |
ISBN 9780190603038 (epub)
Subjects: LCSH: India—Economic conditions—21st century. |
India—Economic policy—21st century. | India—Foreign relations—21st century. |
India—Forecasting.
Classification: LCC HC435.3 N56 2017 | DDC 330.954—dc23
LC record available at https://lccn.loc.gov/2016017261

1 3 5 7 9 8 6 4 2

Printed by Edwards Brothers Malloy, United States of America

For Sevanti

Contents

Emerging Realities

India and the World

Looking Ahead

Acknowledgments

THIS BOOK BEGAN as a joint exercise with Vijay Joshi, the well-known economist, author, and emeritus fellow at Merton College in Oxford, who proposed the idea over a lunch, in January 2012. Eventually, it became clear that our two writing styles would not fit well, and we decided, amicably, to do separate books. Vijay was a reassuring sounding board for testing ideas and a valuable source for suggestions on readings and new lines of thought. Were it not for him, this book would not have been written.

Thanks are due also to the Jawaharlal Nehru Memorial Fund, which helped with the generous Nehru Fellowship for 2013 and 2014. Mahesh Rangarajan, director of the Nehru Memorial Museum and Library, kindly extended the hospitality of a room for quiet work.

Over the years of my work as a journalist, I have benefited from conversations with a range of Indian economists spanning two generations: Vijay Kelkar and Surjit Bhalla, Montek and Isher Ahluwalia, Shankar Acharya and Rakesh Mohan, plus Bimal Jalan, Nitin Desai, Kirit Parikh, Suman Bery, Deepak Nayyar, Subir Gokarn, Urjit Patel, Arvind Subramanian, Devesh Kapur, and many others. Editorial meetings at *Business Standard* provided a stimulating forum for freewheeling discussion, enriched by the presence at different times of Ashok Desai, the late Sudhir Mulji, Deepak Lal, Ajay Shah, Shubhashis Gangopadhyay, Shyam Saran, Sanjaya Baru, T. C. A. Srinivasa-Raghavan, and others. Track II dialogues that Tarun Das organized provided opportunities for interaction with decision makers in half a dozen countries and provided new perspectives.

To Uday Kotak I owe much, personally and professionally. For the purpose of this book, I must thank him in particular for the clarity of his analysis and insights with regard to banking and related areas. Thanks are due to Bharat Sheth and Naresh Kotak for generous hospitality in Mumbai and Kodaikanal. Colleagues at *Business Standard* helped in different ways; my thanks to my long-term compatriot A. K. Bhattacharya, who was always ready to help when asked, and also to Sanjay Sharma, Surinder Sud, C. E. Narasimhan, Dillip Satapathy, and Raghuvir Badrinath. Others who helped include Ajit Balakrishnan, Pradipta Bagchi, Arun Bharat Ram, Steve Biegun, Naresh Chandra, Raj Chengappa, Tony Jesudasan, Ranjan Mathai, Prasad Pradhan, Atul Punj, Jayadeva Ranade, and Ajai Shukla.

Specifically for this book, I have met James Abraham, Arjun Asrani, Venkatesh Babu, Abhijit Banerjee, Chandrajit Banerjee, Nancy Birdsall, Robert Blackwill, R. C. Bhargava, Tejpreet Singh Chopra, Venugopal Dhoot, Arunabha Ghosh, Jamshyd Godrej, Ashok Gulati, Gajendra Haldea, S. Jaishankar, Amitabh Kant, the late Surinder Kapur, Satish Kaura, Lars-Olof Lindgren, Sunil Mehta, Rinku Murgai, Nandan Nilekani, Baijayant "Jay" Panda, G. Parthasarathy, P. S. Raghavan, Raghuram Rajan, S. Ramadorai, Jairam Ramesh, Kishan Rana, G. M. Rao, M. Govinda Rao, Shashi Ruia, Manish Sabharwal, Shyam Saran, Nik Senapati, Ajai Shukla, and Gautam Thapar. The defense officials, diplomats of various countries, company executives, and government officials who met on condition of anonymity have my thanks too, as do those too numerous to name whom I met on visits to factories, shipyards, laboratories, educational establishments, and elsewhere. If I have forgotten to mention anyone who deserves notice, I offer my apologies.

For critical comments and feedback on the manuscript, I am grateful to Shankar Acharya, Surjit Bhalla, Ramachandra Guha, Bimal Jalan, Pratap Bhanu Mehta, Leela Ponappa, Shyam Saran, Chiki Sarkar, and of course Vijay Joshi. The responsibility for mistakes and shortcomings remains mine, of course. The folks at Penguin Random House in India and Oxford University Press in New York have held my hands through the publishing process. To them, to Catherine Clarke and her colleagues at Felicity Bryan, and my assistant, Mahinder Singh, enormous thanks.

Finally my wife, Sevanti, bore the brunt by living with someone who was even less helpful around the house than usual, and who spread out books, reports, and papers all over the study that she vacated, then a second room, and a third, before it was all done and mailed to the publisher. For that and everything else, this book is dedicated to her.

Turn of the Tortoise

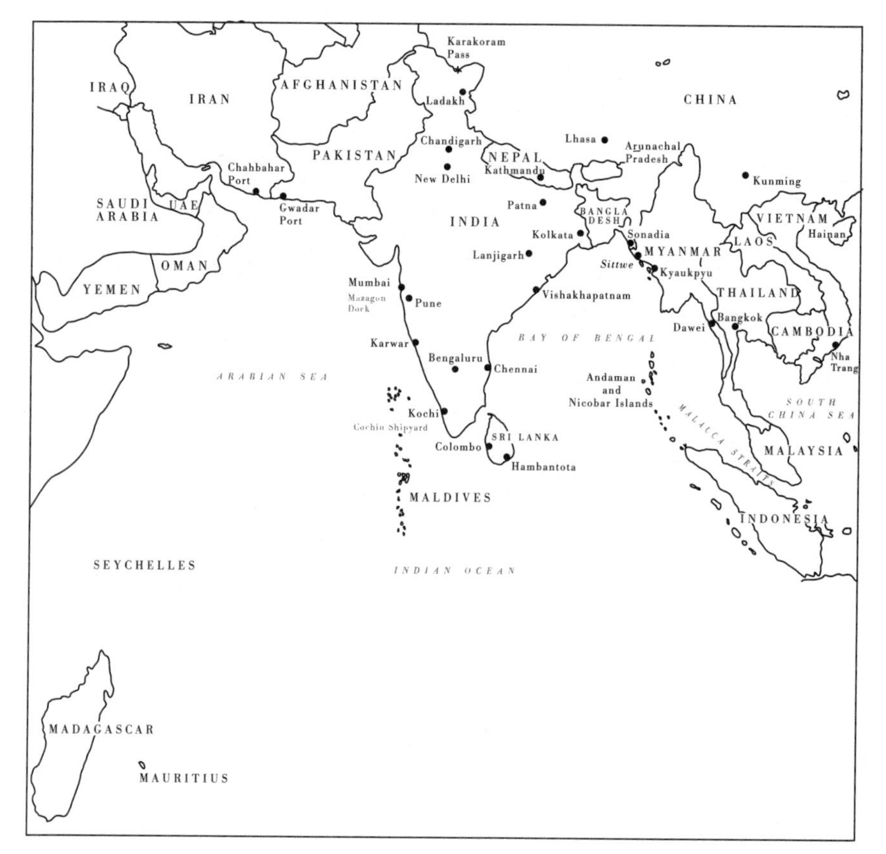

Map of South Asia

Source: Courtesy of Penguin India

We're (Not) Like That Only

1

A Question of Size

COMMENTARIES ON INDIA sometimes mention that in the first half of the eighteenth century, the country accounted for a fourth of the world's total income (gross world product, or GWP). That compares with about one-fortieth today. The old glory did not mean much; it was mostly a matter of the size of the population. In the pre-industrial age, incomes did not vary hugely across countries; if a country had a larger share of the population, it accounted for a greater share of world GDP. Such income variations as did exist left the average Indian poorer than the average European of the time.

Economic size therefore tells us only a part of the story. Even in the 1870s, a frequently famine-ravaged India could claim to be the world's second-largest economy, next only to China. It was bigger than its imperial ruler, Britain, and accounted for an eighth of GWP at the time. But the lack of development and capabilities (human, industrial, technological, institutional) told a more material story. India's per capita income at the time, according to the economic historian Angus Maddison,[1] was three-fifths of the world average and only a sixth of prosperous Britain's.

Today, as a free country, India seeks its place under the global sun even as it strives at home to abolish large-scale poverty and achieve broad developmental goals. Its international heft has increased as its economic size and domestic market have grown. From being the twelfth-largest economy at the time of the Western financial crisis in 2008, India was in seventh place in 2015,[2] overtaking three developed economies (Spain, Canada, and Italy) as well as Russia and Brazil. Over a quarter century, the country has more than trebled its share of world trade and multiplied manifold its foreign investment inflows—and outflows too, for that matter. The growth of its middle class has meant that some of its markets have grown to world scale—the second-largest market for mobile phones and for powered two-wheelers (motorcycles, scooters, and mopeds), for instance. Martin Wolf of the *Financial Times* called it a "premature superpower"[3]—a country that has gained in economic size while still being low income, and struggling to deal with the most basic issues of poverty and the debilities that are mass poverty's side effects.

India's poverty has reduced in scope and scale but remains widespread, blighting the lives of at least a fourth of its people, probably more. Still, there has been progress: India has moved from the World Bank's list of low-income countries to the lower–middle income category,[4] where it will remain for the foreseeable future. If it doubled its per capita income over the next decade, it would be a star performer on the world stage and become the world's fourth- or fifth-largest economy, in nominal dollars (it is already the third largest, when counting in dollars adjusted for purchasing power parity). But even then, its per capita income would be only what neighboring Sri Lanka already enjoys, and a third of today's global average of a little over $10,000. It is more than likely that India would continue to account for the largest share of the world's poor.

If India counts regardless, the explanation for India's importance is its size: the scale and potential of its domestic market, of its population (the second largest in the world), and its landmass (the seventh largest), located such that it dominates South Asia and is the largest country abutting the Indian Ocean—through which passes half of the world's trade and 70 percent of its petroleum shipments. Size therefore is crucial to India's perception of itself, past and present, and to the world's perception of India. Even when the country accounted for only half of 1 percent of world trade, it was a negotiator to contend with in world trade talks—for reasons that went beyond the fact that its diplomats were fluent in English.

Size helps preserve India as a democracy; it is too big and too complex for any one person to so dominate the whole land as to render the law and institutions ineffective, or at least to do so for any length of time. But some of India's states are as big and populous as countries, and many politicians and their progeny do dominate state politics for long periods. On occasion, they have acquired such local power that it appears they are, de facto, beyond the reach of the law. If these states did not belong to the larger India, dictatorships could well have flourished—as they did for differing periods in the smaller countries that broke away (Pakistan and Bangladesh). The dynamic of a large political union that is actually a federation of states with different and criss-crossing identity markers has helped preserve Indian democracy.

The awareness of its size has made India commit policy errors. Successful small countries find it easy, indeed necessary, to focus on export markets because their internal markets are too small to support scale production. Both South Korea and Taiwan tried industrial development through import substitution before deciding to focus on export markets. But India is big enough to offer the potential of a large domestic market; inevitably, that became the focus of policy. The difference between exporting units and those with a domestic market orientation is that the former have to be competitive, the latter not necessarily so. In India's case, the inward focus became so pronounced that the country became an economic prison, functioning behind high protective walls. It therefore evolved into a market for mostly shoddy, usually overpriced goods that would not sell anywhere except in other countries that were similarly starved of quality goods, such as the Soviet Union, which at one stage was India's largest trade partner. Size therefore has led India into various policy cul-de-sacs from which it has been trying to extricate itself.

One could argue that the complications wrought by size have prevented India from becoming like the rapid-growth economies of Southeast Asia, such as Thailand. Tamil Nadu and Gujarat (states of India; Gujarat has a similar population to Thailand) may have grown as rapidly as some countries of rapid-growth Asia (RGA) did, but Bihar and Odisha would bring down the national growth rate. The RGA countries grew by more than 7.5 percent annually in the decade leading up to the 1997 Asian financial crisis, while Gujarat in 1991–2001 also grew at 7.5 percent. In the following decade, when the RGA countries were not rapid-growth anymore, Gujarat accelerated to 10.2 percent annual growth, matching two of the original Tiger economies, South Korea and Taiwan, in their best years.

Size is the main reason that India is portrayed as the third-highest emitter of greenhouse gases (GHG), though at 1.7 tons of CO_2 it has one of the lowest emission rates per head among the large economies.[5] Further, it ranks lower than the global average on emissions per unit of gross domestic product (GDP), calculated using purchasing power parity (PPP) dollars.[6] In a country ranking by the International Energy Agency using the latter measure, India was among the twenty smallest emitters out of 140 countries, and below the world average. If India were twenty-nine different countries, in the way that the European Union has twenty-eight member countries, the charge of "third-largest emitter" would simply not exist because each "country's" emissions would be tiny.

Confusion about Objectives

Size is what has led India into confusion about objectives. A poor country has no limit on the number of things it wants to get done; and if you are a large country, you naturally think you can or need to do it all. Smaller countries try to keep things simple and focus on a few objectives: do what it takes to succeed, like becoming a regional financial center (Singapore even changed its time zone to make itself attractive to currency traders), or focus on dominating the world in silicon chip fabrication units, like Taiwan.

In India, however, it was not enough to set up, for example, a massive solar-power-generating capacity because there were other objectives to be served. The solar cells and panels would have to be made in India, even if that meant higher costs. Textile units were fine, but small-scale weavers had to be protected, so they paid a lower electricity tariff or no tariff at all. Entrepreneurship was to be broad-based, so small-scale units paid a fraction of the excise duty that large units did, so India became one of the few countries (if not the only one) where television set assembly and the manufacture of air conditioners were predominantly in the small-scale sector, till the government offered a level playing field for all units. Preexisting employment in activities like making shoes and matches had to be protected, so mass manufacture was banned in these and more than 800 other industrial sectors while China established volume production and took over the world market in shoes, toys, and other items. The same situation existed with the employment-intensive garments trade. Industrial units, the official prescription said, should preferably use domestic technology; if not, technology transfer should be provided. Factories must be set up in backward areas (which, almost by definition, were not the ideal locations from the viewpoint of efficiency). And so on.

If multiple objectives are pursued simultaneously, compromises have to be made on the main objective—mathematically, it is impossible to maximize more than one function. The result has been that none of the objectives was achieved to any degree of satisfaction. Indeed, the end result was the opposite of what was intended, as India failed to industrialize like the countries of rapid-growth Asia, most of which focused on simple policy objectives. Instead, India became heavily import-dependent and ran large trade deficits. There were bizarre contrasts: the country could not make a halfway decent razor blade or fountain pen even as it built atomic power plants and sent rockets into space.

The problem at root was confusion about goals and tools. Was industry meant to produce things or develop backward areas? Was state ownership an objective or a means to an objective? Were subsidies the answer to poverty or one among several ways of achieving income transfer from the rich to the poor? Was the creation of work an end in itself or was employment the by-product of a properly functioning economy?

The confusion and resultant mistakes in policy have meant that India is the last major poor country on earth, the Galápagos-size tortoise that has been left behind by the mostly smaller, speedier countries of RGA and other regions. One hesitates to introduce new animals into a debate that already features tigers, elephants, and dragons, and also the lion that is the mascot of the "Make in India" program, but the well-known fact is that the "hares" of RGA have raced ahead, while India, the "tortoise," has fallen behind. This is not just on the income metric. South Korea moved from a literacy level of 22 percent in 1945 to 87 percent by 1970,[7] while India in 2015 was aiming for 80 percent.[8] And it is not only in the economy where China has outpaced India by a mile; its health and education attainments of two decades ago are what India is struggling to achieve today. If that isn't tortoise speed, what is?

Different League Tables

Even so, size will shape India's destiny. If only 30 percent of its people enjoy discretionary spending power, its middle class would be larger than the population of all countries other than China. Many product markets therefore would reach world scale quite quickly. India's market for automobiles is already the world's sixth largest,[9] though less than 5 percent of households owned cars in 2011.[10] The country became the largest exporter of rice in 2012 and 2013,[11] accounting for between a quarter and a third of world rice exports, and it could become an agricultural power in world markets if policy supported that goal.

Because of India's size and potential, the tendency is to compare it with other large countries—like Brazil, though that country has seven times India's per capita income. A cottage industry has come into existence, comparing India with China (whose economy is now five times as large as India's); it is not compared with Iran (India is five times its size). There is good reason for this tendency to push India into a higher league than it has attained, but the exercise can result in misleading comparisons. Discussions of how India missed the bus include facile comparisons with countries like Japan. For instance, it is often said that India and Japan began making cars at about the same time, in the 1950s (car production in Japan was banned by the Allied Occupation until 1950), but only Japan built a world-leading car industry by the 1970s.

This ignores the two countries' very different capabilities and histories. Japan defeated the imperial power that was Russia in a war in 1905 and began making trucks in the inter-war period; by the 1930s it was an expansionist colonial power that was building aircraft carriers to do battle simultaneously on two fronts, with the United States and Britain. India at the time had two small steel mills and is only now building its first aircraft carrier.

It is easier to understand comparisons with South Korea, whose per capita income in 1950 was not much more than India's but today is fifteen times larger. It is, of course, true that Korea's population had better health and education levels than India's at the starting point in 1950. But if life expectancy in India reached Korea's 1950 level of fifty-four years only in 1978, surely that had to do with India's failures. By Maddison's calculation, Korea in 1950 had per capita income that was 24 percent higher than India's—a quite small early-bird advantage that does not explain how South Korea took off on the trajectory that it did, while India did not.

There are complex reasons why countries follow different tracks, but little doubt that India has not performed to its potential, even as other countries have. Much of the commentary on the subject looks at industrial, trade, and currency policies—all of which are important. But few take note of the vital ingredient that was equality, introduced in these countries through sweeping changes in land ownership and agrarian relations—in Communist China, US-administered Japan, South Korea, Taiwan, and elsewhere. These changes were accompanied crucially by quick successes in creating an educated workforce, which helped to equalize opportunity in rapidly growing economies. As for health, while all low-income countries saw life expectancy improve from thirty-six to sixty-two years in the three decades to 1990, India's number moved reluctantly from forty-one to just fifty-eight.[12] The leader had managed to become the laggard.

This is not the place to explore the reasons for other countries' successes. Our immediate purpose is served by noting that Japan and South Korea were the early "hares" that set the pace, along with Taiwan. Soon they were to be followed by a fourth speedster, China. Each of these four achieved two to three decades of scorching growth, averaging 8 percent and more. In Japan's case, the growth rate was fractionally under 9 percent for the three decades after the Second World War, while Taiwan averaged 8.7 percent for three decades after 1952. South Korea managed 8 percent from 1962 to 1989, and China had 9.9 percent annual growth for three decades up to 2010. During much of this period, India averaged a tortoise-like speed of 3.5 percent, accelerating to no more than 5.5 percent after 1980 and then maintaining that new speed for close to a quarter century before accelerating further in the 2003–13 decade to 8 percent.[13]

While India continued to hurry slowly, the smaller countries of rapid-growth Asia had their shining moment in the decade that led up to the 1997 Asian crisis. Countries like Malaysia, Thailand, and Indonesia averaged annual growth of more than 7.5 percent. After 1997, though, all these economies lost steam. In contrast, India picked up momentum after 2003 and went on to clock its best decade—though remaining noticeably slower than China.

Starting Handicaps

So why is the country still a global laggard when it comes to income and poverty? The answer is now a forgotten fact: most of the countries of RGA took off from starting blocks much farther down the track than India did. It is not without reason that the global byword for poverty and hunger midway through the twentieth century was India, not Malaysia or the Philippines. It is instructive, therefore, to look at the picture that emerges if one compares India not with the successful countries of Asia, which mostly had a better starting position, but with the ones that were at India's level of poverty and human development indicators in 1950.

Maddison has done just such a comparison, studying sixteen South Asian and East Asian economies starting from 1950. India had per capita income that put it in the bottom third of even this list, along with Nepal and, yes, China. The countries of the original six-nation grouping that is the Association of Southeast Asian Nations (ASEAN), that went on to become part of rapid-growth Asia, enjoyed income levels in 1950 that India would not reach for nearly two decades and more. None of these more prosperous countries had to battle the disabilities of widespread grinding poverty, disease, hunger, and other abysmal indicators of human development to the extreme extent that India did. Taiwan had a higher per capita income in 1965 than India does half a century later. When economists talk of Sri Lanka's (and neighboring Kerala's) model of development, it is worth remembering that India reached Sri Lanka's 1950 level of per capita income only in 1989.

As it happens, India has outpaced the poorer countries of Indo-China listed separately by Maddison. And out of the fifty-seven African countries reviewed by him, only diamond-rich Botswana started with an income level lower than India's and ended with higher per capita income in 2001.[14] Indeed, once India had reached the 1950 starting point of the more prosperous Asian countries, it began to do better than the rest of the world taken together. It may not be flattering to the Indian ego—puffed up easily, and yet vulnerable—to be told that the country did better than the most poorly placed countries, but that is what India too was at the time. Indeed, it would have been considered on a similar footing if not for its size. In the World Development Reports of the time, India in 1979 was ranked the fifteenth-poorest country on per capita income, in a list of 124, poorer even than Malawi and Rwanda. In the International Monetary Fund's World Economic Outlook database of countries ranked according to per capita income for 2014, India still features in the bottom quartile (142nd out of 185).[15] To move up from there to the median position (the 93rd rank), would mean more than trebling its 2014 per capita income of $1,626 to Thailand's level of $5,445, and would be the work of one generation.

Still, the country's poor position at the outset did not automatically mean that policymakers had to make wrong choices, and be slow or reluctant to learn from either their own mistakes or from success stories elsewhere. Perhaps a combination of interest groups (upper castes, business, big farmers, and bureaucrats),[16] intent more on preserving the status quo than on bringing radical change, made it impossible within a democratic framework of populist politics to do anything other than muddle along with suboptimal compromises. Whatever the reasons, India trailed the rest of the world in the speed with which it improved its human development indicators and economic performance, all the way to 1980 and right up to very recently.

India therefore has never been one of the "miracle" economies. It never met the "rapid-growth" criterion set by the World Bank's Commission on Growth and Development: GDP growth at an annual rate of 7 percent or more for more than twenty-five years.[17] In India's best twenty-five years, from 1988 to 2013, it managed average annual growth of 6.4 percent (calculated in constant 2005 dollars). Importantly, though, the balance had begun to shift, for if you thought that rapid-growth Asia did better than India in this quarter century, you would be only partially right. Remember that more than half this period falls into the post–Asian crisis phase, when many East Asian countries slowed down. And so, according to World Bank data, India's GDP multiplied 4.76 times over this period.[18] China (whose economy multiplied tenfold) and Vietnam (5.24 times) did better, while Malaysia was close to the Indian performance (growing its economy 4.31 times). As for South Korea, Thailand, Indonesia, and Taiwan—they all grew slower than India over the latest quarter century.

This is very much the tortoise story in the fable—the slow starter gaining steadily over time. And there is good reason that the "hares" have slowed down—economies tend to ease up once they reach a certain level of productivity and prosperity. India, being a perennial laggard, has plenty of room to make up before it gets to the point the others have reached. Most significantly, it has barely begun to shift the bulk of its workforce from low-productivity agriculture to higher-productivity activities in manufacturing and services. So the tortoise must keep going.

Momentum, More Than Speed

The defining change, though, is the shift in relative momentum—which is a combination of speed and weight, or mass. Even if growing at less than "miracle" speed, India's large economic weight (as the seventh-largest economy) means that it has gained greater momentum than most of the other countries. This is reflected in the figures on how much a country contributes to world economic growth. In the 1980s, India was the thirteenth-largest contributor to world growth, improving to ninth in the decade of the 1990s. Then, in successive five-year periods from 2000, India's rank on the metric of incremental GDP went from tenth to fifth and then sixth. For the coming five years, it is projected to be the third-largest contributor to world growth, after China and the United States, which have occupied the top slots in the last three quinquenniums. The tortoise is closing the gap.

India's game, therefore, is greatly influenced by its size. Greater speed of growth is desirable, but what defines its place in the world is its momentum—a $2.2 trillion market growing at perhaps 7 percent annually. As it happens, the difference between the desirable 7 percent "miracle" growth and the 6.4 percent growth that India has shown it can deliver over a quarter century is not hugely significant. The higher growth rate, if sustained over a decade, would make the economy only 6 percent larger by 2025. Over a longer period, up to 2040, 6.4 percent annual growth would take India's GDP to about $9 trillion; at 7 percent growth, it would be $11 trillion. Either way, India would have become the world's third-largest economy, in nominal dollars, some years before 2040.

However, India may—or may never—be the fastest-growing economy for a sustained length of time, as Japan, South Korea, and China have been at various stages over the past seven decades. The pessimist would say it is a society whose different strands work at cross purposes and which is therefore unable to muster the single-minded determination required to emulate these other countries. And yet, India has shown the ability to keep going, indeed to accelerate. Even now, there is much that India can do with little trouble to improve productivity, and much ground that it can cover before it hits any productivity barriers. Maintaining and even improving on its past record of growth should not be intrinsically difficult—though of course there can be no guarantees about the future.

Since Indians swing between pessimism about their country "getting its act together" and premature triumphalism about what has been achieved, the sober truth is that the past record is one of successes existing alongside disappointments. The country may not have attained all the Millennium Development Goals set for 2015 by the United Nations (UN) General Assembly, but it has met a few (including important ones like reducing poverty by half), and missed some others by only narrow margins. While maternal mortality has been reduced by 60 percent, infant mortality has been more than halved—both with 1990 as base year—and literacy has been raised from 52 percent in 1991 to 74 percent in 2011. The country has changed in ways that most people are not conscious of as they go about their daily lives, especially the detractors who complain about the government and its many shortcomings. It is by no means the best country record to boast of, but momentum is being built in different ways. Size helps.

External Impact

That brings up the external impact of India's size, present and future. Power is always relative, and India's economic ascendancy will help it break free from South Asian constraints, even if a nuclear-armed Pakistan with some characteristics of a rogue state continues to present both irritants and substantive challenges. The real constraint for India is the growing presence in the larger Asian region of a much greater power in the form of China, keen as it is to undermine India's dominance in South Asia and the Indian Ocean by arming and backing satellite powers in the region, including Pakistan, and by making a determined push elsewhere into India's immediate neighborhood. The hard fact is that India's rising international profile will not match China's ascendancy, so it will have to play a complex strategic game or fall under China's shadow. China therefore features at different points in this book—first, to show how futile it is to bracket the two countries together.

Beijing set the stage for a new phase in its strategic outreach when, in or around 2013, it gave up its earlier pretense to "the peaceful rise of China." But that move also showed the limits of its power as the rest of Asia pushed back against Beijing's revanchism. Recognizing this, China made a tactical withdrawal from some of its more aggressive postures in the South China Sea and its island disputes with Japan, only to reach out more expansively and also more assertively in 2014 and 2015. Other powers are wary; Japan and India have been drawn closer together, and the United States has warmed to India. By virtue of its size, India should be the default choice as China's counterweight in Asia; the smaller countries of Southeast Asia (some of them locked in territorial conflict with Beijing) and larger ones like Australia would especially wish India to play such a role. This puts India in a sweet spot, as the acceptable rising power of Asia. India is non-threatening to most countries in East Asia because, while it seeks a larger role, it is not displacing any other power. Nor does it seek to overturn the established order. It wishes to maintain the status quo in power relations, unlike irredentist China, which would like to rewrite the rules. The problem will arise if India does not deliver to potential. The default choice could then become the defaulting power.

Anything resembling a gang-up against China, even if it may have been contemplated, is already impossible because China is changing the game. By getting all the major economic powers of Europe to become part of its proposed infrastructure bank, it has stuck a finger in America's eye. It has demonstrated that it will not be held hostage by the West in existing bodies like the World Bank and IMF (the US Congress had blocked for years a modestly higher vote share for China as well as for India). By reaching out to countries in the broader region with its revivalist "Belt and Road" initiative over land and sea, China has also demonstrated for the first time that it can and will act in the interest of developing wider regional commons—but with itself at the center of new networks and institutions—all this at a time when America's treaty allies in the region are no longer sure of effective US support.

India is always conscious that it is the weaker power in relation to China, and therefore vulnerable—or at least defensive in its stance. Understandably, the country's diplomats do not see any advantage in conflict with Beijing; they know that (as in the past) India will be alone if hostilities break out. Some of the pages that follow look at the unequal competition between the two countries for natural resources and markets in Africa and Central Asia; the option of cooperating rather than competing; India's troubled armaments program that undermines its strategic goals; and how China might decide before long to challenge India's naturally preeminent position in the Indian Ocean.

The Scope of Inquiry

This book is an attempt to understand where India is, midway through the second decade of the twenty-first century, why it has emerged as it has, and what the coming decade might bring. It is not all economics and there is no prediction of future growth rates. Hardly anyone had forecast either the rapid economic acceleration from 2004 or the sharp slowdown of 2012, or for that matter the oil price collapse of 2014. Especially after the official statistics were revised to transform the expected 5.5 percent growth in 2014–15 to an estimate of 7.3 percent, forecasting has to be discarded as a fool's game. The attempt, instead, should be to understand why things went wrong for India recently, including the reasons the shine has come off the country's vaunted private sector.

Looking ahead, the chapters that follow explore some important economic and social themes. By what alchemy does growing inequality coexist successfully with surging aspiration? What is the actual size of the emerging neo-middle class (indeed, how do you define it?) and what are its implications for the economy and for politics? What are the many ways in which the government is trying to improve itself, even as it continues to flounder in all the old ways? A chapter examines whether India is finally in a position to put an end to absolute poverty, and how such a task might be addressed. There is also an attempt to understand how an India with real weight might deal with the rest of the world. More important, how will the rest of the world deal with India—other countries will of course be much more demanding of India in every global forum. Is India ready?

Some fundamental questions are raised, such as how to correctly assess the cost to the environment of a growing economy, and the merits of focusing not on income growth (that is, GDP) but on what is happening to the country's balance sheet, which would include its natural assets. Viewed this way, much of what is conventionally recorded as growth is seen to disappear. So what should the country be doing differently? And is there something that should keep Indians awake at night? Perhaps. A good candidate would be the steady descent from a country with abundant water to one that is water-stressed, and in the future water-scarce.

Indian politics is full of surprises. Narendra Modi might have sought to break free from Congress-style welfarist politics, yet he may get pulled back into it. There has been much talk of India's billionaires, but do you know that a member of Parliament (MP) you might not even have heard of is worth more than the entire British cabinet? More surprises come when you try to assess India's corruption—how big or small is it? A greater number of important politicians are in jail or out on bail than you would have imagined possible, but does that mean the situation is getting worse or that more people are getting caught?

As you may have divined, this is not an "India superpower" book, waving the national flag for an emerging middle class whose soul has apparently been long suppressed and now finds utterance in nationalist jingoism. Nor is it an unalloyed "private sector good, public sector bad" kind of book. It is not shy of accepting India's many failures; instead, it argues that despite the failures, and the many frustrations of living with their consequences, India has held together quite well and its record has been rather good. It could have been much worse, and of course, it could have been better. In exploring the themes that it does, the book does not merely restate known positions in familiar debates, though you may find some viewpoints predictable. What it tries to do is say some things that are new.

This is not an ivory-tower exercise, because real-life stories are there, leavening the arguments. It is broad spectrum because India is broad spectrum. And it does not give you a cleanly drawn picture, because India is messy and complicated. At the end, if the book has helped you understand India a little better, put before you some plausible narratives, and offered enjoyable and occasionally illuminating reading, it would have served its purpose.

WHAT HAS OFTEN been said about India has also been said about Brazil: that it is the country of the future and will remain so. But then, many forecasts have also been made about how India's time has come, only for the tide to ebb again. Recall the famous signs all over Davos put up by the Confederation of Indian Industry (CII), announcing "the world's fastest-growing, free-market democracy," shortly before the India story imploded. At some point, though, the optimistic chaps who have kept shouting about India's time having come will be proved right, though perhaps not for the reasons they had thought.

This book comes at a time when China is slowing down, its workforce shrinking, and its economic model going through wringing change—but also at a time when China is asserting itself abroad. How India performs at this juncture will determine many outcomes. I would not bet that India will be "shining," as a government hoping in vain for re-election declared once, for there will almost always be clouds in our imperfect sky. What is true is that the country is well positioned to reach for some of its long-sought-after goals, like the slow-moving tortoise that at long last sees some end points in sight. It would of course be ideal if India could hasten its progress. But the important point is that India does not have to do anything out of the ordinary or seek to become what it is not. It just has to keep making steady progress over the ground to be covered. This is not too much to ask, which is why it may happen.

2

The Last Great Frontier

INDIA IN 2014 had less than a sixth of the global average per capita income, a level lower than that of Laos, Zambia, and Sudan.[1] It is the poorest large national economy in the world, with the lowest per capita income among the forty economies that account for 90 percent of world GDP. This will change only slowly. Even a decade of 7 percent annual economic growth (translating into 5.7 percent annual growth in per capita income) will only help India to reach today's per capita income of the next-poorest economy in the list of forty, which is the Philippines (2014 per capita income of $2,865, against India's $1,626). In 2025, India will almost certainly still be the poorest large economy in the world.[2]

That is why the country is full of potential. The theory of backwardness,[3] multi-country experience, and common sense all tell us that the room for economic growth is greater from a relatively low-income starting point, though all countries may not make use of that room. A late starter can learn from other countries, use technologies that already exist, and "catch up."[4] Thorstein Veblen called this the "advantage of relative backwardness."[5] Rapid economic growth by a catch-up country means that many product and service markets can grow, in even the short space of a decade, in multiples, not just percentages. But poor countries also function sub-optimally, so opportunity comes in a package deal that includes many challenges. Anyone who seeks to glean India's future would need therefore to understand four questions: what works in India, what doesn't, why, and whether it can be fixed.

This chapter addresses in capsule form a broad range of the most important economic issues: what has and has not worked in India; the missing pieces in the reforms program that must be addressed to sustain rapid economic growth; the key question of how to create employment; and how programs and policies should be directed at the base of the pyramid. These and other issues are explored in greater depth in subsequent chapters.

People, Markets, Policy

A useful way to understand what works, and what does not work so well, came from the chief executive of one of the largest, most diversified engineering companies in the United States (and the world). He observed during a visit to India that his company had succeeded every time it bet on the Indian people, less so but with good success when it bet on the Indian market, and least of all when it bet on Indian policymaking and policymakers. Go through the experience of the leading companies and sectors in India and the broader relevance of that three-set analysis becomes evident.

Business success has come most of all from employing India's educated manpower. Software services, the big story of the past couple of decades, and pharmaceuticals are the obvious examples. There are also less-talked-about cases, like the country's record in building and launching rockets and satellites, notable because these have been done on surprisingly small budgets. Satellites need thousands of engineering man-hours of testing before launch, and (as the software service companies recognized) engineering man-hours come relatively cheap in India. For that reason, but also because of the quality of engineers, leading international firms like Intel and Shell, General Electric, and SAP have housed research centers in India. Some of them do frontier research in places like Bengaluru. Meanwhile, IBM has three-quarters of its global employee strength of 400,000 in India; Accenture employs more than a quarter of a million people in the country.

It is not just engineers and the people who do back-office work—whose ranks include lawyers and accountants, not just call-center staff. Indian managers have also proved their mettle. International companies in fields as diverse as financial services and consumer-goods marketing have Indian managers working for them in countries around the globe, and have benefited from doing so.[6] Some of the managers have gone on to become global corporate chieftains—in companies such as Microsoft, Pepsico, and Google.

If its educated middle class is India's biggest business asset, the Indian market is not a distant second—and not unrelated to the first. The many companies selling consumable and durable consumer goods have notched up average annual sales growth of 15 percent and more over the decade to 2015. That means they quadrupled their business over ten years—creating such phenomena as a billion-strong market for mobile phones. India's car market is the world's sixth largest, and its domestic aviation market the fourth largest.[7] Regional aviation hubs to the west and east of the country are being built or expanded partly on the strength of growing Indian traffic. Already you can sit in Doha's spanking new airport and watch nine different flights leave for various Indian cities within the space of an hour. With the International Monetary Fund (IMF) forecast about the country continuing its run as the world's fastest-growing large economy, the importance of specific markets can only grow—even in unlikely product categories such as diamonds, for India is now the world's third-largest domestic market for diamond jewelry. Alexandre Ricard, head of Pernod Ricard, the French liquor giant, sees India as the company's fastest-growing market, and about to replace France as the third largest.[8]

As the domestic market has grown, companies and their shareholders have prospered. The combined market value of companies listed on India's stock market has gone from $125 billion in 2002 to $1.58 trillion in 2015.[9] Global companies that came to nibble have ended up taking big bites of the market. India has become the fourth-largest market for Sony and the second-largest market for Vodafone's data traffic. It accounts for about 10 percent of Samsung's mobile handsets, while Suzuki in 2013–14 made more money in India than in Japan.[10] So India's people and its markets have delivered. What about the third category, government policy and executive action? It would of course be a serious mistake to assume that the success stories have had nothing to with the government. The dramatic growth of the mobile phone industry is a result of enabling policy. The creation of the educated middle class is a result of the stress on higher (and specifically technical) education. Much of the recent economic growth is because of reform measures announced in 1991. Government policy and action have certainly been factors contributing to the success stories.

Still, if a company's business depends directly on government decisions, the result is often frustration, sometimes setbacks, even outright failure. A torturous and expensive bidding process for 126 fighter planes can wind along for eight years and end up as an order for thirty-six aircraft—and the subject of further negotiations. Whether it is clearances for mining projects or the pricing of natural gas, government purchase contracts or time taken for dispute settlement, the uncertainties involved in operating in India are high. Most companies, when asked, talk of being frustrated by policies and procedures, arbitrary decisions like massive retrospective tax demands, sweeping court judgments, the risk of cronyism, and occasionally scandal. Yet the companies stick around; there are few large economies left where you can hope to double your business every five or six years. India is the world's last great business frontier—and, perhaps inevitably, has some of the flavors of a frontier country.

Looking at the three-set perspective of people, markets, and policy lends coherence to the otherwise puzzling story of how India has been among the better-performing economies in the last quarter century, even as it has been among the most difficult places in which to do business—as ranked by the World Bank year after embarrassing year. India has suffered grievously from failures in the policy area, but it has coped regardless because long years of steady growth have combined with the development of educated manpower to create a substantial market as well as a growing middle class and neo-middle class. These have proved to be semi-autonomous drivers of domestic investment and magnets for global firms.

The result, as noted in the previous chapter, is that India is estimated to have become the seventh-largest national economy in 2015. It has the potential to become the fourth largest by 2025—overtaking Germany, Britain, and France. With the new basis for calculating GDP showing higher growth rates than earlier numbers did (an average of 7.1 percent for the three-year period 2013–16,[11] against less than 6 percent postulated earlier), it would be a signal failure if the country did not now sustain 7 percent annual economic growth for the medium-term future. A $2.2 trillion economy growing at 7 percent annually would make the country the third-largest contributor to world economic growth, and it could retain that position for the foreseeable future. The country has barely begun moving up the income ladder, so it is many years away from reaching a stage when it would ordinarily be expected to slow down.

But anyone who makes the facile assumption that India's continued rapid economic growth is assured just because it is feasible or plausible, should think carefully about the slowdown of the recent past. Any number of things can go wrong. Countries that lose momentum, as India did after 2010–11, often find it difficult to regain the old speed. The world economy is not what it used to be, with growth plunging from about 5.5 percent in the fat years to 3.4 percent and less in the lean ones. That would act as a constraint on any country's ambitions. Besides, India has found it difficult to introduce the kinds of reforms it now needs. If the required changes are introduced, there is no reason that annual growth of 8 percent and more should not be achieved—rivaling what rapid-growth Asia managed to do in the 1980s and '90s. If not, the downside risks are not to be dismissed lightly, since the country has already witnessed a plunge from 8.9 percent growth to 5.4 percent in two short years to 2012–13.

Product Markets and Factor Markets

Having looked at what works and what does not, the question to address is *why* some things don't work. The answer comes from looking inside the portmanteau term that pops up over and over again in any conversation about the country: reforms. It is a catch-all word that encompasses more than most such words. So a useful approach is to think in terms of key categories: product markets (for cars, phones, or steel) and factor markets (that is, the four factors of production—land, labor, capital, and entrepreneurship/technology). India has substantially reformed the first group except in agriculture and agri-businesses like sugar and fertilizer, and introduced little real or positive change in the second group.

The reforms that were introduced in 1991 focused primarily on product markets. They opened up the country to international competition by abolishing import controls and lowering tariffs. Capacity restrictions on domestic producers were removed; more players were allowed to enter and compete in product and service markets. Some, like airlines and telephone services, were no longer reserved for government-owned companies. Before the opening up of the economy, India's tariffs used to be among the highest in the world. The peak rate of customs duty was dropped from over 200 percent in 1991 to 65 percent in 1994. Even after the correction in tariffs, customs duty collection in the mid-1990s was as high as 30 percent of imports. That is now less than 10 percent, and even lower on non-agricultural imports. The results of opening up to the world have been greater trade orientation and therefore rapid growth of trade, better products in the market, greater consumer choice, low inflation for manufactured products, more foreign investment, and of course faster economic growth.

What went mostly unreformed in 1991 and later were the four factor markets. This was not for lack of trying, because governments have constantly obsessed about policy issues relating to land and labor. Both are intensely political subjects. The clash of strong interest groups, the failure to apply clear principles, and the role of intermediaries seeking to protect their positions or to cash in on insider advantage—all of these have kept the rules complicated and unsatisfactory.

The rules governing land, in both town and country, are complex, opaque, and prone to misuse, and therefore they create plenty of room for rampant cronyism and corruption. Land title records suffer from poor record-keeping, are mostly not digitized, and therefore are often unclear or contestable, and capable of being manipulated. Rules about who can buy and who can sell, and on what terms; what purposes the land can be used for; how much one can build on a piece of land; what taxes will apply—all these and more are subjects of complex rules that have created a non-transparent market and interfere with proper price discovery. In cities like Mumbai the biggest rackets involve land, creating a politician–builder mafia nexus and artificial scarcities that drive up housing prices to largely unaffordable levels. In the countryside, distrust flows from a long history of unequal contracts in which farmers got a very short end of the stick. Rules and laws have been changed and then changed again in cities, states, and the country as a whole, often creating fresh points of contention. The fiercest legislative and political dispute of 2014 and 2015 involved new rules for the land market that were introduced in 2013.

When it comes to labor, the reformistas have argued for a quarter century that the country's laws are the most restrictive and counterproductive in the world, some of the key provisions dating to Indira Gandhi's leftist days in the 1970s and '80s. Since the more restrictive laws apply only to what is considered the organized sector (units that employ ten workers or more), there is a bias against crossing that threshold—which therefore limits the size of the organized sector and creates an unusually large unorganized employment market. Other laws that prevent downsizing or closure when a business takes a downturn or becomes unviable discourage employers from hiring. Once again, the effect is the opposite of what is intended, because employment in large factories is retarded.

As clear as this logic may be, those already employed in the organized sector view the prospective changes as diluting the protections available to them (against retrenchment, for example, even if it comes with increased financial compensation). That makes the trade unions speak up against change. Politicians hesitate for fear of losing votes. Even the Modi government, armed with a parliamentary majority in the Lower House, has been reluctant to act, leaving state governments to seize the initiative if they wish.

It is not just the tight constraints and lack of flexibility that the laws impose on employers; there is also multiplicity (forty-four separate central laws, plus state laws), with each law having its own compliance requirements and visits by labor inspectors who need to be kept happy. The one change that the Modi government has introduced is for companies to self-certify under many of the laws, thereby reducing the role of inspectors. While this runs the risk of false self-certification, it is easy to see that such procedural change is not enough; the laws themselves need change.

The primary achievement concerning the third factor of production, capital, has been its accumulation through the rapid growth of savings—facilitating investment that has fueled growth. The country doubled its investment-to-GDP ratio from 12.8 percent in 1955–56 to 26.0 percent in 1990–91, and then raised it further to a peak of 38.1 percent of GDP by 2007–08 before it fell back to 34.2 in 2014–15[12] as accumulated problems began to surface. This was in part the result of large investments getting stuck in infrastructure projects that became unviable or subjects of dispute or (in the case of power stations) victims of soaring fuel costs or scarcity. Recovery has been slow because clearing the logjam has not been easy, and the resultant stress on corporate balance sheets and banks' asset quality has restricted fresh investment.

If investment rates can be kept high and lead to increased output, then rapid growth is assured. At a ratio between incremental capital and output of 4:1, 32 percent of GDP invested should deliver growth a quarter of that—that is, 8 percent. If capital is used badly, the capital–output ratio climbs and growth falls. A ratio of 5:1 at the same level of investment delivers growth of only 6.4 percent. The efficiency of capital use and therefore of capital markets is vital.

From the perspective of reform, the market for capital has moved toward greater efficiency. Interest rates are market-determined, no longer controlled by fiat; and there is easier access to international capital. Also, the private sector has been allowed entry into banking, insurance, and asset management. But in a financial system dominated by banking rather than bond and equity markets, it is a constraint that 70 percent of the banking system is still with government-owned banks, whose lending decisions are sometimes influenced by political cronyism, and (more important) whose risk-assessment capabilities are poor. This lethal combination has led to high levels of stressed assets (bad loans or those that might go bad); the ratios are as much as three times as high as for the leading private banks. Not only is this a waste of capital but it also clogs the credit system, hinders further lending, and raises the need for fresh doses of banking capital—and the government does not have funds to provide this.

Privatizing banks, like rationalizing labor laws, is politically taboo—although the private banks with 30 percent of the market now make more profits than the public sector with 70 percent. In this situation, an effective bond market would serve two purposes—improve long-term funding for infrastructure projects and allow corporate borrowers to access debt directly and more cheaply from the money market, bypassing banks. But the bond market is hobbled by many factors. Because fiscal deficits are high, governments borrow a great deal to pay their bills. The money market is therefore dominated by government securities. Restrictions on free trading in these securities mean there has been no hope so far of a true corporate bond market, though the government has recently promised one.

As for entrepreneurship, the fourth factor of production, India has always been rich in its entrepreneurial gene pool, and there has been a widely reported flowering of young entrepreneurs trying their hand at start-up operations—as in contemporary high-tech areas such as chip design. But, according to World Bank findings, getting all twenty-five permissions required to start construction can still take more than five months, and an electricity connection more than two months (both in Mumbai).[13] Threading through all the processes for dealing with an export container costs a third more in Mumbai than in China, and even more in Delhi.[14] Worst of all, enforcing a contract can take four years.[15] Cumbersome and often pointless laws, rules, and procedures are widely recognized as being among the most frustrating in any country.

As should be obvious, reforming complicated factor markets is far more difficult than freeing product markets. The latter can often be done at the stroke of a pen—as with abolishing industrial licensing or lowering tariffs. In contrast, reforming factor markets is more process-driven; involves many more stakeholders at central, state, and local government levels; and is therefore politically demanding as well as time-consuming. If reforms could be accomplished, the result would be substantial productivity growth across the system.

Creating Employment: Looking beyond Labor Laws

A populous, low-income economy grows by exploiting what it has in abundance: labor, which by definition comes at low cost. If you improve the quality of the human resource and apply more capital to production while introducing better technology, you improve output and incomes. Low labor costs have been an essential feature of India's success in diamond cutting and polishing, in the promotion of handicraft exports (even now a large item in the export basket), and in creating a diversified engineering base where labor costs can be massively lower than in wealthier countries with higher wages—car production in India, for instance, has only a 3 percent labor cost, with the hourly wage rate a tenth of the $30 per hour that prevails in the United States.[16]

The big failure has been in education and training—which may be an odd thing to say when the country's biggest asset is supposed to be its educated workforce. The problem is the usual one of dichotomy, and the existence of haves and have-nots: those who receive high-quality school and university education exist side by side with those who are barely taught to read and write, usually (but not only) in underperforming government schools.

Public investment in education has been 3.8 percent of GDP, whereas for Malaysia it is 50 percent higher and for Thailand twice as high.[17] Much of this money goes into teachers' salaries, but teacher absenteeism is high and motivation levels low—and that is the heart of the problem. Although about a fifth of the relevant age cohort now attends post–high school courses that deliver degrees or diplomas, the average Indian in 2015 had barely five years of schooling—a figure that was lower than for Zambia and Ghana, both poorer countries.[18] Not much is learned in those five-plus years. Countrywide surveys[19] have shown repeatedly that about half the students in class five are not able to do class two level reading and arithmetic. After the government allowed two states (Tamil Nadu and Himachal Pradesh) to join the Programme for International Student Assessment (PISA), their performance was shown to be the worst among all participants other than Kyrgyzstan. Indeed, the average class eight student in the two Indian states was no better than a class three student in South Korea. Yet these devastating results of domestic surveys and international tests elicited no answering response from the educational establishment, including ministers. Their priorities seem to lie elsewhere.

Meanwhile, both productivity and incomes will go up substantially if more people can be moved from low-paying agriculture to higher-paying industry and services—a key transition that the country has barely begun. Indeed, skill development is one of the big government programs of recent years. But acquiring job-related skills without the benefit of a basic education is a challenge—it is hard to be a fitter or an electrician at a construction site if you don't know basic arithmetic and can't read simple instructions on a product pack. The intended transition, moving large numbers currently engaged in agriculture and related activities to industrial and service employment, will be impossible if the quality and extent of education do not improve.

There is much room for expanding employment in manufacturing, but the potential is often overestimated and the time frame condensed. Goals such as getting manufacturing to grow from 17 percent of GDP to 25 percent by 2022 are not much more than pipe dreams. Further, contrary to much of the commentary on the subject, manufacturing will not be able to directly absorb the numbers that it once might have done because of increasingly greater factory automation. India has 22.3 percent of its workforce engaged in the secondary sector (manufacturing, mining, construction, electricity, etc.), compared to just 28.7 percent for China, which is the great success story in manufacturing.[20] So, it is quite likely that the bulk of India's workforce will continue to be engaged in agriculture for the foreseeable future—as indeed is the case in China, where 36.7 percent of the workforce was still engaged in the primary sector in 2010. Most of the spillover of the workforce from agriculture will be absorbed by services of different kinds, some of them created as downstream activity by the expansion of manufacturing.

This makes the employment challenge more complicated than simply developing the manufacturing sector—especially since increasing automation and new technologies will make not only manufacturing but also software services and back-office work less manpower-intensive than it has been. There is a reason that China is becoming the principal maker and user of robots, and why India's leading software services companies like Infosys and Tata Consultancy Services are taking a fresh look at market focus and strategy—to move away from what has been termed the linear approach (more software engineers create more revenue) to the platform approach, where revenue generation is not manpower-intensive.

What commentators often ignore while discussing employment is the enormous untapped potential of Indian agriculture, to be realized through crop diversification into more labor-intensive and higher-value products like fruits and vegetables, and the application of better technology and farming practices. Paddy output per hectare, at about 3.7 tons, is 20 percent short of the global average and barely half of China's. One reason is that Indian farmers are not using the latest strains of high-yield varieties (growing them is also more employment-intensive) or adopting new methods of cultivation that require less water. It's the same with maize. Traditionally backward Bihar has made rapid strides in maize output after switching to hybrid varieties. Output has gone up to more than 4 tons per hectare, against the national average of 2.5 tons; the United States manages 7.7 tons per hectare and China 5.9 tons.[21]

Gujarat did with cotton what Bihar has done with maize—productivity quadrupled to 750 kilograms (kg) per hectare in a quarter century to 2007–08; overall, the decade from 2003–04 saw the state's agriculture grow at 7.6 percent,[22] or about twice the national average. Madhya Pradesh did as well as or better, and now follows Punjab and Haryana as the third-largest contributor of grain to the public distribution system.[23] The truth is that India can hugely increase the productivity levels on its farms, continue to comfortably feed itself, become an export powerhouse if it wishes to, and in the process raise both employment and income levels substantially in the rural areas—while also (because of gains in output per hectare) freeing land for non-agricultural use. These issues rarely figure in the ceaseless debate on economic growth and reforms, although changes in agriculture will directly affect half the workforce.

As for manufacturing, there is plenty of scope for developing sectors that are employment-intensive and internationally competitive—especially as China has started moving out of some labor-intensive industries because its wage costs have risen substantially in the wake of its rapid economic growth. Hourly manufacturing sector wages in China went up from $0.22 in the early 1990s to $1.15 in 2006; in roughly the same period, India's went from $0.34 to $0.53.[24] The current monthly wage in Shenzhen is 2030 yuan[25] (about $327), compared to the stipulated minimum wage in Delhi of Rs 10,478 ($166) for a skilled worker. Chinese wages are significantly lower in Fujian and even Beijing, but so are they in India's southern states. As a rough rule of thumb, wages in India would appear to be about half those in China. In industries where labor is an important element of cost, India therefore can conceivably out-compete China—the ready-made garment industry is the most obvious example.

However, there are more than two fish in the sea. There is lower-income Bangladesh and also similar-income Vietnam and higher-income Philippines, all of them making better use of the opportunity provided by China's rising wages. This, combined with the fact that Chinese garment exports continue to be seven or eight times India's, should tell the country that labor cost and policies are by no means the only issues to be addressed.

India has a rich tradition in textiles, plenty of cotton, and low wages, so it has no reason to be satisfied with a 4 percent share of the $350 billion global garment export business. But while the country should seek to improve on that performance, it would be a mistake to base manufacturing strategy on just low labor costs, and employment strategy primarily on manufacturing. Indeed, the bigger challenge may not be changing labor laws; it may be the continuing inability to provide efficient infrastructure, like a contemporary transport system (good roads, fast and clean railway services, efficient ports) and assured power supply at reasonable prices. These impede domestic efficiencies and export competitiveness—especially for manufacturing activity.

It is not that nothing has changed. The country today has better roads than it did a decade ago, some efficient private ports, and good voice communications networks. But it will probably take another five years before further significant improvement becomes visible in infrastructure—especially in the railways (through the long-promised freight corridors) and in providing assured, quality electric power without either breaks in supply or voltage fluctuations. It bears noting that these are all areas where primarily the state has failed.

Addressing State Failure

Since the principal failures so far have had to do with policymaking, regulation, and sectors dominated by government companies, some important lessons must be drawn from the experience of the last six decades. The obvious point that must strike any observer is that governments have tried to do a great many things, from running watch and scooter factories to making shoes—all unsuccessfully. They continue trying to run airlines, telecom companies, hotels, and banks—all of which have found it difficult to compete with private competitors, losing ground to the latter when they come on the scene. Meanwhile, too little government attention is paid to core areas like law and order, education, and health—too few judges, too few teachers who teach, too few hospital beds; also too few trade negotiators and too few policemen, especially those with proper training. It should be obvious that there are many things the state does inadequately or badly, and many tasks that the state has needlessly taken on itself. The cold truth is that the tasks taken on by the state, viewed in their entirety, are beyond the capacity of the Indian state to deliver.

State failure is not necessarily fatal. The unintended benefit that has flowed from government sector underperformance is that government has had to cede ground to private players out of practical considerations, even when there is no new ideological conviction (which remains broadly left-of-center in the political world). In sector after sector once reserved for government-owned companies, private players are now either dominant or on the ascendant. The last quarter century's experience has shown that when the private sector is asked to provide telecom services, run airlines and airports, build and run ports, undertake banking, distribute electricity, and even undertake water supply, the result is usually (though not always, for there is no shortage of private banks and airlines that have failed) a substantial improvement on what the government was doing until then. In a crucial difference from the public sector, when private enterprises fail it is usually possible for them to quickly cut their losses.

Jawaharlal Nehru had wanted the public sector to "occupy the commanding heights of the economy," a phrase borrowed from Soviet communism, but the public sector's long-term failure to generate enough surpluses and to attract funds for investment has meant that its share of investment has plummeted from over half of the national total to a fifth or less. It is the private sector that is now generating surpluses and successfully attracting the savings of the household sector to undertake investment. The public sector is still dominant in energy, transport, and financial services, but it would seem to be only a matter of time before that too changes—half of new power-generating capacity commissioned in recent years has been in the private sector.

The limitation is that private players can replace government companies, not government itself. Providing purely public goods like law and order and the administration of justice are tasks that only the government can perform, but the attention of governments is frequently diverted to many non-essential tasks. The parallel problem is that providing merit goods, like maintaining irrigation systems and introducing new agricultural technologies, ensuring proper public health coverage and at least a minimal social safety net, carries management challenges that seem to have no solutions in the Indian operating environment. Effective service delivery is hampered by the absence of a carrot as well as a stick, severe understaffing, poor training and motivation, and outdated procedures. These are the issues to which the state's attention must turn, though they may be less glamorous than, say, running an airline—even a bankrupt one.

As a broad rule to be followed, governments should shed non-essential activities that other agencies can undertake and focus on what they alone must do. Most people would argue that other than providing public goods, the government should also arrange for merit goods like health and education, especially to those at the bottom of the pyramid. A minority would say that these too should be provided by private agents: if the poor have to be helped, the government should only pick up the bill through initiatives like public health insurance, while the actual administration of medical care is left to private hospitals. Such an approach of "buy, don't make" may or may not work well in practice. Until proven so, particularly in the case of tertiary medical care, there would be merit in the government continuing to run, indeed to expand, the network of public hospitals to which the poor mostly turn. This is because of the extent of malpractice evident in private corporate hospitals and their evident lack of interest in treating poor patients. The existence of a functioning alternative, if it can be created, would encourage otherwise deviant private providers to operate more honestly.

So the first broad lesson for improving governance is that governments must focus their energies on providing public goods and (at least for the time being) some merit goods as well. While this would address, and partially reverse, the problem of mission creep, there is no one in Indian politics who actually believes in making governments focus on the essentials alone and shedding the rest. One of the slogans on which Narendra Modi fought his 2014 election campaign was "minimum government, maximum governance," but nothing that he has done in his first two years as prime minister suggests that he will in fact minimize government or address serious administrative reform. In his broad approach, he is as interventionist and maximalist as anyone else.

The second bad habit of those running governments is to meddle with prices, usually in the name of helping poor people who can't afford market prices. However, long experience has shown that subsidies usually get captured by the middle class—as has happened in India. Most of the large subsidy bills have been for goods consumed mostly by the middle class—diesel and cooking gas, electricity, and fertilizers. Also, price controls discourage producers (there has been virtually no investment in fertilizer capacity for more than a decade, as imports have grown), while subsidies create market distortions—like the widespread adulteration of diesel with kerosene and the equally widespread diversion of subsidized cooking gas from the intended home market to the commercial market. Replacing subsidized gas cylinders with a cash subsidy paid into bank accounts has unearthed 30 million bogus gas connections (a fifth of the total!).[26] Subsidized foodgrain supply has been shown to suffer similarly from widespread leakages to the open market and costly overheads: ten years ago it cost Rs 3.65 to deliver a rupee's worth of benefit through the public distribution system, according to the Planning Commission.[27] There should be better ways of taking care of the poor, without distorting markets and prices.

Finally, the advent of information technology presents opportunities for bettering governance (like digitizing land records and improving tax administration) and safety net payments (electronic transfers to bank accounts, physical or virtual), and enhancing the citizen interface in countless ways—all of it low cost and cost saving since it would replace more expensive methods. Indeed, there is almost nothing that the government does that cannot be improved with the use of information technology. The overall impact could be transformational.

Different Approaches to "Inclusion"

A key issue to consider has to do with what is called inclusion: taking care of or helping the poor. The state's approach from the early 1970s, when Indira Gandhi announced a "crash" program to create employment, has been based on the belief that the normal growth process will not deliver inclusion. That may have been a reasonable thought when per capita income in a very poor country was growing at less than 1 percent annually, as was the case at the time. Many other initiatives have been taken since then to benefit those below the official poverty line. Midday school meals have worked well. Election campaigns have been fought and won on the promise of subsidized grain and other free programs.

As an illustrative and illuminating example, the Tamil Nadu government in 2015 listed the following items as being given free to some or all residents of the state: twenty kilos of rice per family; mixers, mixer-grinders, and electric fans; school education with laptops, books, bicycles, school uniforms, footwear, and so on; milk cows and goats to people below the poverty line; marriage assistance up to Rs 50,000 plus four grams of gold; paddy crop insurance for farmers affected by drought; electricity to handloom and power-loom weavers; sanitary napkins for rural adolescent girls; plus pension and other payouts.

Such "welfarist" populism is now ingrained deep in the political system; every party in every state promises more free benefits at every election—free electricity, bicycles, laptops, TV sets, and so on. In addition, nationally there was the adoption of a "rights" approach after Sonia Gandhi acquired influence over government policy during the 2004–14 decade when the Congress-led United Progressive Alliance (UPA) was in power. The right to employment, right to food, and right to education were all enacted as law and were to have been followed up by a universal, government-paid health insurance program ("right to health"), but elections intervened and resulted in a change of administration.

The problem is that the road to real inclusion does not get paved with free benefits. Inclusion is best attained through capacity enhancement (as through genuinely universal education, that is, not just class attendance but also real learning), and by satisfactory employment for those joining the workforce each year. These therefore should be the two central objectives. The evidence of the rapid-growth years of 2004–12, as revealed by the assessments of a decline in extreme poverty during that period, is that rapid economic growth is in itself a good part of the solution to poverty. But those who talk of growth and those who talk of rights go to different conferences and address different audiences; the result is a dialogue of the deaf. The politicians go to neither and do what they think will win votes.

A social safety net is desirable in any caring society, and necessary if the costs can be afforded. India should have one. Properly designed, it might grow in a few years to ensure that extreme poverty is finally abolished. As calculations in a subsequent chapter show, this is not immediately feasible financially, but a beginning can be made. Still, the primary method for delivering inclusion should be the core economic process of growth and development, appropriately designed to be employment intensive.

Conclusion

There are many things that need to be done if India is to realize its manifest potential: to become and continue to be the world's fastest-growing economy, and to double per capita incomes in a decade (which means growing GDP by more than 8 percent annually). The reforms of the 1990s have given the Indian market a certain momentum and size, along with the growth of the middle class. These twin strengths can now act as semi-autonomous growth drivers, in the absence of major disruptions. But reform of factor markets and improvement of governance standards are central to the question of whether India can sustain rapid growth for the medium-term future. In any case, economic growth alone is not enough; the system has to mend underperforming sectors like education, and deliver jobs as well as an inclusive society.

The main failures of the Indian system have been primarily government-related. Governance and economic performance will improve only if key reforms are undertaken. For instance, the welcome focus on manufacturing as job creator is nevertheless not a complete solution to the employment problem. Changing the product mix and increasing productivity in agriculture will probably do more to create rural jobs and grow incomes in the immediate future, while the development of manufacturing will mean going beyond the business of changing labor laws and competing with higher-wage China.

The essential tasks on which the government has been failing will be done better if (as is argued in a subsequent chapter) the government creates separate service delivery agencies that are not subject to government behavioral norms; these agencies can be given specific goals and then monitored on relative performance. The need is to shrink government and re-imagine it as a reformist policymaking and monitoring body. It should shed its superfluous tasks and focus laser-like on essential public goods and selected merit goods.

The temptation to interfere with price signals should be resisted because of all the market distortions it creates. Information technology should be used to upgrade government processes and the citizen interface, as has happened in the issue of passports, the booking of rail tickets, and to some degree in tax administration. Finally, as outlined in the first chapter, policy should be kept simple and focused.

This is quite a lot to ask, because no political party has anything close to such a program of action. There is an easy way out because business-as-usual, along with incremental reform, will still deliver what the country has managed in the last quarter century: about 6.4 percent annual economic growth, and therefore slightly more than 5 percent increase in per capita income. India's ascendancy will continue on the strength of such performance. But a more radical action plan is needed if the country wants to double its per capita income in a decade and approach a level near what Egypt, for example, already enjoys. Given the history of what other countries have managed to do, this should not be beyond India's capacity.

3

Not Twins and Not Alike

UNTIL QUITE RECENTLY, the generally accepted narrative for India and China was of two Asian powers, both of them large, populous, and poor; both free after long years of feudal subjugation; and now rising together. When that storyline began to come apart because China had raced far ahead, there was much talk of India learning from China's successes—how the latter had achieved manufacturing prowess, made a success of its special economic zones, attracted so much foreign investment, and so on. Somewhere along the way, the commentators forgot that China and India are very different countries; have very different histories, cultures, and systems, and consequently are two very different peoples. So what one country does successfully, the other might not be able to copy—for 101 different reasons. Trying to make Indians do what the Chinese have done may be a bit like the European experiment of the moment: asking the Greeks to be like the Germans. It may happen, but don't bet on it.

Rewinding to the start of the story, it is true that when the two old nations started off anew in the middle of the twentieth century, both suffered from the blight of large-scale poverty and low incomes. Their different political systems led observers to talk of two systems (communism and Westminster-style democracy) in competition on a continental scale. With a population that was 50 percent larger than India's in 1950, China had a 10 percent bigger economy; in effect, India had a higher per capita income. By 1958, though, per capita incomes of the two countries had broadly equalized.

Through the next two decades, despite their being marked in China by the destructive madness of the Great Leap Forward (1958–62) and then the sustained chaos of Mao's Cultural Revolution (1966–76), the two economies did equally well or badly—which does not, therefore, say very much for India. By the time Deng Xiaoping's Four Modernizations began in China in 1978, per capita incomes of the two countries were still equal, with China having 50 percent higher GDP because of its larger population.[1] Importantly, though, China by then had achieved greater equality as a society while India's efforts in that direction had failed—if they were ever seriously attempted. China's infinitely greater political and social mobilization, plus its Iron Rice Bowl, had translated into better numbers on nutrition, literacy, and health while India's evolutionary approach, dependent on the unconvincing exertions of a post-colonial bureaucracy, had delivered poorer results on these fronts. These differences were to be distinct advantages for China when under Deng its focus shifted to efficiency and growth.

By the time India began its economic reforms in 1991, China's economy had become twice India's in size. To Indian observers at the time, this did not seem significant. Indeed, there was a tendency among them to question the veracity of some of the improbable numbers that China had begun to report—like 14 percent GDP growth. As the years rolled by, though, the gaps became too big to be ignored. By then, India was already two decades and more behind China on key indicators, and it has not closed the gap since.

Two Rising Powers—Indeed!

It was Jack Welch who as chairman of General Electric (GE) visited New Delhi in September 1989 (a year before India plunged into a foreign exchange crisis that triggered economic reforms) and declared famously that he saw India and China as the big new markets of the future. Soon the term "Chindia" came into vogue, in India if not China, to bracket the two countries together. But a quarter century after Welch homed in on the two countries, GE's China business had vaulted to become three to four times the size of its India business, even as China's GDP had grown to five times India's. China became the world's second-largest economy in 2010, five years ahead of a 2003 Goldman Sachs forecast.[2] By 2014, it had become the world's largest economy if measured by purchasing power parity (PPP), as also its leading exporter and manufacturing power. Two Asian giants may be rising at the same time, but that does not make them equal today even if their economies were of broadly comparable size in 1980.

In the two decades that straddled the turn of the century (coterminous with India's post-reform period), China's income grew at the astonishing rate of 10.5 percent annually, while India managed 6.6 percent. In the preceding decade of the 1980s, growth had been even more unbalanced—10 percent for China and 5.4 percent for India. While India struggled with trade deficits,

China's trade surpluses helped it build up foreign exchange reserves that are twice India's GDP. China dwarfed India on foreign investment flows; its success gave strength to the yuan, whereas the rupee steadily lost ground. India may have been a country on the ascendant, but in the quarter century since India kicked off its economic reforms, it yielded almost unrecoverable ground to China.

If the Indian economy were to grow henceforth at an annual average of 9 percent, it would take nearly two decades to get to China's current size (in nominal dollars). China's literacy rate in 1991 was 78 percent, whereas India's was just 52 percent. Twenty years later, India's literacy rate was still only 74 percent while China had moved ahead to 95 percent. It was the same with life expectancy. China's in 1991 was seventy years; twenty years later, India could boast of only sixty-six years.[3] Even if India were to take the lead in the pace of economic and social progress, while China slackens off, as has begun to happen, it will be around 2035 before India is where China is today—and China is not resting on its laurels. The economic and strategic power imbalance is therefore a reality for at least the first half of the twenty-first century.

Most of India has wakened only fairly recently to the disillusioning reality that the narrative of "two Asian giants rising simultaneously" is long past its validity date. By the end of 2010, China had annual steel consumption that was more than eight times India's, and six times India's car sales. It was building 1,000 megawatts of fresh power capacity every week,[4] compared to 400 megawatts by India.[5] It accounted for more than 40 percent of the world's consumption of copper,[6] more than half of the total aluminum;[7] and it had half also of the skyscrapers[8] being built in the world. Naturally, it was also emitting much greater quantities of greenhouse gases, but India's climate change negotiators (still hostage to the Chindia mindset) decided to make common cause with China at the Copenhagen Summit in 2009.

Meanwhile, China had built more than 9,300 kilometers (km) of high-speed rail track, with another 14,000 kilometers under construction, to handle trains running at faster than 200 kilometers per hour (kmph). The superfast train journey from Beijing to Shanghai (1318 km) takes less than five hours. Even the standard train takes only ten hours. In embarrassing contrast, Indian Railways' premier "superfast" Rajdhani Express from Delhi to Mumbai (a comparable distance) takes the same sixteen hours that it did in 1969, when the service was launched. Indian policymakers and businessmen can barely begin to understand the creation of an ecosystem that has also enabled China to account for 60 percent of the world's production of zippers, 70 percent of its toys, nearly a third of its garment trade, and a growing if not dominant share of information technology (IT)-sector hardware and solar photovoltaic cells. Before China's economic slowdown in 2013–14, the *increase* in its steel consumption was more than India's total annual steel consumption of 76 million tons.

Can Greeks Become Germans?

And so, the question has often been asked, what lessons can India learn from the Chinese success story? Can they be applied to India—or is the national genius, or DNA, so different that copycat strategies won't work? It is when one confronts these questions that the similarities, assumed on the basis of size, scale, and (once upon a time) income level, are seen to be superficial. The historical and cultural differences between the two entities, and therefore their political and economic choices, are more substantive factors. China's geographical core has been a centrally administered empire for a couple of millennia, whereas India's history mostly comprises multiple feuding monarchies. China is overwhelmingly Han, while India is a polyglot nation with every kind of diversity: ethnic, linguistic, religious, caste. China has a long experience of being run by a merit-based bureaucracy; India does not. China has a sense of destiny (the Middle Kingdom with a mandate from heaven), history, and continuity, while India's history is the cause of current political contestations. Chinese nationalism is unifying, while some kinds of Indian nationalism are divisive.

Differences in the modern era are equally substantial. China became a one-party dictatorship while India imitated Westminster democracy. China's rulers emerged hardened from a civil war and could take the tough decisions about breaking down old ways of doing things in order to create a new reality, whereas India won its freedom through non-violence, so its leaders were inclined to make the softer choices. China mobilized its masses to bring about revolutionary change, whereas India sought change through laws passed in Parliament and implemented by a bureaucratic setup inherited from colonial rulers. China began under Mao by emphasizing change in the countryside while India under Nehru sought industrialization; it is therefore ironic that the country that has successfully industrialized is China. For good measure, China achieved rapid progress on the key human indicators while India did not. China began reforming its economy in 1978 with a sense of national purpose; India's reforms since 1991 have been halfhearted at best and without much political conviction. The end results have thus been very different for the two economies; China has become a global power that casts a shadow over India's regional status.

The two countries' paths to development have been almost polar opposites. For a long time, China was seen to have a better macro story than its micro story: that is, its state performed better than individual companies. India in contrast had an underperforming state that failed to deliver the basics, while its entrepreneurs (usually from the traditional trading castes) ran a better-performing private corporate sector. China therefore attracted more foreign direct investment in job-creating new factories, while India attracted portfolio investment in existing companies. In recent years, following sweeping reform of its public sector, China's micro story has improved as well, though in general corporate governance norms remain superior in India.

China achieved what it did by throwing resources on an unprecedented scale into the development of infrastructure, by offering factory owners swarms of workers with no real rights to industrial action or collective bargaining, and by keeping its currency artificially low in order to capture export markets while suppressing local demand. It operated an opaque banking, financial, and pricing system in which outside observers found it hard to understand cost structures; also by stealing or copying technology from foreign firms that invested in China; and by achieving exceptionally high productivity norms on factory floors.

India is not about to do any of these; it couldn't even if it wanted to. While the Indian state has never been able to deliver adequate physical infrastructure (electricity, roads, ports), the existence of a capital market meant that the relationship between capital investment and increased output (the incremental capital–output ratio) has always been better in India than in China—that is, it can achieve similar rates of economic growth with the use of less capital. At the same time, the attempt to apply private-sector efficiency to building infrastructure (through public–private partnerships) has resulted in problem-ridden contracts, bad investments, stalled projects, and debt-laden balance sheets.

Taking away the collective bargaining rights of industrial labor, as China has done for all practical purposes, would be unthinkable in a multiparty parliamentary democracy with a long-term left-of-center bias. A mercantilist currency policy to keep the rupee cheap is ideologically taboo among Indian policymakers who buy into mainstream orthodoxy about not manipulating the exchange rate; in any case, the policy is not without its costs if pursued for any length of time. India's politicians, in turn, have often confused a strong currency with national strength—as some Bharatiya Janata Party (BJP) politicians did during the 2014 election campaign. Meanwhile, the wholesale theft of industrial technology is impossible in a country with an independent judiciary.

Importantly, the combination of large-scale production and very high productivity, which seems to have an East Asian patent, appears to be a leap too far for India. Chinese workers are better educated and better fed, and they seem to take willingly to the monotony of repetitive shop-floor work. Those in charge of India's National Skill Development Corporation report, in contrast, that young Indian men show a marked preference for training that will help them get white-collar jobs, even if manufacturing work pays more. Anecdotal evidence suggests that they are willing to take as much as a 50 percent cut in pay to switch from blue- or brown-collar to white-collar work (such a preference could be linked to caste and status; among other things, it improves prospects in the marriage market). Similarly, whereas young, single women in China are willing to move far away from home and stay in dormitories located next to factories, their Indian counterparts prefer to stay at home and get bused to work. This is slower, costlier, and less efficient, and it results in higher absenteeism.

The Chinese system has fewer checks and balances, so the alignment of objectives is easier, with coordinated action to follow. In India the two major political parties can agree on the need for a new law, yet each will try to stop the other from getting it passed in Parliament. Much of Narendra Modi's initial legislative thrust and policy stance were on issues that his party had opposed when in opposition (higher foreign investment in the insurance sector, a border settlement with Bangladesh, the goods and services tax, majority foreign investment in organized retail trade, and so on). Even more ironically, its principal political battle after it formed the government was to try to undo something it had voted in favor of when in opposition (the 2013 land acquisition law).

The separation of powers between legislature, executive, and judiciary makes getting project clearances a complicated hurdle race. This is especially so when populism comes easily to politicians seeking votes and legislatures pass unrealistic laws. The executive is rule-bound rather than results-oriented, and the judiciary given to overreach, issuing sweeping judgments that sometimes show a divorce from economic logic. The result, as Singapore's Lee Kuan Yew declared tersely a few years ago, is that "Indians talk while Chinese do"—a remark that drew raucous laughter in the Singapore business forum where Lee was speaking.

Two Outlier Countries

The different trajectories of the two countries show up most clearly in their successes and failures. Both countries have put in place industrial policy. But where Deng Xiaoping declared that it didn't matter whether a cat was black or white so long as it caught mice, India had many more demands of the industrial cat, not just the simple business of catching mice. It should preferably be government owned, located in an industrially backward area, be small scale in its operations, and use indigenous mice-catching technology as well as capital equipment. Inevitably, India hobbled its manufacturing sector while China became the world's factory. China also became the world champion in its ability to focus on an objective, while the intricacies of Indian thought processes resulted in multiple objectives for every move, invariably failing to achieve the main one. Even a scooter factory that had stopped making scooters was supposed to keep going, or jobs would be lost.

In the meantime, revolutionary China placed emphasis on school education while, in the initial decades, de-emphasizing university education. India, ruled mostly by the upper castes during the initial post-Independence decades and even later, adopted a brahminical approach: it neglected school education (one reason for the slow improvement in its literacy rates) while building quality institutes of higher learning. China therefore created an educated industrial workforce while India built a comparative advantage in white-collar work. These were to prove fateful choices. By 2013, manufacturing accounted for an enormous 33 percent of China's total economy (or GDP), while India's was barely half that, at 17 percent. Most of rapid-growth Asia had manufacturing shares that were larger than India's.

This pattern showed up in trade numbers too. China's merchandise exports were ten times its export of commercial services. India's ratio was 2:1, while the global average was between these poles, at roughly 4:1. China was the world leader in the export of merchandise and numbered second in services; India was a poor nineteenth when it came to merchandise exports, but a healthy sixth for services exports. India's share of world merchandise exports, at 1.66 percent, was half its 3.3 percent share of world services trade.[9]

When India tried to copy China's special economic zones, the results were very different, resulting in farmers' protests over land grabs, court actions to undo the land acquisition, the planning of new cities instead of production centers, and not one large new manufacturing enclave or cluster.

The ironic situation, though, was that China and India had total export-to-GDP ratios that were not very different: 25.2 percent for India,

26.4 percent for China. But these numbers were achieved through very different routes and told very different stories. China was an outlier in one direction, India in another. Indeed, among the twenty-five largest exporters of commercial services, all countries with the solitary exception of China had per capita income that was at least eight times India's. In effect, the country had arbitraged the low cost of its white-collar manpower to grab a bite from the rich countries' cake. Interestingly, a McKinsey Global Institute survey of 2005 reported multinational businesses saying they would hire only one in ten Chinese graduates, compared to one in four Indian graduates—in part because of the latter's better knowledge of English and communication skills.[10]

The scale of India's failure in manufacturing, and consequently in merchandise trade, has to be fully understood. Taiwan, with a population less than 2 percent of India's, exports almost as much merchandise as India does.[11] In recent years Bangladesh has become a much bigger exporter of garments. If India had been as successful in merchandise trade as it has been in services exports, that is, if it had captured a similar share of world trade, it would have exported twice as much as it did in 2014–15, at $311 billion. It would then have replaced France as the sixth-largest exporter of merchandise, and been ahead of South Korea as well.

India's failure to do better in manufacturing and merchandise exports has come at a heavy price in terms of jobs. The garment business, for instance, generates about a million jobs for every $2 billion of output. In the tech sector, the ratio is a million jobs for $10 billion in output. The difference in employment intensity is a factor of five. Success in the tech services sector is simply not a substitute for job creation in labor-intensive manufacturing. China has benefited enormously from its focus on manufacturing; India has a serious employment problem because it has failed on that front.

As for the future, India's plan for "Make in India" lists twenty-five sectors, a mix of low-end and high-end manufacturing (garments and electronics, aviation and tourism, solar energy equipment and defense items)—all areas that China has already mastered. Meanwhile, China has reportedly listed ten priority sectors for 2025. These include new information technology; high-end, numerically controlled machine tools and robotics; aerospace equipment; ocean engineering equipment; advanced railway traffic equipment; new materials; and biological medicine.

Anyone want to try to copy Chinese-style manufacturing?

Quick, Slow . . . Quick?

4

Enterprise Losing the Plot

LIKE MANY ECONOMIES around the world, India never had a better expansion period than during the five-year period 2003–08. The rate of economic growth averaged a record 8.7 percent, the previous best being 6.9 percent during 1995–2000. Business boomed, and poverty levels fell faster than ever before as agriculture too did exceptionally well. Wages and salaries rose rapidly, fueling a surge in the demand for cars and homes. Tax revenues were buoyant. Admittedly, inflation was high, and the global commodity price surge showed up in rapid import growth. But the country's foreign exchange reserves more than trebled on the back of massive capital inflows, even as the rupee strengthened against the US dollar.

Three years later, the mood had begun a downward swing. The growth rate plunged from an average of 9.5 percent in 2005–08 to 5.4 percent in 2012–13, and buoyancy left the system as fresh investment suffered. In 2013, the rupee also took a sharp plunge as global investors fretted about the future course of the country. Commercial bank credit had been growing at over 26 percent during the boom years of 2003–08, but dropped to single-digit numbers by 2014–15. An impatient press talked of policy paralysis in the government, but business was half-paralyzed too.

One can try to understand this story from several perspectives: the domestic backwash effects of the lead-up to the 2008 financial crisis and the Great Recession that followed; a discredited and exhausted government on its last legs as it approached elections at the end of a decade in office; and the mistakes that businessmen made as unbridled enthusiasm got the better of good judgment. Since the "India story" had been seen essentially as the flowering of Indian enterprise, the business prism is particularly inviting—especially as it is business issues that have delayed and then slowed the recovery long after there has been a change of government. And one might as well begin with the largest business house in the country, Tata.

Tata Goes Global

The year 2006 was an exciting one for Tata. Its automobile arm, Tata Motors, was busy designing a car that had made headlines around the world before anyone had set eyes on it, because the Nano promised to be the cheapest car ever made—at a pre-tax price of Rs 1 lakh ($2,500 at the time). At around the same time, Tata Chemicals bought a US chemicals company for a billion dollars and made two British acquisitions. Tata Power spent another billion dollars or thereabouts for stakes in two Indonesian coal mines and contracted them for their cheap coal to fuel the company's giant 4,000 megawatt (MW) power project at Mundra on the Gujarat coast.

That wasn't all. The group's hotel company acquired luxury properties in New York, Boston, San Francisco, and Sydney. It also bought a minority stake in the Orient Express Hotels chain before launching a $1.2-billion bid for the company. Tata Motors topped all these with the purchase in 2008 of the British Jaguar and Land Rover marquees from Ford, for $2.3 billion, after having made smaller acquisitions in South Korea and Spain. But the biggest prize was bagged by Tata Steel, which outbid a Brazilian rival and sealed a deal in January 2007 to buy the Anglo-Dutch Corus Group for $12.04 billion. Tata Steel's production capacity went up with the acquisition from less than 4 million tons to 25 million tons, taking it from fifty-second to fifth in world steel rankings. The group became Britain's largest industrial employer. Among all the Indian business groups that had stepped out confidently onto the global business scene, Tata had made the boldest moves. In all, the group had invested over $16 billion in thirty-seven cross-border acquisitions, after which 58 percent of its turnover came from outside India.

Before long, though, many of the bets started to come unstuck. The Nano project got caught in a land dispute in West Bengal. The state's main opposition politician Mamata Banerjee (who became the chief minister in 2011) went on a twenty-five-day fast, demanding that some of the land acquired from farmers be returned to them. Tata Motors continued to build the plant, but after close to two years of attrition it threw up its hands; the company dismantled the factory and replanted it at the other end of the country, in Gujarat. To add injury to insult, once-eager buyers soon shunned the car, which was seen as underwhelming. Sales were equally underwhelming.

Tata Power found that using its Indonesian coal was no longer feasible as global coal prices went from $50 to $140 per ton and Indonesia imposed minimum export prices. The coal became unaffordable and crippled the power plant at Mundra. The hotel company saw the value of its international acquisitions fall and abandoned its bid for Orient Express Hotels before putting its minority stake on the block. In telecom, the group tried to hedge technology choices in an uncertain regulatory environment and remained a bit player, thereby missing arguably the biggest business opportunity of the decade. Then its Japanese partner, NTT Docomo, decided to exit at half its 2009 investment price of about $2.6 billion, even as the company lost about a billion dollars in both 2012–13 and 2013–14 (at the then prevailing exchange rates).

Tata Steel Europe (as Corus was renamed) went through successive rounds of job cuts as the world economy struggled with recession and slow-down; part of the capacity acquired in Europe was sold or put on the block; jobs were shed. Loans had to be renegotiated to get longer repayment periods. Overall, the group's debt had piled up, reaching $30 billion in four companies whose net profit totaled barely $3 billion. If the group could still think of fresh investments, it was only because its software services arm, Tata Consultancy Services, continued to thrive, accounting for 80 percent of the profits of the group's listed companies and about 60 percent of its $114-billion market value. It also helped that the Jaguar–Land Rover acquisition had worked out brilliantly, riding on the back of record sales in China.

Still, write-downs on overseas investments were announced, totaling more than $3 billion in the four adventurous companies—Tata Steel, Tata Motors, Tata Chemicals, and Indian Hotels. Many assets were sold or put on the block to reduce the burden of debt: part of the coal mine investment, a 50 percent stake in Dhamra port on the eastern coast, and a two-thirds stake in a telecom company in South Africa, among others.

Hubris or Bad Timing?

So was it hubris or bad timing for the global gambit? The answer had to be, both. Tata's ups and downs were no different from the boom and bust that much of Indian business went through in the go-go years and the crisis period that followed. Like Tata, one ambitious business group after the other (GMR, GVK, Mittal, Essar, Anil Ambani, DLF, Jaypee, Lanco, Bhushan) embarked on projects abroad and at home, using large sums of borrowed cash. Many of them were investments in infrastructure with long-term payback periods. Some had dangerously high debt-to-equity ratios, of 5:1 and more. As with Tata, the projects of many of these and other business houses were undone by global commodity price swings, the economic downturn as India's GDP growth rate virtually halved to 5.4 percent, and the whimsicality of the country's evolving regulatory environment.

This last was not insignificant. The coal and iron ore mining sectors and downstream industries like power generation and steel were thrown into crisis when scandals led courts to order that iron ore mines be shut across the board and coal mining licenses canceled. More than 100 telecom licenses that had been issued in controversial fashion were also canceled by courts, rendering fruitless the billions of dollars that businesses (including international companies) had invested.

As the country's mood swung from unreal optimism to frustration over a deteriorating business environment, a real estate boom evaporated in the wake of excess supply and sharp business practices by developers that put off customers. Job losses dented the consumer mood and car sales went flat. The stock market was virtually moribund for four years. Banks—the largest of them owned by the government—which had compounded businessmen's mistakes by lending on the basis of poor risk assessment, paid the price. In 2013 and 2014, they had to restructure loans that amounted to more than 7 percent of their corporate debt portfolio (Rs 1.8 trillion out of Rs 25 trillion). Non-performing assets climbed further to Rs 5.8 trillion by March 2016. The government-owned banks (which accounted for 70 percent of all banking) saw their stressed assets balloon to become nearly as large as the capital invested in them. Fresh credit, especially to industry, slowed to a crawl.

The IMF weighed in to say in 2014 that more than a quarter of corporate debt was held by loss-making companies, while almost 30 percent of debt was with companies that had a very high debt-to-equity ratio of 5:1 or more. Financial stress tests showed that the shock scenario for Indian companies in 2013 was the second highest on record, marginally better than in 1999.[1] Many large business houses had become so saddled with debt that the only thought on their minds was to sell assets and repay the loans. Progress was slow. Sales curves flattened, so over four long years up to 2014–15 the manufacturing sector saw average annual output grow at no more than 1.5 percent.[2] It did not help that problems with coal and gas supplies as fuel for new power stations, like that of Tata Power, rendered mostly inoperative a slew of stations with a combined generating capacity of 30,000 megawatts. These represented investment of about Rs 1.5 trillion.

Many projects had been launched jointly with the government and were termed public–private partnerships, or PPP. When these ran into trouble and disputes arose, the projects got stuck halfway—putting at risk much of the investment that had already been made. Fresh investment dried up—and caused sharp drops in the production of capital goods. The government-owned banks in particular needed large doses of fresh capital, which had to come from a government already struggling to reduce its fiscal deficit. The infrastructure project crisis was driven home when some large road-building projects for which the government invited bids found no takers.

The problem found reflection in the changing ratio between turnover and assets for the fifty leading companies that constitute the Nifty 50 stock market index. This climbed from 2.97 in 2002–03 to a peak of 4.41 in 2006–07 before falling back to 2.62 in 2013–14. During the high-growth years, 2003–09, the ratio fluctuated between a low of 3.41 and 4.41; it dropped below 3.00 in 2009–10 and then kept falling.[3] In other words, a lot of new capital had been invested, but it was not generating much business. Result: stressed balance sheets and heavy debt overhang. The inevitable denouement was that investment itself slowed down. Corporate capital formation as a share of GDP fell dramatically in the low-growth years.

In late 2014 came a policy about-turn. The government noted the double bind of the corporate sector's inability to invest because of an excess of debt, and banks' inability to lend because of the bad loans on their books. It announced that the answer was fresh investment by the government and by public-sector companies, some of which were sitting on large piles of cash simply because they had done little in the go-go years. It was a way out of the cul-de-sac that was the opposite of everything the country had come to expect and believe in, after 1991.

Public, Private . . . Public?

The story of India's ascent to economic stardom in the wake of the sweeping economic reforms that were launched in 1991 was the story of the rise of India's private-sector companies. Unshackled after decades of ideology-driven restrictions and bureaucratic regulations, they proved their worth handsomely. The de-licensing of industrial activity (thereby removing capacity restrictions), abolition of import controls, slashing of import tariffs, and opening up of different sectors to private investment heralded a new era. Manmohan Singh, India's Oxbridge-educated finance minister in the early

1990s, borrowed a phrase from the economist John Maynard Keynes to say that businessmen's "animal spirits" had been unleashed.

In sector after sector that was opened to private investment, businessmen put in the shade the established, government-owned companies. In telecom, aviation, and banking, these legacy companies were shown up by new entrants from the private sector, some of which quickly became market leaders (inevitably, some also went belly-up). In areas of emerging strength for the economy, like software services and pharmaceuticals, companies like Infosys and Sun Pharma did much of the running. In telecom, private firms accounted for more than 90 percent of consumers in 2015, growing from nothing in 1995. Private airlines, once again starting from nothing, accounted by 2013 for more than 80 percent of passengers, even as the domestic aviation sector grew sevenfold in two decades.

International firms that came to the country as it progressively opened up, like Suzuki and Hyundai in cars, LG and Samsung in consumer products, and General Electric and United Technologies in a range of engineering industries, set market performance benchmarks that served as magnets for later entrants like Ford and Volkswagen, Vodafone and Lafarge. Energy giants like BP and Shell established business outposts, while IBM and Accenture established leadership positions in business process outsourcing (BPO). On occasion, the business in India grew to overshadow the parent company's home business—as happened with Suzuki, the Japanese small-car maker that pioneered the automobile revolution in India in 1983. Thirty years later, Suzuki's Indian company accounted for about half the Indian market of 2.6 million passenger vehicles annually and was remitting royalty and dividend payments from India that together were greater than the profits from Suzuki's Japanese operations. The same was true for a while of Cairn India, the oil producer, vis-à-vis its Scottish parent before the Indian subsidiary was sold. While these were exceptions, most companies saw the Indian market become steadily more important in their global operations—and even more important for the future.

By the time the economy soared to record growth rates in the new century, the private sector was firmly in the driver's seat. It was not that successful government-owned companies did not exist, especially in the oil, coal, power, and financial sectors, where some of them continued to enjoy de facto monopolies. Indeed, some government-owned firms continued to be counted among the country's most profitable, while Oil and Natural Gas Corporation, Coal India, and State Bank of India featured among firms with the highest market capitalization on the stock market. But their usually sedate performance faded into the background as the private sector surged ahead. Private-sector companies also became for the first time the largest providers of jobs in the corporate sector.

None of this could have happened without the presence of a large entrepreneurial class, and some outstanding businessmen (some of whom, it must be said, leveraged their special relationships with politicians and governments in order to bend rules their way). Individual success stories therefore were very much a part of the macro mosaic. Mukesh Ambani built the world's most complex oil refinery and the largest such single-location installation; as a result, he enjoyed industry-leading refining margins.[4] N. R. Narayana Murthy of Infosys and others were central to why the information technology (IT) services sector captured the imagination of the business world, growing from $0.5 billion in 1991 to a $118 billion business by 2015, most of it exports (the numbers exclude e-commerce and hardware business).[5] Mahindra & Mahindra, led by Anand Mahindra, became a manufacturer of small utility aircraft, bought SsangYong Motor Company in Korea in 2011, and set up assembly plants for tractors on three continents.[6]

In consumer goods, the Godrej clan, Harsh Mariwala of Marico, and the two promoters of Emami competed successfully against global giants like Unilever; some of them bought brands and businesses on different continents as they ventured out globally. The unassuming Dilip Shanghvi's Sun Pharma emerged from nowhere to become the country's most valuable pharmaceutical company, with revenue of over $4 billion and market capitalization of $33 billion;[7] Shanghvi himself became the wealthiest Indian. Sunil Mittal's Bharti emerged from the fierce telecom scrum as the country's largest operator. Meanwhile, Tata Advanced Systems was making cabins for Sikorsky helicopters, fuselage and wings for Dornier, and components for Lockheed Martin's C-130J transport aircraft.[8]

In a country whose companies had been known all too often for shoddy products, new levels of competition forced change. Soon a succession of companies was winning the Deming Prize[9] for total quality management (or TQM). The list included TVS and Rane, Tata Steel and SRF. The last of these transitioned from the plain Jane business of tire cord to specialty chemicals, using technology developed in-house, and saw both sales and margins soar. Innovation had been another weak feature of the Indian industrial scene. As at SRF, this began to change while some companies experimented with what came to be called frugal engineering—though its most famous example, Tata's low-cost Nano car, had to be repositioned and re-launched after it failed initially to find favor with customers.

Many start-ups flourished, but some inevitably failed as businessmen entered what for them were unexplored waters. A bunch of new private airlines went bankrupt one after another in a demonstration of Joseph Schumpeter's theory of creative destruction,[10] even as Indigo stuck rigidly to its low-cost formula and emerged as a comfortably profitable market leader in a thin-margin business. Some new private banks failed or were merged into older banks (Global Trust, Times, Centurion, etc.); however, HDFC Bank surfaced as by far the country's most valuable, and Kotak emerged twelve years after becoming a bank in 2003 with a market capitalization of more than $19 billion. Four private banks, all started after 1991, were now counted among the five most valuable in the sector. Satish Kaura's medium-scale Samtel progressed from the disappearing business of making cathode ray tubes for TV sets to doing complex avionics and display systems for fighter aircraft.

As testimony to the flowering of the country's entrepreneurial spirit and mood of optimism, fresh graduates from the elite Indian Institutes of Technology (IITs) and Indian Institutes of Management (IIMs) began to start their own businesses instead of automatically settling for assured careers at consultancies and investment banks. Flipkart positioned itself as India's answer to Amazon and in the latter half of 2015 was valued at $15 billion, though that number slipped later. Housing.com did the amazing feat of hiring forty-five IIT graduates in campus placements barely a year after the company had been founded by another IIT graduate. Flipkart, Snapdeal, and the rest were, like other such start-ups, growing rapidly while still to earn a return on investment—tempting some observers to warn of a bubble in the making; but there was no shortage of funding, even if in some cases the valuation multiples shrank. Quick to recognize the new trend, Narendra Modi announced a "start-up India" program with government funding and tax incentives.

If the face of Indian business had changed, so too did the faces of Indian business. It helped that many of the new faces that emerged were (for a while) fresh, clean ones, not bearing the shop-soiled names that had flourished in the old "permit raj."[11] These were people like the founders of Infosys, who were all engineers and with a fetish for honesty as well as a yen for philanthropy—as was the case with Azim Premji of Wipro. The fifty companies featuring in the Nifty 50 index in 2015 included about a dozen ventures that did not exist or were too small to count when economic reforms were launched in 1991. The ranks of India's rupee billionaires showed too that the majority of the biggest were self-made—people like Dilip Shanghvi and Sunil Mittal and Rahul Bhatia of Indigo. Narayana Murthy of Infosys and Uday Kotak of Kotak Mahindra Bank were successively declared "world entrepreneur of the year" at the annual jamborees organized in Monte Carlo by the accounting and consultancy firm Ernst and Young. The land of snake charmers and begging bowls had begun to look like a land of opportunity.

The story went beyond successful businessmen who attracted the klieg lights. The shift of corporate power showed in the macro numbers too. Private corporate savings (that is, profits) had been less than 1 percent of GDP back in 1950–51, and also less than half of public-sector savings at 2.1 percent of GDP in that year. The numbers swung even more toward the public sector during Nehru's socialist high noon, and later in the wake of Indira Gandhi's statist push when she nationalized entire sectors of business—insurance and banking, coal mines and textile mills, and also a raft of engineering companies making everything from railway wagons to bicycles. By 1976–77, therefore, private corporate savings were still only 1.3 percent of GDP, while public-sector savings had soared to more than four times as much, at 5.6 percent. The pendulum swung back only slowly, as the first modest reforms in favor of markets took place in the 1980s. It was only around 1990 (just before the big-bang economic reforms of 1991) that the private corporate sector caught up and then pulled ahead. A decade and a half later, in 2004–05, the private corporate sector's savings were at 6.5 percent of GDP while the public sector now languished at 2.4 percent. The tables had been well and truly turned. But in the slowdown that followed, private corporate savings dipped back to no more than 3.9 percent of GDP.

Crucially, the private sector was much better at tapping household savings, which at all times were the largest component of national savings. So when it came to securing money for investment, from 2004–05 onward the private corporate sector's role in fixed capital formation was three times that of the public sector. There was no doubt about who now occupied Nehru's "commanding heights." It showed in the soaring values on the stock market; the total market value of all listed companies multiplied tenfold in fiteeen or sixteen explosive years, going from $125 billion in 2001–02 to $1.4 trillion in early 2016.

For perhaps the first time in the history of any large economy, the private sector even became central to the task of building the country's physical infrastructure—roads, power stations, ports, and airports. Deficit-hobbled governments either did not have the money or their agencies had been shown to be incompetent at project management. In power generation, the private sector accounted for more than half of the new capacity created after 2001, after having been virtually shut out of the sector till the mid-1990s. Gautam Adani established what quickly became the country's largest port, at Mundra; bought Dhamra port; and contracted to build a new deep-sea port at Vizhinjam in Kerala. Private companies, in partnership with government counterparts, now ran the airports in four of the five most important cities and built new terminals, even as they bid and won airport projects in countries as far afield as Turkey and Indonesia. From the passengers' point of view, Indian airports ceased to be smelly embarrassments and became confident statements of a new India; the biggest at Delhi and Mumbai featured regularly in lists of the best-run airports in the world. Growth thus meant developing new capabilities for new business groups that emerged from the sidelines, like GMR and GVK. Larsen & Toubro set up a shipyard and submarine design center and was making hulls for submarines, while Godrej's engineers built equipment for atomic energy plants and parts of rockets and supersonic cruise missiles. Private construction companies bagged most of the contracts in the highway program.

The global push that businessmen began to make, as Tata did around 2006, was taken by many as the clinching proof that India's businessmen had arrived. Outbound investment ranged between $15 billion and $20 billion annually for five years during the days of heady growth, expanding in some years to 60 percent of investment inflows. The cumulative outbound total crossed $100 billion.[12] Indian companies accounted for the fifth-largest (in 2011–12) and then the third-largest (in 2012–13) number of foreign investments in Britain.[13] Bharti bought a fifteen-country telecom business in Africa for $10.7 billion in 2010,[14] and the risk-taking Ruia brothers at Essar acquired or set up a number of businesses overseas: a 12-million-ton oil refinery at Chester in England and a 50 percent stake in a 4-million-ton unit in Kenya, where they also had a telephone company, coal mines, and a BPO business. There was a 4-million-ton steel plant in Canada, a mine and pelletization plant in Minnesota, and a rolling mill in Indonesia. Stakes were bought in oil exploration blocks in three countries.[15]

Videocon, a manufacturer of consumer durables, began investing in new oil fields. It bought a 10 percent stake in the Rovuma gas field in Mozambique in 2008 and struck gold as Rovuma was declared one of the largest new gas fields to be discovered. Videocon, along with the government-owned Bharat Petroleum, also invested in much bigger oil and gas fields in Brazil. In the search for energy sources, ONGC Videsh and others invested in oil and gas fields as far afield as Russia's Sakhalin peninsula, Sudan, Brazil, and Australia—though (as in Sudan) not always with happy outcomes.[16]

The Avantha Group was another investor overseas. Memorably, it acquired in 2005 a troubled electrical transformer manufacturer in Belgium, saving jobs. A grateful local populace in the town of Mechelen organized a celebration while a local church's bells pealed the unfamiliar chimes of India's national anthem. Avantha eventually sold the Belgian company as the group ran into headwinds. As with Tata, Mittal overpaid for his African acquisition, which proved to be a drag on the group's balance sheet for many years. These and other Indian groups learned valuable (and costly) business lessons through their overseas forays, even as there were spin-off benefits from the engagement of global firms with India.

What Went Wrong?

So how did what looked like a story of successful enterprise go so badly wrong for India's vaunted private sector, to the extent that the government felt economic revival would happen only if the public sector stepped in to become lead investor again? There is no one reason; several factors were at work, starting with the fact that businessmen tend to make mistakes in the good years because of overweening optimism. Typically, they take on too much debt and are forced to apply painful correctives in the lean years. It happened once earlier, when uncalibrated optimism in the first flush of post-reform enthusiasm led during years of rapid growth (1994–97) to excessive gearing. It took the best part of five years for companies that had gorged on debt to digest it, restructure capital, reduce costs, and emerge in 2002 with healthy balance sheets and a new appetite for growth in a low-interest-rate environment. History had now repeated itself, and the process of digestion and restructuring was under way. It would not be done overnight.

The difference this time was that the crisis sector was infrastructure, with widespread effects through the economy. Investment in the country's under-provided physical infrastructure had doubled—from 3 percent of GDP to 6 percent—and the talk had been of taking it all the way to 10 percent, in imitation of China. Inevitably, businessmen had gone where the money and opportunity were. This had meant moving from business-to-consumer sectors where markets functioned (as in cars, pharmaceuticals, or consumer durables) to business-to-business areas where policy formulation and government contracts were key to success. The risk of sub-optimal decisions was higher and ticket sizes bigger. The scope for inflating project costs and siphoning off cash was also greater—doubtless one of the incentives for some of the fireflies attracted to the flame. It is telling that banks lent for highway projects at an average of twice the costs assessed by the National Highway Authority of India.

Second, private companies had moved into the resources sector, previously closed to them. By their nature, extractive industries are more likely than not to be sources of conflict and political engagement, especially when the rules have not been properly thought through and regulation is mostly absent or regulators suborned. Third, these projects tended to be of longer duration, with the attendant increase in uncertainty and risk. Finally, companies ventured overseas without fully understanding the dynamics of other markets, often overpaying for the assets acquired. The systemic problem this time, unlike in 1997, was that since it was infrastructure development that had gone off track, the ensuing problems had greater spread effects through the system.

Roiling markets added other complications since markets move ahead of government processes, especially in the always problematic resources sector. Thermal coal prices, for instance, had been around $25 per ton for many years up to 2003. As Chinese demand grew and grew, the price roller coaster began. Price per ton fluctuated between $45 and $65 between 2004 and 2007, then surged to $190 a ton in the summer of 2008. After the financial crisis, the price crashed to $65 in early 2009 before peaking again at $140 in 2011. Once China slowed down, the price was back at $50—still twice the level of 2003. As markets fluctuated, coal mining moved from being a not particularly attractive business to a hot sector, and then cold again.

When India allowed the private sector to undertake the captive mining of coal (by power stations and steel mills, for their own consumption), there was no great rush for mining leases. By the time the leases were issued, coal was beginning to look like black gold—but the leases were still issued as of old, without charge and with no clear rules for choosing from among applicants. Businessmen smelled a gold mine and applied for mines in multiple company names; some with barely a postal address to their credit were among those allotted coal mines. It was classic cronyism as ministers, their relatives, parliamentarians, and newspaper owners were among those caught in the crossfire that was to follow.

An alert civil servant, P. C. Parakh saw the push for easy money growing early on, in 2005, and suggested that coal mines be auctioned to the highest bidders.[17] His minister opposed the idea vehemently and, in a pattern that was to become familiar, Prime Minister Manmohan Singh opted for the path of least resistance. The scam hit the headlines with full ferocity when the government's auditor submitted a report that estimated the notional loss to the government (in auction prices forgone) at a stratospheric Rs 1,85,591 crore. It seemed an outsize estimate till the government, acting under court orders, auctioned thirty-two of the mines and attracted bids that, over thirty years, could potentially yield state and central governments a total of Rs 2,00,000 crore, but over an extended period of time. In all, 204 coal mine licenses had been canceled, but the remaining mines were relatively small. Meanwhile, Singh and Parakh were summoned by a trial court as people accused of corruption for favoring a particular businessman in the allotment of one of the mines.

There was a similar story in iron ore. Till 2003, China (producer of nearly half the world's steel) was importing iron ore fines at $11 per ton. As with coal, iron ore prices began climbing toward the end of 2003, doubling by 2004 and then trebling again by 2007, crossing $60 before soaring to the $100 mark in late 2009 and peaking at an astonishing $187 in early 2011 before falling back partially to about $130. Sesa Goa (later Sesa Sterlite), India's largest private iron ore mining and exporting company, saw its stock price climb from Rs 2 per share in 2002 to Rs 180 in late 2013, before falling back.

That gives some idea of how much money iron ore exporters were making. Smart operators were tempted to break the law and move into areas for which they did not have a mining lease, in the process also cheating the state government of royalties. The politics of iron ore export took over the southern states of Karnataka and Goa. The most infamous operators (but not the only ones) were three Reddy brothers in Karnataka, sons of a police constable. They had dabbled in local politics and small businesses in Karnataka's Bellary district before getting their first mining lease in 2004, just as iron ore prices started climbing. They used that to mine in areas for which no lease had been given, getting immunity through their political connections. Iron ore barons also managed the extraordinary feat of illegally exporting 3.5 million tons of confiscated iron ore lying at Belekeri port on Karnataka's Karwar coast—a scam that would have been manifestly impossible without political cover.

With their newfound riches, the local iron ore miners acquired vast mansions, fleets of luxury automobiles, private aircraft, and helicopters. They organized flashy weddings and hired private armies for protection and enforcement. One of the Reddy brothers had a gold throne said to weigh fifteen kilos (33 pounds). More important, they could bid for serious political power, including ministerships in the state government. They nearly brought down the BJP's uncooperative chief minister, B. S. Yeddyurappa, before he sued for peace. Nemesis finally caught up in the guise of a state ombudsman's report. Two of the three Reddy brothers went to jail for different periods, and some close relatives faced arraignment, while Yeddyurappa (indicted by the ombudsman on an unrelated issue) walked out of the BJP. The party lost power in the state following the 2013 assembly elections. A chastened Yeddyurappa soon returned to a BJP that was glad to have him back. Scams often cause only short-term political damage in India.

If the problem in coal was that the government was caught totally off guard by changing market realities, which made nonsense of its mine allocation rules, the issue in iron ore was that the mining sector was poorly regulated and there was no effective oversight, while state governments were mortgaged to miners. In the sale of the radio spectrum used for mobile telephones, only the "convenient" aspects of the sector regulator's recommendations were adopted by the minister.

In their different ways, these showed how political operators could team up with business cronies to extract or hand over vast amounts of "economic rent." All three were also a part of the process of learning how to deal with and regulate businesses that had hitherto been public-sector monopolies and which now had major private players. As Raghuram Rajan wrote in a syndicated newspaper article shortly before he moved from being the government's chief economic adviser to the governor of the Reserve Bank, "Because India's existing economic institutions could not cope with strong growth, its political checks and balances started kicking in to prevent further damage, and growth slowed."[18] That was a polite way of saying that scandals brought the government to a virtual standstill.

Economic growth slowed as the accumulated problems took their toll on investment and on consumer spending habits. Gross capital formation in the private corporate sector nearly halved in five years, from 17.3 percent of GDP in 2007–08 to 9.3 percent in 2012–13. Haunted by sustained inflation and interest rates that were lower than inflation (hence negative "real" interest rates), households doubled investment in unproductive gold, to 2.6 percent of GDP. Bank credit growth had been running at an average annual rate of 25 percent for six years of rapid growth, and then at 20 percent for another four years, but dropped to 9.2 percent, the lowest in living memory. India's vaunted private sector had tripped, and tripped badly.

5

Cronyism in an Arbitrary State

INDIA'S SUGAR INDUSTRY is, and has always been, among the businesses most susceptible to government intervention. With its roots in agriculture, it is politically sensitive, and governments have routinely intervened in everything from the price of cane to the selling, marketing, and distribution of sugar. Mill owners came to terms long ago with having to buy peace with state-level politicians. Even then, the owners of sugar mills in the northern state of Uttar Pradesh (UP) were not prepared for what was to come their way after a newly elected state government sought political brownie points by announcing, in 2012, unusually high prices for the cane that mills buy from farmers.

Overnight, the industry had become unviable. One financial quarter after the next, leading mills like Balrampur, Simbhaoli, Mawana, and Bajaj Hindustan reported losses that, taken together for a year, ran into billions of rupees. When this situation persisted into a second year, mills that feared further losses refused to crush sugarcane at the start of the crushing season. Agitated farmers, their ripe cane beginning to dry out in the fields, took to halting traffic on highways. Faced with a potential crisis, the government resorted to a medieval trap. Even as mill owners were called to a meeting in the state capital of Lucknow, government officials were preparing arrest warrants for some of the sugar barons (it is illegal to refuse to crush cane during the season). Information leaked and the target businessmen went into hiding, as policemen armed with warrants began knocking on the doors of their homes.

Eventually, the businessmen buckled. Accepting an offer of loans to tide them over the immediate liquidity problem, mills started crushing cane even though they were headed for certain losses. The crisis had been papered over with palliatives, but reform of the sugar sector's pricing rules remained unaddressed. Many mills did not (or could not) pay farmers—another criminal offense. Bank loan repayments became overdue, bringing another set of penalties. And so, at the start of a third season of operating under unviable conditions, policemen were out with arrest warrants once again, looking for the mill owners. An angry mill owner, who closed the shutters on his mill and fled the country just hours before the police knocked on his door, said he understood why so many of his compatriots had decided to invest overseas rather than in India. One offered to hand over his sugar mills to the government for free or to be set up as a farmers' cooperative. Stock market valuations had in any case collapsed, so giving away a mill would not have been much of a loss. By the summer of 2015, the government was offering Rs 60 billion as bank loans to the cash-strapped industry so that farmers could be paid for their cane—another palliative because the dues to farmers had crossed Rs 200 billion. Still, the industry began to see a small recovery in its fortunes as market prices rose.

The sugar industry is not alone when it comes to being subjected to irrational policies by governments and politicians. A good part of the reason the country was virtually stopped in its tracks starting from about 2010–11 had to do with the troubled relations between businesses and the agents of the state—trouble that took many forms: questionable methods for granting access to scarce resources, whether assets in the ground like bauxite and iron ore or in the ether like the radio spectrum; kickbacks for dispensing government purchase contracts; arbitrary granting or withholding of approvals, whether environmental clearance for a project or a plain investment decision; extreme interpretations of complicated tax laws, invoking massive penalties; or overcorrection for past failures, as when the Maharashtra chief minister Prithviraj Chavan stopped all building clearances in Mumbai for a year, while he cleaned up the building rules—bringing the real estate business in the city to a halt. All of these raised the cost of doing business in the country. Given the open democratic system, every now and then an issue would erupt as scandal, leading to criminal investigation, arrests by the police, parliamentary inquiry, high-decibel media coverage, protracted disputes in court—and often, while the drama played out over months and years, a halt to decision making.

The history of the second United Progressive Alliance (UPA) government could be written as an elaboration of these problems: the telecom license/spectrum scandal, the coal mine allocation scandal, the controversies over environmental clearances, numerous cases of what came to be called "tax terrorism," and public outcry over contracts given out for the Commonwealth Games of 2010. The tax cases alone were eye-popping because of the numbers involved and also because some of them invoked issues that went back many years. The government defended its right to impose taxes retrospectively, and demanded Rs 110 billion from Vodafone on an offshore business sale, Rs 210 billion from Nokia for withholding tax on royalties paid to its Finnish parent, Rs 50 billion from IBM, and so on (a dollar was worth about Rs 45 at the time, so even in dollars the tax demands were in billions). The most egregious was a tax of Rs 60 billion demanded of Shell on the ground that a wholly owned Indian subsidiary issued underpriced capital to its overseas parent. Shell said with reason that the demand was in effect a tax on foreign direct investment and, like some other companies, took the matter to court.

Vodafone won its case in the Bombay High Court; in an effort to signal a new regime, a newly elected Modi government chose not to go in for an appeal. Further, it promised to put an end to retrospective taxation, but that did not prevent the tax authority from imposing a fresh Rs 202-billion tax on Cairn, the oil company, for the sale of a business eight years earlier. Soon after, the taxman asked foreign portfolio investors to pay tax on profits for six years up to 2013–14—the bill could run to an astronomical Rs 400 billion, it was said. The government initially declared that this was not retrospective taxation, only a legacy problem; the finance minister even spelled out all the good things he could do with the money.[1] But as shivers ran through the stock market and foreign investors began pulling out money, the tax numbers were quickly pared to Rs 6 billion, and then the whole thing was shelved.[2] A former adviser to the finance minister disclosed that the tax notices to foreign institutional investors ran counter to understandings that had already been reached with them through a consultation process in 2013.

The Hunter Hunted?

In the relationship between businessmen and the state, the role of hunter and hunted seems to be interchangeable. Ordinarily, he who pays the piper is supposed to call the tune. But every year, after the finance minister presents the government's annual budget to Parliament, businessmen rate the budget on TV news shows and in the newspapers. India has had no shortage of poor budgets, but there is no year in which the overwhelming majority of businessmen did not rate the budget at 8 on a 10-point scale or better. Brave, and rare, is the businessman who rates the budget at 7 or less. A quarter century after the start of economic reform that was supposed to reduce the role of government in business, businessmen still want to ensure they don't cross the sovereign's path.

Yet it is business that is the main source of funding for political parties; when elections approach, party treasurers start making phone calls. Chief ministers of state governments run by the large national parties often have targets—the amount of money that must be delivered to the party treasurer in New Delhi every month. A political party has fallen on truly bad days if it loses control of important states. In their more candid moments, businessmen and politicians will tell you that there is no direct quid pro quo associated with election funding, other than gaining goodwill. Specific favors from the government in power require separate payment, but on such occasions it is never clear how much of the money stays with the minister or intermediary who collects the funds and how much goes to the party. Public-sector companies are useful too, as sources of patronage and funding—an important reason that there is great reluctance to sell or shut down even the most problematic ones.[3]

The result is a complex relationship between politicians and businessmen, and of course bureaucrats (who, at the end of the day, have to put their signature on a file that allows a questionable decision to go through). While there is plenty of evidence of businessmen bending policy to suit their specific purpose, they are always aware that political power trumps financial power—hence the obsequiousness at budget time. But matters are more complicated since politicians developed greater financial awareness and realized that they were getting relative pennies while businessmen were becoming billionaires. Some, therefore, became businessmen themselves. Rajeev Chandrasekhar, who ran a telecom business before selling out to become an investor (including investments in the media) and a member of Parliament, told James Crabtree of *Financial Times*: "We have a completely unique phenomenon in India, which I call political entrepreneurship, that has taken root in the last five to six years. . . . They [the politicians] are saying: 'We don't want briefcases full of cash and Swiss bank accounts and all that any more. We want to own businesses ourselves. We want equity stakes.' "[4] In turn, businessmen have sought influence and power by joining political parties and entering Parliament. This fusion of business and politics has given India its oligarchs, people who wield financial as well as political clout.

Media power has added spice to the mix. Mukesh Ambani of Reliance (which has featured in its share of controversies) is believed by many to be India's most powerful businessman. He first bought and then took charge of a media company that owns a number of regional-language TV news channels before folding that into investment in a multimedia business that ran mainstream business and English news channels. He then entered a financing arrangement with the promoters of another TV news company that effectively gave him partial ownership rights whenever he wanted it. Another businessman with varied interests, Subhash Chandra, owns the Zee TV network as well as a newspaper in Mumbai. Chandra openly aligns with the BJP and in 2016 entered Parliament with its support. Many businessmen have taken minority stakes, with no obvious control or influence, in a variety of media companies, like Kumar Mangalam Birla, who is a shareholder in the India Today multimedia empire. Gautam Adani, a go-getting businessman widely considered to be close to Narendra Modi, is a passive investor in India TV, promoted by the pro-BJP Rajat Sharma.

Kalanithi Maran runs the Sun TV news and entertainment network across southern India and is the grandnephew of M. Karunanidhi, patriarch of a southern political party, the Dravida Munnetra Kazhagam (DMK). His brother Dayanidhi Maran's story is instructive in exploring the links that cut across business, government, and the media. A first-term member of the Lok Sabha whose party (the DMK) was a member of the ruling coalition in New Delhi, Dayanidhi Maran became the cabinet minister in charge of telecommunications in the first Manmohan Singh government, in 2004. He had to resign in 2007 (over another matter), and now faces charges in court for setting up an illegal telephone exchange at his Chennai residence and for arm-twisting a Chennai businessman to sell his telecom company to a Malaysian businessman. The latter was simultaneously investing in the media business owned by brother Kalanithi at, it was said, an exaggerated price. Later, the government seized Rs 7.4 billion of Dayanidhi's assets, which he alleged was an illegal action. The case remains to be decided, but no one has asked how Manmohan Singh gave Dayanidhi charge of a sector where his brother had business interests, despite the obvious conflict of interest. The links between politics, business, and the media became even murkier when the new government's home ministry held out against renewing the Sun TV group's licenses, citing security issues—a stance that was not shared by either the information and broadcasting ministry or the attorney general to whom the matter was referred. Every TV company would now ask itself questions about its vulnerabilities, hardly a situation that would encourage a free media.

In Andhra Pradesh, Chief Minister Y. S. Rajasekhara Reddy died in a helicopter crash in 2009. Soon his son Jaganmohan Reddy emerged into the limelight as a substantial businessman with several companies, including an ambitious newspaper venture, and then broke away from the Congress to float his own political party. Like Maran, he later faced charges of accumulating no less than Rs 13.4 billion of ill-gotten wealth—allegedly obtained from businessmen for whom his father had done favors. Assets worth Rs 8.6 billion were seized, and he spent time in jail before being bailed out. Here, too, the case is winding its way through court.

It remains to be seen whether these cases stand up to judicial scrutiny. What is interesting is the narrative that shows through the charges: that those at the helm of political parties, or in charge of state governments, extract more than their pound of flesh, either in return for favors granted or through extortion. Often, when the political wheel turns, they get a hard blowback. Populist promises that are sought to be delivered at the cost of companies, as with Uttar Pradesh's sugar mills, make news only tangentially. Businessmen in turn seek protection or advantage by straddling the line that separates business and politics, by financing politicians and political parties, and using media ownership as an additional weapon—of defense, perhaps, or to offer airtime to politicians at election time. The Saradha Group, enmeshed in a financial scandal in West Bengal, also ran a newspaper that had its political biases.

The Roots of Cronyism

The intertwining of business and politics began decades ago, with the socialist desire to control business and limit individual wealth. Through long years of statist intervention, businessmen learned to circumvent the infamous "permit raj" or "license-permit raj." Policies designed ostensibly to curb the power of big business produced contrary results: the largest business houses pocketed the greatest number of licenses to set up industrial units (smaller businessmen found it impossible to negotiate the labyrinth of government regulations). Price controls on everything from paper to tires, and from cement to soap, meant that government decisions could make or destroy businesses, even as black markets of these products flourished. Lobbying with the powers that be in New Delhi became an essential feature of most businesses—and you not only lobbied for yourself but also to put down your competitor. Stringent import controls gave birth to a vibrant smuggling industry that survived because it had political links, while extortionate income tax rates (up to 97 percent at one stage in the early 1970s) made tax evasion a growth industry—and being a tax official a very lucrative career option.

The foundations for the business–politics nexus and for taxmen's rapacity had thus been laid in the 1960s and '70s—a period when it was illegal to produce more than allowed by your industrial license. But businessmen realized that licensing constraints also limited competition, and high import tariffs were a protective wall that allowed them to keep markets to themselves and make comfortable profits, especially if helpful tax laws had provisions that allowed those profits to stay free of tax under certain conditions. Many businesses became flabby operations, prospering despite turning out shoddy goods at high cost. When economic reform followed in the 1990s, some of the business houses that were unprepared for competition dropped by the wayside as markets acquired a cutting edge. Still, policies were often more business friendly rather than market friendly. Whom the government liked or disliked, or whom you had cultivated over the years, could make a difference.

When reforms removed controls on production capacity, imports, and selling prices (among others), elements like environment rules became the new playground for whimsical government conduct, a new kind of license–permit raj. It may have been coincidental, but when the Congress was in office, the businessmen whose projects ran into trouble on environmental grounds invariably happened to be those aligned with parties other than the Congress. Later, when the BJP took office, the businessmen to face the fire were people like the former Congress member and steel magnate, Naveen Jindal. Indeed, Jayanthi Natarajan, briefly environment minister in the Manmohan Singh government, disclosed later that she used to get instructions from Rahul Gandhi (the Congress vice president) on specific projects awaiting environmental clearance—a claim that the Congress quickly denied.

Conglomerate Power

Part of the problem is the structure of India's corporate sector. It is no accident that some of the more influential business families have focused on industries and sectors where the business–government interface is important—the terms of a mining lease, a highway franchise, or a power purchase contract—or where heavy capital investment gets financed by government-owned banks, with the terms of the loan often restructured midway. They have mostly kept away from technology-based sectors and branded consumer goods, where the marketplace usually offers a level playing field and where the rules are clearer.

These families have demonstrated entrepreneurial flair, of course, and have smart businessmen who understand cost control in commodity businesses, or they wouldn't have survived. But all too often when it comes to policymaking, the interests of seventy-five business families have trumped those of 750 million consumers. If they make bad business decisions, more often than not the company "promoter's" interests (that is, shareholding) are protected, while lenders (usually state-owned banks) take the hit—which makes nonsense of the notion of equity being risk capital. Like the keiretsu (and earlier the zaibatsu) in Japan and the chaebol in South Korea, these businessmen have built political relationships over long years, acquiring not just market power but also power over the political system that makes policy. Across East Asia, governments have patronized local businesses as national champions but simultaneously enforced the discipline of facing international competition. In India, crony capitalism flourished for long years behind protective walls and built a high-cost economy full of shoddy goods produced in sub-scale factories. The price was paid by consumers.

There has been enough reform in the past couple of decades to put market power into consumers' hands. But in commodity sectors and natural resources like mineral ores, government intervention has continued to be a critical element, and lobbying can still be vital for business success. Penetrating the government system takes place at several levels. At the top, political deals are made; in the middle, friendly officials get placed in key slots and are bought off with relatively small favors like a preferred posting or the financing of a child's education overseas; and at the bottom lowly functionaries leak vital government documents that provide an inside track on policy formulation. An honest person in such a den will find herself surrounded, and soon resigned to the status quo. The dense and interlocking network of political, social, financial, and media relationships results therefore in a smooth capture of the system. But when it gets in your face—as happened during the term of the second Singh government—it can cause a political, media, and public reaction that spins rapidly out of control. In the case of the Singh government, it led to the electoral rout of 2014.

The bending of the system takes many forms, and it does not always need money. Favors can be justified on the basis of public purpose, like protecting domestic industry (an easy sell to most Indian politicians) or some other social good. Corporate hospitals cornered prime pieces of real estate in return for their promises—almost never fulfilled—to offer free or subsidized treatment to the poor; some did not even build the promised hospitals. When questioned, one hospital said it had promised free treatment, not free beds or sheets.

Reliance's founder Dhirubhai Ambani had an elemental energy about him and, among other things, built a legendary reputation for being able to get suitable government policy passed for his purpose, but it was not just him. Under the supposed threat of Chinese motorcycles and scooters swamping the Indian market, the import duty on these was kept higher than the "peak" customs duty—suggesting some effective lobbying. And recently, when private power companies made wrong bets on fuel (imported coal prices went up sharply), the Modi government's initial response was to ask state-owned Coal India to supply them with cheaper coal (by reducing the quantum that Coal India was auctioning at a higher price).[5]

Sacrificing the interests of state-owned companies to keep businessmen happy is not unusual. Praful Patel as the civil aviation minister was accused of making state-owned Air India vacate flight slots that were quickly taken up by its private-sector competitor, Jet Airways, and of bartering away too many rights to carriers from the Arabian Gulf; Patel has pleaded innocence and responded by taking an accuser to court for defamation. During his successor Ajit Singh's time, Abu Dhabi was given the freedom to operate more flights to and from India, curiously just when that emirate's airline, Etihad, was buying into India's second-largest private carrier, Jet Airways. Meanwhile, whenever governments offer loan write-offs to poor farmers, there is an outcry. But when businessmen run into trouble, the outcome is often different. State-owned banks, frustrated in their efforts to get Vijay Mallya's Kingfisher airline to repay loans, converted part of the loans into equity—but at Rs 64.48 per share when the prevailing market price was Rs 40 and headed lower. The systemic result was what someone called a "festival" of loan write-offs—known more formally as corporate debt restructuring, or CDR. Through the business slowdown of 2012–15, companies that had borrowed from banks negotiated deals that included moratoriums on repayment, reduced rates of interest, and fresh funding.

Fresh CDR cases (admittedly unavoidable to some degree during a business downturn) grew from Rs 700 billion each in 2012 and 2013 to more than Rs 900 billion in 2014, taking the cumulative total to Rs 3,800 billion. In the two-year period up to December 2014, while bank loans to large industry grew by Rs 3,400 billion, fresh CDR cases were of Rs 1,700 billion (or half as much!). At that stage, the outstanding CDR loans of Rs 2,700 billion constituted an astonishing 12.9 percent of all bank loans to large industry (Rs 20.9 trillion). This was separate from bank loans restructured in bilateral deals between individual banks and borrowers—some of which involved ever-greening of loans by simply rolling them over. Tellingly, the failure rate on CDRs rose in two years from 24 percent to 41 percent.[6] A 2015 report by CRISIL, the credit rating agency, put the failure rate for restructured loans in 2011–14 at 40 percent. Religare Research put the expected failure rate in 2015–17 at 50 percent of restructured loans.[7]

The Reserve Bank cracked down on an obvious regulatory loophole and changed the rules on the provisioning required for restructured loans.

Less than a week before that deadline, twenty-three banks approved a particularly large CDR deal—a restructuring of loans and guarantees totaling Rs 75 billion for Pipavav Defence, an additional funding of Rs 45 billion, a two-year moratorium, and a reduction in the interest rate from 14 percent to 11 percent. The company promoter's contribution to the deal: Rs 1.6 billion.[8]

Poor risk assessment capabilities and even poorer banking practices had led to state-owned banks commanding stock market valuations that were almost always lower than book value, sometimes less than half the book value. It was a signal that investors did not trust the accounts of the banks to be telling the full truth. In comparison, most private banks enjoyed valuations that were two to three times book value, sometimes even higher. Addressing the issue, Narendra Modi called bank chiefs to a meeting and promised an end to "phone calls" to bank chiefs (read political interference in loan decisions).[9] Then his government said it would offer fresh capital to only the better-run state-owned banks;[10] the rest would have to fend for themselves (which would be difficult, given their low valuations on the stock market) or shrink their business. It was the first application of market discipline to government-owned banks, and a step to get only the healthier banks to grow. Then the government relented, took a softer line by agreeing to recapitalize all government banks, and made this a part of a broader package to change the way banks were run.

More effective pressure on the banks to change their behavior came from the Reserve Bank, which felt that enough delaying had gone on, and asked that banks make full disclosures of all stressed assets by March 2017. From early 2016, banks started announcing sharp increases in problematic loans. Banks had resisted fuller disclosure, fearing loss of public confidence; instead, this greater openness increased faith in the banks and some of them saw their share prices increase.

A Low-Trust Society

India is at a halfway point where underperforming institutions coexist uncomfortably with overzealous ones, creating stress, conflict, and loss—especially when venality or whimsicality in one is matched by self-righteousness in the other. As an example, the country has no effective way of regulating mining practices. As another, the Supreme Court issued a sweeping order to cancel 122 telecom licenses—hitting amidships a company like Norway's Telenor, which had bought into one of the companies that had been issued a license. It invested $1.1 billion for a two-thirds stake and then a further billion dollars to build the business. Overnight, the company had no business left.

Second, the setting of rules is defective. Legislation is often poorly drafted and can create as many problems as solutions. The law on nuclear liability ran counter to standard international practice, and the one on land acquisition left the business world saying that the processes involved would inordinately delay projects. Contracts for complex projects that underestimated project risks have led to disputes or renegotiation. Private contracting parties are known to overbid in order to cover unforeseen risk, raising project costs. The resolution of disputes is slow; the delay often does more harm than the original infraction.

Third, within the government, the incentive system is perverse. There is no penalty for inaction or delay in decision making, but quick decisions meant to speed things up might invite trouble for the result-oriented official in case a decision goes wrong. Tax officials, under pressure to meet revenue targets that are set unrealistically high, feel obliged to take the most extreme positions when determining tax liability, and then appeal every negative verdict all the way to the highest court. Both arbitration and the courts involve slow processes, which are to the advantage primarily of the intermediaries: arbitrators and lawyers.

Fourth, bureaucratic obstructionism has been honed into a fine art, indeed a way of life. Anyone with the power to say yes or no becomes a gatekeeper who has to be placated; the spoils system is institutionalized such that, in many offices, the income is shared up and down the hierarchy so that everyone is compromised. Refuse to play ball and you might be sent to manage the archives.

Finally, there is a pervasive lack of the trust that is at the heart of any smoothly functioning system. Politicians mistrust markets, which reciprocate. Governments mistrust businessmen's motives, while businessmen try to figure out whether an obfuscating bureaucrat is being conscientious or just angling for a payoff. The media are supposed to be a skeptical watchdog, but new ownership patterns and financial pressures have disempowered many. The man in the street simply says *"Sab chor hain"* (everyone's a thief)—the stance that helped a new formation, the Aam Aadmi Party, sweep state polls in Delhi in 2015, winning sixty-seven of seventy seats; its election symbol is a broom. The courts have been sounding like the Red Queen, decreeing "Off with their heads" (all iron ore mines to be closed, all telecom licenses to be canceled, all coal mine allocations to be scrapped). Put it all together, and the system is manifestly dysfunctional.

Writing two decades ago, Francis Fukuyama compared what he considered low-trust and high-trust societies, arguing that it was the latter that do well economically.[11] Only societies with a high degree of social trust are able to create large, efficient, and flexible organizations, which Fukuyama associated with economic success. Trust also lowers administrative costs and improves institutional reliability. Low trust leads to dishonesty; the result of pervasive sub-optimality is that everyone tries to game the system.

But countries also get a chance to refresh and reboot. With a new government in office in 2014, the narrative of widespread and pervasive corruption paused as everyone concerned took the measure of a strong prime minister who had campaigned against corruption. Indeed, the Modi government's first couple of years in office were notably free of scandal. But unless the funding of political parties and elections comes aboveboard, problems will inevitably recur.

How Projects Get Stuck

One of the common themes of the economic slowdown has been that industrial projects did not get moving. Studying some of the biggest among them shows why. The London-based Anil Agarwal learned the hard way that access to mineral resources in India could mean getting embroiled in politics. His Vedanta group decided to set up an aluminum project in Odisha, a state whose people are as poor as its bowels are rich in mineral deposits, including bauxite, which is the main raw material for making aluminum. Vedanta's was to be perhaps the largest industrial-cum-mining project in Odisha in more than three decades. Tens of thousands of crores' worth of investment hung in the balance as controversies raged for years over everything from land acquisition to the size of projects and the environmental damage resulting from mining activity. In Agarwal's case, the environment ministry, and later the Supreme Court, refused to give permission for mining bauxite from a hilltop—which is where bauxite is usually found—in the state's Lanjigarh area, chiefly because the local tribals (mostly animists) believed that their god Niyam Raja lived on top of the mountain.

The case had become a cause célèbre, in part because Vedanta was already a controversy-ridden company. Rahul Gandhi, seeking to build for himself a pro-poor image, visited Lanjigarh more than once and declared to the tribals that he would be their soldier in Delhi. At the remote mountain site of one of his meetings, there still lay half-buried in the grass the plastic seat of a Western-style toilet, erected hurriedly in a bamboo hut, apparently for the use of the princeling politician. Civil society activists, homegrown as well as international, saw in the fight between mining company and local tribals a real-life manifestation of James Cameron's allegorical film *Avatar*. However poetic, though, it would be misleading to see in the local Kondh tribals' poverty-stricken lives any of the lyrical qualities of *Avatar*'s Na'vi. On the one hand, it was undeniable that bauxite mining would be disruptive in a pristine world of forested hillsides watered by crystal-clear streams and cooled by a gentle breeze. On the other, the project would give the state government thousands of crores of rupees each year as revenue from royalty and mining cesses (taxes), not to mention other general taxes. According to one reckoning by a senior state government functionary, such receipts from the state's stalled mining and metals projects would double the government's revenue; at least some of that money would probably have been spent to improve the lives of tribals who ranked low on any human development indicator.

After a decade of waiting, Agarwal finally conceded that it was a mistake to have started the investment. Company spokesmen suggested conspiracy: global aluminum giants wanted to prevent Vedanta from emerging as a challenger in the world aluminum market, using India's abundant bauxite; or the Congress government in New Delhi was spiting Anil Agarwal, who was seen to be politically aligned with the Odisha state government, run by a regional party. Whether conspiracy or not, Agarwal conceded defeat.

He was not the only one. POSCO, the Korean steel company, waited for a decade from 2005 for permission to set up an iron ore mining project linked to a 12-million-ton steel plant and related port project in Odisha. The investment rivaled Vedanta's. But there were disputes over acquiring land from protesting landowners and occupants, delays in getting environmental clearance, and then the rules changed on how mining contracts could be given. By 2015 the company was pretty much ready to pull up its tent and leave. For all practical purposes, Odisha's two largest investment projects were dead—along with a joint venture between the government-owned Odisha Mining Corporation and the international mining giant Rio Tinto to extract iron ore, which had been in limbo for more than fifteen years. With these and other projects gone, the state government would be substantially poorer because of large revenue streams that would now not materialize, civil society activists would go looking for new battles against industrial and mining projects, and the poor in one of India's poorest states would be left to their poverty. It was arguably the worst of all outcomes.

Businessmen get fed up too. There have to be many things wrong with an environment in which entrepreneurs prefer to invest overseas rather than in their home market. Quite a few have also shifted residence overseas, becoming non-resident Indians; as many of them confess privately, life and doing business are much easier elsewhere.

Embarrassing Rankings

The World Bank's annual rating of countries on *Doing Business 2015* featured India in a miserable 142nd place, in a list of 189 countries. More tellingly, India ranked a poor sixth among eight South Asian nations. The ranking is a composite of scores on ten issues: what it takes to start a business, deal with construction permits, get electricity, register property, get credit, protect investors, pay taxes, trade across borders, enforce contracts, and resolve insolvency.

India did quite well on getting credit (though most small and medium businesses might disagree) and protecting investors—reflecting the steady improvement in the supervision of capital markets. But it was close to the bottom in getting permits for construction (an area in which builders and politicians have built a powerful nexus in many cities and states, using deliberately opaque and complicated rules) and enforcing contracts—almost certainly because of the inordinate time that courts take to dispose of cases. On some parameters, India featured at or near the bottom of the list. The World Bank's listing has become an annual exercise in naming and shaming the country.

On Transparency International's Corruption Perceptions Index, India did better, ranking 85th in a list of 174 countries in 2014 (the 2013 rank was 94). While judgments on such matters are subjective, and the sample of respondents is skewed to international businessmen, India was perceived as less corrupt than China (ranked 100th) and Russia (136th) but worse than South Africa and Brazil (ranked 67th and 69th, respectively).

At the end of its second five-year term, the scandal-plagued Manmohan Singh government finally started work on a project to address the ease of doing business (or lack of it) in the country. Taking note of the World Bank's list of multiple clearances required for getting started or shutting down, and for everything in between, the industry ministry zeroed in on digitization as the way to improve the country's unflattering rankings. As conceived, some 200 clearances (or "services," as they were christened) could be applied for online. Each application would be tracked and no applicant would have to visit a government office. Questions on an application would have to be posed digitally, there would be an electronic trail, and delays in giving approvals would require explanation. The project, in the works for more than two years, eventually got going in a skeletal fashion in early 2014 with a couple of clearances online. The Modi government picked up the threads, launched its eBiz initiative, and declared it a mission objective to improve the country's score to 50 in the World Bank rankings. It's going to take some doing, not least because many of the issues lie outside the control of the central government and are with state and local governments and the courts. Still, the initial efforts met with some success because for both doing business as well as reducing corruption, the rankings improved a few notches.

Government Capabilities, Institutions, and "Good" Capitalism

If the experience of the past couple of decades has taught India anything, it is that private entities cannot compensate beyond a limited extent for the failures of the government. The government's ability to deliver on a wide variety of fronts has to be improved substantially, especially when potentially transformational projects have been drawn up for building transport networks, industrial hubs, communication backbones, and new urban centers. A railway line from Jammu to the Kashmir valley should not be promised for completion in five years and be less than half-done after thirteen years. Three state-run companies were to lay a national optical-fiber network by the end of 2013; yet by March 2015 less than 10 percent of 250,000 gram panchayats (vvillage-level local government) had been connected.[12] The failures of the public health and education systems have been fully and repeatedly documented.

It is possible to circumvent public-sector failures by asking private companies to lay the fiber network and to expect private educators to pick up the slack—though these face accusations of charging exorbitant fees and of making false claims to get certification. It is useful to remember that it is precisely the decision to ask the private sector to take on the task of building infrastructure that has caused so many companies to be mired in heavy debt and stuck with disputes over half-finished projects. The risks in such long-gestation projects with multiple uncertainties are high, the likelihood of deviation from the intended results therefore almost certain, and a logjam guaranteed if there is no effective mechanism for resolving disputes quickly. In any case, the effective provision of "merit goods" like public health services and "public goods" like clean air, as well as tasks like the regulation of infrastructure sectors that are thrown open to private investment (many of them natural monopolies where market discipline is not feasible), are to be done primarily or only by public agencies. If government capacities are not improved when it comes to setting rules, regulation, supervision, and dispute settlement, if not also project execution and service provision, the country is setting itself up for more systemic failures. At its root, the issue that arrests a country's development is the lack of institutional capacity—as Daron Acemoglu and James A. Robinson have powerfully argued.[13] All too little attention is being paid to this fundamental issue as governments of every hue seek to appoint party loyalists to head important public institutions.

As for oligarchs and crony capitalism, William Baumol and his co-authors wrote many years ago about bad capitalism and good capitalism.[14] The first category, they said, included state-directed and oligarchic capitalism; the second included "big-firm" and entrepreneurial capitalism. Indians will disagree among themselves on the virtues of state-directed capitalism. Some will contend that it has worked well in many East Asian economies, but those are corporatist states whereas India remains anarchically individualistic. It is hard therefore to disagree with Baumol's conclusion that an economy runs smoothly when there is a healthy combination of entrepreneurial and big-firm capitalism. Both, fortunately, are more visible in India now than ever before.

Big firms can tap into economies of scale, finance innovation and research, invest in more efficient processes, and in general contribute to improving system productivity—if they are made to function in a competitive environment and properly regulated. The country needs many more such firms. Meanwhile, entrepreneurial capitalism is flourishing in some sectors: e-commerce ventures and the tech-oriented businesses are examples. Products flowing out of in-house research have made a difference to enterprises in the fields of pharmaceuticals and automobiles. But technology-driven innovations remain relatively rare. India needs much more of both big-firm and entrepreneurial capitalism.

As for state capitalism itself, it is alive if not well. The Modi government is not averse to selling state-owned companies if the alternative is closure, but it is focused more on making them efficient, something previous governments have attempted and failed. The real problem with privatization is that most of the people with the money to buy large state-owned companies are those running the conglomerates—and that would hardly be an improvement in terms of market structures or power balance. A second set of buyers would be foreign companies, but selling them large state-owned companies would be politically impossible.

To its credit, the Modi government has moved to clean up the interface between business and government. The scandals over handing out scarce natural resources (like mineral ores and radio spectrum) as largesse to favored ones are unlikely to recur because auctioning has been accepted as the way to go. In the effort to get legacy issues out of the way, the government has enacted a new bankruptcy law, and another law to simplify dispute settlement between private and government parties. It has also announced an end to retrospective taxation—though this is still to be seen. When the promised new laws on bankruptcy and dispute resolution materialize, they will hopefully address some of the issues that have destroyed the business environment in recent years. But laws are only as good as their effectiveness, and in India it is easy to block them through bureaucratic maneuvering and dilatory court procedures. Reform of judicial processes has to be an essential element of broader reform, but judges who are eager when it comes to pronouncing *obiter dicta* from the bench are surprisingly blind to the fundamental problems of the justice delivery system. Some obvious solutions to reduce inordinate judicial delays—ending the practice of repeated adjournments, reducing the time provided for oral arguments, and relying more on written submissions, or grouping similar cases—await widespread adoption.

Other than public sector and institutional failure, India's business environment has been poisoned by oligarchic capitalism—business conglomerates that try to gain power over the political executive, even more than seeking market power in any specific industry. It is no surprise that some fifteen conglomerates account for troubled bank loans that represent a major part of all stressed banking assets. Conglomerates with the ability to influence rule-setters have been present particularly in the infrastructure sectors, and have also moved purposefully into new areas that are being opened up—including defense manufacture where the quality of government interface is crucial. It is useful to recall what Dwight D. Eisenhower said as he left office as US president in 1961. He used his final address to warn against the development of a military–industrial complex that influences government policy. In India, regulatory capture is already a familiar phenomenon.

Raghuram Rajan and Luigi Zingales, while arguing the obvious point that markets cannot function without the very visible hand of government regulation, listed four pillars on which to build policy and regulation: avoid the concentration of productive wealth in a few hands; create a safety net for the people (not companies) who lose out in competition; keep borders open for international competition; and keep driving home to the public the benefits of competitive markets.[15] It is hard to improve on that to-do list, but it is also harder to deliver than to prescribe.

6

Manufacturing

A HANDICAPPED SECTOR

THE HOLY GRAIL of India's industrial policy has become the "revival" of the manufacturing sector or, more correctly, its faster growth. The generally accepted narrative is that unlike most other countries, India has been unable to use its abundance of cheap labor to make the natural transition from the primary sector of the economy (agriculture) to the secondary sector (industry, especially labor-intensive manufacturing, but also construction, electricity, mining, etc.). Instead, India has developed its tertiary sector (services) somewhat precociously. Consequently, the share of manufacturing in GDP has hovered around a fairly low 17 percent (out of a total secondary sector share of more than 30 percent), while services account for 51 percent.[1] One of the Modi government's signature programs, therefore, is to "Make in India."

If this thesis about India's failed manufacturing thrust is correct, other emerging-market economies should have a bigger manufacturing sector. They do, but mostly in East Asia and in the transition economies of Central Europe. In the first category, manufacturing in three economies (South Korea, China, and Thailand) accounts for more than 30 percent of GDP, while in another three (Indonesia, Malaysia, and Philippines) it is at 20 percent or more. In Central Europe, the major economies (Czech and Slovak Republics and Hungary) are in the 20–25 percent range. Among the rich economies, only Germany has a manufacturing sector that accounts for more than 20 percent of GDP. However, quite a few developing countries, across three continents, have roughly the same percentage as India or even lower, countries like Turkey, Brazil, and South Africa.[2] So it is not true that India's manufacturing sector has been uniquely dwarfed. However, it remains true that India has missed many opportunities for developing manufacturing activity—opportunities that East Asian countries took advantage of.

More than relative shares of GDP, the real worry has been about the skewed distribution of the labor force across sectors. Some 47 percent of India's total workforce of about 500 million people remains engaged in agriculture and allied activities (fisheries, dairying, poultry, etc.). This is usually low-income work, so they generate only 18 percent of GDP. The remaining 53 percent of the workforce generates the remaining 82 percent of GDP. But this is not as unusual as it might sound. In Thailand, one of the most successful manufacturing countries, those in agriculture continue to represent 40 percent of the workforce. In China, despite its considerable success in building a factory sector, 35 percent of its workforce is still engaged in agriculture, generating about 10 percent of its GDP.[3] Like it or not, the transition away from agriculture as the primary source of employment is going to be slow, even if labor-intensive manufacturing activity flourishes.

In India, the ratio of non-agricultural to agricultural income (82:18), and of non-agricultural to agricultural labor, shows that the average income generated per head in non-agricultural occupations is more than four times what it is in agriculture. The most practical way to raise income levels at the bottom of the pile, therefore, is to move workers from agriculture to industry and services (though that may not reduce inequality).[4] Hence, we see the crucial importance of industries such as those producing ready-made garments, which involve labor-intensive manufacturing and create large-scale employment if done in organized factories where productivity and therefore wages are usually higher than in the unorganized sector.

Man-Made Hurdles

India so far has had much more of unorganized than organized manufacturing—an imbalance that is largely the result of policy biases. The official statistics say that barely 12 million people are employed in the private, organized sector and fewer than 30 million in all organized activity (about 6 percent of the total workforce).[5] These numbers, widely used and cited, may underestimate the reality; it is curious that membership of the Employees' Provident Fund Organisation, restricted to employees of units with at least twenty people, is about 50 million. The organized sector, consisting of units that need only ten employees (twenty, if no electrical power is used), must logically employ even more, while those employed by various governments are another 10 million or more. A 60-million figure would mean that 22 percent of the non-agricultural workforce is engaged in the organized sector. While appropriate policies need to be evolved, statistical confusion must be addressed as well.

Whatever the statistical truth may be, employers are disinclined to hire workers because of the rigidities introduced in the labor market by the government—regarding flexible labor practices (important for seasonal industries), women working the night shift, restrictions on overtime work, and restraints on employers to retrench and close down unviable units. An employer who cannot lay off workers if business slows down is unlikely to hire in the first place and will try to automate as much as possible—precisely the opposite of what a judicious labor policy in India should achieve.

It is not an accident that the labor-intensive product segments where India has had notable success do not involve factory-based manufacturing as traditionally understood. One example is diamond cutting and polishing—which employs about a million people, mostly organized into small (<10) worker units and generates exports of about $25 billion. The availability of low-cost workers and the quick adoption of new technologies have together propelled the country to global leadership in the business and helped Indian diamond traders compete with and in some ways displace the once-dominant Jewish businesses in Antwerp's diamond trade. Cutting and polishing typically add between 60 percent and 100 percent to the value of a rough diamond. According to trade sources, the cost of the operation in India is only 60 percent of that in China (a rising power in the business) and even less in relation to costs in other countries. The availability of low-cost labor has helped also in the export of handicrafts, another large export item. An important component of this category is the labor-intensive business of weaving hand-knotted carpets.

However, neither carpet weaving nor diamond cutting is mainstream "manufacturing" activity, which has been hobbled not just by labor policy but also industrial policy. From the 1970s, the government reserved hundreds of manufacturing sectors for small-scale companies. These reserved sectors included precisely the sectors where China cornered world markets by setting up large-scale production, such as making garments, shoes/leather goods, and toys. Indian manufacturers were prevented by law from competing in these sectors and tapping the efficiency gains from large-scale manufacture, leading to bizarre consequences. Garment exporters were forced to set up dozens of units under different names to get around the size restrictions, but they would still be unable to fully exploit the economies of scale.

India was perhaps the only country where the manufacture (more correctly, assembly) of TV sets was in the small-scale sector, creating a hothouse clutch of import-dependent companies that basically indulged in "screwdriver manufacture" by importing sub-assemblies from East Asia and screwing them together in sheds. Naturally, they were unable to stand up to import competition when the market was thrown open. Even the manufacture of room air conditioners was dominated by small-scale units, which got special rates of excise duties and could therefore outsell larger companies. Small-scale power-loom weaving and finishing outfits (some of them with just a single loom or a single crimping machine) got special electricity rates or even free power in states like Maharashtra and Tamil Nadu, putting large, organized-sector weaving mills (that paid better wages) out of business. A garment exporter who was interviewed for this book pointed out that the polyester cloth he imported from China was made from polyester chips exported to that country from India!

Even after import licensing was abolished and global giants could sell their produce in India, production within the country continued to be reserved for small-scale units—who, naturally, could not compete. The markets for many consumer products were soon dominated by imported goods. The small-scale reservations went slowly, as did some (not all) of the aberrations in excise rates and power tariffs; the reservations finally disappeared only in 2015—twenty-four years after industrial and import de-licensing were announced as part of the 1991 package of reforms. By then, India had missed many manufacturing opportunities.

Less important than labor policy and small-scale reservation, but significant inhibitors nevertheless, were three other policy hurdles. The first of these was the policy on industrial location. The logic of export-oriented units would ordinarily prompt companies to locate factories near ports and other transport hubs, for ease of moving inputs and the final output to and from the factory—the cost of an export container unit could go up 20 percent if it had to be transported inland. This explained why China focused on its coastal zones for developing export-oriented industries. But policy in India was inward-looking and dictated that units be set up in industrially backward areas. There was of course a reason why these areas were backward—they were inaccessible, or unsuitable for locating industry because of distance from either raw materials or product markets or both. The biggest tax concessions were given to the most difficult-to-reach areas in hill states like Sikkim, because they were seen as the most disadvantaged. These then attracted investments from companies that looked solely to exploit the tax loopholes. If the tax law was changed, companies pulled down shutters virtually overnight. Such artificially stimulated industrial centers continue to flourish in places like Himachal Pradesh's Baddi, across the state border from Punjab.

A bizarre oddity, since abolished, was the freight equalization policy. This decreed that steel be offered at the same price everywhere in the country, irrespective of location and transport costs. This instantly disadvantaged eastern India, which has a great deal of iron ore and coal, and where much of the country's steel capacity has been located. Logically, downstream engineering units should have been set up nearby, but the freight equalization policy took away eastern India's location advantage, and its once-flourishing engineering sector went into decline for this and other reasons.

Finally, there was the issue of choice of industries. The East Asian countries focused on the logical step of setting up light, labor-intensive industries, since what a poor economy has is a surplus of labor. In contrast, India chose to emphasize capital-intensive heavy industry. In this, it copied Soviet Russia, which had a very different resource mix: it had surplus land, not labor, and it needed heavy industry for mechanizing farms and for making weapons to fight wars.

Overriding all this, the critical difference between industrial policy in India and some of the East Asian countries was that while some were like India and started with import substitution, they switched focus quickly to export markets. This helped their industries stay competitive. India (in part because of a larger domestic market) stayed much longer with its import-substitution policy, in pursuit of which it set up high tariff walls and subjected imports to tight licensing. Protected domestic manufacturers lost their competitive edge, and with that all hope of winning export markets—at a time when world trade saw sustained rapid growth and presented a massive opportunity. The country's share of world merchandise trade dropped from about 2.5 percent at Independence in 1947 to less than 0.5 percent four decades later.

Permeating the entire system was the bureaucratic maze that was the veins and arteries (often clogged) of the government system. You entered that bloodstream at your peril. Everything that a manufacturer needed to do required multiple clearances from a plethora of government offices.[6] Before the reform process began, it was a Kafkaesque world whose black humor escaped only the bureaucrats and politicians who operated the system. As Jagdish Bhagwati and Arvind Panagariya wrote, India had become a "laughing stock" around the world: "Could anyone take seriously a country that would not let companies expand licence capacity and would prevent diversification of production?"[7] It was a world in which a five-year-old car fetched a higher price in the resale market than a new car because the latter's price was controlled by the government; importantly, new cars were accessible to government employees by special quota.

Many, not all, of these absurdities have been removed in painfully slow stages, starting from the mid-1970s when tax rates began to be lowered from the heights they had reached, and followed in the 1980s by such innovations as the "broad-banding" of industrial licenses: if you had a license to make one kind of product, you could also make a related one. The sharp break came only in 1991, with sweeping de-licensing and deregulation. Unfortunately, the bureaucratic maze has survived. Where old controls went, new ones were introduced. In 1998, the then finance minister Yashwant Sinha promised an end to the "inspector raj." But a policy statement issued in 2011 (two full decades after 1991) recognized that the average manufacturing company had to comply with seventy laws, face multiple inspections, and file as many as 100 returns in a year. Bear in mind that these returns were being filed (or not filed) by small and medium enterprises that accounted for 45 percent of manufacturing output and 40 percent of merchandise exports.

To its credit, the Modi government has introduced some amount of self-certification, but an army of inspectors still exists to check on the implementation of many rules—including the requirement that every factory or establishment maintain a "lime register" detailing when the last lime coat had been applied to the factory walls (lime being an old precursor to contemporary paint). Since no one can possibly follow all the countless rules, there are numerous opportunities for inspectors to make some quick money. If an employer allows staff to work part of the time from home and therefore does not maintain an attendance register, it runs foul of the Shops and Establishments Act.

Manufacturing and Services: Four Differences

If policy has been the primary constraint in the way of manufacturing growth, what lessons can be learned from India's success in service sector activity and exports, and can they be applied to the manufacturing sector? One explanation put out sometimes is that the government did not "interfere" with sectors like software services, characterized as a "quintessential example of India's rise," while the counterproductive attention that the government paid to manufacturing led to the stunting of that sector.[8] This is only partially correct, because the tech sector did not grow independently; rather, it was built on a foundation provided by the government. It is the government that set up the key institutes of technology that produced the leaders of companies like Infosys and HCL; the government (as well as private organizations) set up other engineering colleges that produced the bulk of the tech manpower. Bengaluru, which has become India's "Silicon Plateau," emerged as a tech city because the government housed a series of technological and scientific facilities there, like the Indian Space Research Organization and Bharat Electronics. And of course it was the government that provided the satellite communications links that facilitated the birth of a business that could base itself in India and serve customers halfway around the world. So it would be more correct to say that government action was supportive of tech exports but invariably counterproductive when it came to manufacturing activity and merchandise exports.

A key explanation for success in one and failure in the other is that India had no domestic market for the software services that existed in the United States and elsewhere. The tech companies that started up knew from the beginning that they would have to serve a global market and face global competition; this was different from manufacturers, for example, of cement or paper, who could afford to be satisfied with the pickings in the domestic market, especially if they came with tariff protection.

A second key difference was that the primary resource for the tech sector (trained engineers) and for business process outsourcing (other low-cost white-collar employees) came cheap by international standards and gave companies in the sector a massive cost arbitrage opportunity. In contrast, manufacturers faced a cost disadvantage. Das's point is entirely valid that India's industrial infrastructure was inefficient, insufficient, and far from inexpensive, putting manufacturers at a disadvantage on both efficiency and cost vis-à-vis their counterparts in other countries.

The third difference was that the exporters of business services (including software) plugged into and serviced the leading corporations in the world, even as global firms like IBM and Accenture moved their back-office work to India. Similar intra-firm trade in merchandise, a growing part of world trade, excluded India because the country did not offer scale manufacturing in more than a handful of sectors, if that.

Finally, India has not allowed large retail networks to set up base in India. The sourcing requirements of global retail chains would have encouraged scale manufacture that would have led in turn to export success. With the exclusion of the big firms and big supply chains, the country has found itself relatively excluded from global supply networks—and this has stunted export growth. The World Trade Organization (WTO) quotes the United Nations

Conference on Trade and Development (UNCTAD) in its World Trade Report for 2013 to say that "upwards of two-thirds of world trade now takes place within multinational companies or their suppliers, underlining the growing importance of global supply chains." India, because of its restrictive policies, has allowed the wholesale globalization of production and supply chains to pass it by.

In everyday terms, therefore, India does not have the equivalent of an Infosys or a Tata Consultancy Services when it comes to merchandise trade. Nor has the country made it easy for Wal-Mart or IKEA to set up store chains in India, the way that IBM and Accenture have set up back offices for business process outsourcing. Some of this can still be done, though the political reluctance to allow a free run to large retail trade chains is a constraint. The difficulty is that, unlike in services, India does not have the early advantage in developing merchandise trade, while its still-deficient infrastructure and complicated operating environment for business will continue to be handicaps in the foreseeable future. Also, other low-income countries like Bangladesh and Vietnam provide price competition, especially in employment-intensive industries. If India wants to do better, it has to raise its game or consider different strategies.

"Make in India"

India is once again striving to support the growth of manufacturing with industrial policy. That phrase is now out of fashion in many countries, which have yielded to the belief that markets should be left free to develop. But industrial policy has existed in virtually every country that has enjoyed manufacturing success, starting in the hoary past when the Chinese protected for many centuries their monopoly knowledge of how to produce silk. It was manifest again in how Britain developed its wool-weaving industry in the Middle Ages (by encouraging weaving experts to settle in England, and then by taxing raw wool exports to the weaving center of Flanders). More recently, industrial policy has been practiced by Japan's ministry of international trade and industry, as well as by the rest of rapid-growth Asia, including two of the initial tiger economies, South Korea and Taiwan. India has tried it too, for decades, the crucial difference being that India's industrial policy was essentially import-substituting and used high tariffs as a policy tool that created uncompetitive and capital-intensive rather than labor-intensive industries; this gave birth to lobbies that wanted continued protection.

Strangely, the reborn industrial (or manufacturing) policy of 2011 and the announcement of incentives for specific sectors were focused yet again on import substitution in capital-intensive sectors and the provision of direct or indirect subsidies. Worried that the exploding market for telecom products as well as solar energy panels would lead to enormous import bills, policymakers sought to encourage local manufacture of semiconductor fabrication units, to compete with the world leader Taiwan—an objective that most countries would consider foolhardy. The project also ran the risk of prodding downstream tariff protection for a possibly uncompetitive domestic fabrication unit. Inevitably, as these things go, the government in 2011 offered a handsome 40 percent capital subsidy to the mother industry of silicon fabrication. In turn, domestic solar panel production was pushed as an alternative to imports from the world leader in such panels, China—except that it would add to the capital cost of solar energy installations by perhaps 20 percent. Power distribution companies were asked to buy a minimum amount of solar energy generated from domestic equipment. So, yet again, the government was simultaneously chasing multiple objectives (clean energy but also domestic production), and making cost compromises that could result in that familiar problem: a high-cost infrastructure.

The drive hasn't gotten very far. A couple of local firms showed interest in setting up chip fabrication units, but could not raise the capital required. Four years after the policy was announced, no investment had taken place. And the preference given for local manufacture of solar panels provoked protests from the United States, which has dragged India to the WTO's dispute settlement mechanism. There is also a cautionary tale about such capital subsidies: the government offered one to companies making equipment for generating wind energy. This led to the setting up of many wind farms, but little generation of energy from wind—in part because of the quality of the equipment installed.

The manufacturing thrust has since made a comeback as Narendra Modi's "Make in India" initiative, with its focus on twenty-five specific sectors. Over a home-cooked lunch in 2015 in his Udyog Bhavan office, facing New Delhi's Rajpath expanse, the then secretary for industrial policy and promotion, Amitabh Kant, denied with some vehemence that the program was protectionist, but added somewhat contrarily that electronics manufacture had an 8 percent cost disadvantage which the government would have to neutralize. He also said that sectors like steel faced problems because of dumping by Chinese producers who are faced with surplus capacity (the government later imposed minimum import prices). More positively, Kant also talked of making the country part of the global supply chain, but the government's restrictive policy on the big international retail chains would need modification—and was done in due course.

Kant has a well-earned reputation as a go-getting officer; he created two of India's best-known tourism promotion programs, for Kerala state and nationally, and did the planning and difficult spadework for the Delhi–Mumbai Industrial Corridor. As the man in charge of industrial policy, he said he looked forward to demonstrating some early successes: companies were apparently willing to invest for creating 10 gigawatts (GW) of solar panel capacity. He also listed the policy changes: opening up new sectors (like defense and railways) to more foreign investment; a "quality audit" of about a million small and medium enterprises (SMEs), to pick out the best—and presumably offer them support in various ways; and addressing reverse tariff protection (inputs commanding higher import tariffs than the finished product). Foreign direct investment into India surged in 2015–16 to record levels, and seemed to be headed for further growth in 2016–17.

There has been also the focus on improving India's rank when it comes to the ease of doing business. As detailed in the previous chapter, the intention is to minimize paperwork, reduce the number of approvals required, make the whole process digital (therefore transparent) and time-bound, and expand the scope for self-certification. If it works, some of the rigors of getting clearances for setting up a project should disappear, but many of the issues that give India a poor ranking on ease of doing business lie beyond the pale of the central government.

Planning Big on Infrastructure

Meanwhile, there is the old problem of India's poor infrastructure. The stretched transport networks (rail and road), the routine clogging at ports, and the endemic shortage of grid power that forces companies to generate their own electricity at higher cost (though on a smaller scale than before)—these have been for long years some of the primary constraints when it comes to competitive manufacturing. Other constraints include barriers to the free inter-state movement of goods. The Modi government has worked hard to address these issues, and the energetic exertions of some of his ministers should be expected to make change visible in a few years. But in the absence of overnight solutions, the share of manufacturing in GDP, or the ratio of merchandise exports to GDP, is unlikely to increase significantly for another five years, if not longer. The target of getting manufacturing to account for

25 percent of GDP by 2022 (from a base of 17 percent) looks like a case of vaunting ambition.

Still, some solutions have been in the works for years—like the proposed freight corridors designed to connect industrial centers in the northern hinterland to ports on the western and eastern coasts. The rapid rail services that are planned will use double-stack container cars traveling at three times the current speeds, with intermodal nodes and new urban centers en route acting as manufacturing hubs. The other "great white hope" is the gigantic project known as the Delhi–Mumbai Industrial Corridor that Kant midwifed. This will set up new "smart" townships and special manufacturing zones designed to imitate China's success with the industrialization of its coastal fringe. First proposed in 2007, most of the work so far has been in conceptualization and acquiring the large tracts of land required. The railways are about to start laying tracks for the freight corridor that runs through the industrial corridor, and new industrial townships are being worked on as urban showpieces, to contrast with the country's existing urban centers with all their problems of infrastructure and governance.

"Corridor" is an understatement, as it will cover roughly 10 percent of the country's land area. Typical of what is planned is a new urban center to be located at Dholera on the Gujarat coast; it could become bigger than the island city of Mumbai, complete with its own port and airport, but without Mumbai's endemic curse of stressed city infrastructure. The initial plan had been for a much smaller town, but when Kant as the project boss presented it to Narendra Modi (then chief minister of Gujarat), Modi's response was "Why are you planning small?" Dholera as an idea quickly grew in size.

Meanwhile, many companies are waiting for the chance to get into the large and growing business of manufacturing armaments, reserved until very recently for the public sector but with the bulk of the weapons requirements of the armed forces being imported. The Modi government has signaled a sharp change away from imports to local manufacture, although its specific policy announcements have been confusing, and sometimes moved in a direction away from "Make in India."

The argument has been made frequently that India can move into the export-oriented industries being vacated by China as the latter's labor costs rise. It can, but only up to a point, because there are always cheaper options (like Bangladesh) that crop up when you look at just labor costs. China has the enabling factor of a very efficient infrastructure, which will not be replicated in India in the foreseeable future. Indeed, most producers looking for alternatives to China are not looking at India. Its rigid labor laws remain a handicap, its workers are not always as productive, the infrastructure is deficient, and dealing with the authorities is a nightmare. Almost all countries in East Asia offer easier working environments. If India is to score in manufacturing, the most important lesson it has to absorb is that it has to look beyond relative labor costs.

7

What Works (and What Doesn't) in India

ONE OF THE contentions in this book is that India should look beyond achieving industrial and manufacturing success by copying China, and not assume that it can compete in many key industries purely on the strength of lower wage levels. As spelled out in Chapter 3, the two countries are very different in all the ways that matter, while the similarities of geographical size and large populations are not meaningful beyond a limited extent. Rather than studying China, which has led to failed copycat experiments like special economic zones, it would be more fruitful to study India: how to change its operating environment, then look at what kind of manufacturing has worked in this country, and what has not. Following from that, a strategy can be to back the horses that can run, not the donkeys that can't.

To study what works and what does not, the following five segments look at the country's experience in five kinds of manufacturing/assembly/research work. These are then used to arrive at some guidelines for policy.

No Stitch in Time

The one manufacturing sector where India could have made a bigger splash than it has is of course textiles and related industries. The country is a producer and exporter of the primary raw material (cotton) and has a long and distinguished tradition in fine threads and intricate weaves; it has plenty of low-cost workers to throw into creating ready-made garments, one of the most labor-intensive industries that exist and therefore eminently suitable for a country where the surplus or unused resource is labor. For decades, the textile industry has been the country's biggest industrial employer as well as the largest net earner of foreign exchange.[1] In recent years, the manufacture of ready-made garments has shown that for every rupee of final product, it is more labor-intensive than diamond cutting, any form of engineering, and also back-office business process work.

Unfortunately, misguided policy killed both the historical and the resource advantage that India had. Gandhi's bias against machine-made cloth found reflection in the official policy after Independence. Small-scale weaving was given many advantages over large textile mills, including cheaper or free electricity in some states. When cheap synthetic clothing appeared on the scene, the government taxed it off shop shelves in an ill-conceived drive to protect traditional cotton. And in the policymaker's coup de grâce, garment manufacture was among the hundreds of items reserved for small-scale units. The result: India had thousands of garment exporters, but less than 10 percent of China's exports.

By the time the international trade in textiles and garments was opened up in stages between 1995 and 2005, India found itself stranded while bigger rivals like China and smaller ones like Bangladesh surged ahead. In 2005, India was the world's fifth-largest exporter of garments, a step ahead of Bangladesh. Seven short years later, Bangladesh had moved up to second place, while India slipped in the rankings. In that seven-year period when India's garment exports went from $8.6 billion to $14.4 billion, Bangladesh surged from $6.9 billion to $20 billion, while China went from $74 billion to $154 billion.[2]

Of course, Bangladesh had the advantage of preferential market access that Europe offered to "least-developed" nations, so it has been a more attractive production base—even for exporters from India, who have set up base there. Further, it has only two-thirds of India's per capita income and its wages are correspondingly lower—$68 per month in the garments industry in 2015, compared to more than $100 in India.[3] Since raw material and wages account for 85 percent of the cost, and with duty differentials as an added disadvantage, India is priced out of the bottom end of the market. That still leaves opportunity higher up the product value chain, especially when global buyers are looking for alternatives to the increasingly expensive China.

The only large-scale production that takes place in the textiles value chain is spinning, and Indian yarn is the most competitively priced in the world. The downstream processes (weaving, dyeing and finishing, and apparel manufacture) are where inefficiencies and sundry problems creep in. Rigid labor laws prevent flexibility in manning for a seasonal industry, and hardly any large-scale operation exists that could deliver economies of scale. The country has only three or four garment makers with turnover in excess of $100 million, unlike the leaders in India's tech sector who count their sales in billions of dollars. There is no one big enough in the Indian garment business to be able to put together the resources for world-scale production of the kind that China has managed, although the Indian garment worker, while costing more, was 20 percent more productive than her counterpart in Bangladesh.[4]

The stumbling block is the government. In a strictly seasonal business, India's labor laws come in the way of flexible manning. Nor does the law allow freedom to operate longer shifts (as an exporter explained, workers are more productive toward the end of the day than in the first hour or two). Given these problems, buyers surveyed by McKinsey, the consulting firm, said that while the majority were planning to shift some of their sourcing away from China, they favored Bangladesh, Vietnam, Indonesia, and Cambodia as new destinations. India did not figure in the list.

Garment manufacture can create jobs for millions of people (especially young women) who are coming out of villages with a basic education and the willingness to go through a short training period. India's garment export industry employs 7 million people—or about a million jobs for every $2 billion of exports.[5] That is multiples of what exists for almost any other kind of manufacturing activity. Getting to the size of Bangladesh's garment export industry would add more than 2.5 million jobs. The number would grow to a total of 18 million jobs if India reached Bangladesh's export target for 2020 ($36 billion). That translates into 2 million additional jobs every year for the next five years.

For perspective, remember that the government spends Rs 350 billion annually on its employment guarantee program,[6] creating the equivalent of 7 to 8 million person-years of work.[7] But this is at much lower wages than in the garment industry. Yet the employment guarantee program is politically a holy cow, and the government is unwilling to change it to get garment exports to take off. It is a telling enough comment that the country's most labor-intensive large industry received, between 2000 and 2012, a total of just $1.27 billion as foreign investment![8]

Revving Up Small Cars

It's a different story altogether when it comes to cars—in terms of feeding the domestic market, volume production for export, and attracting foreign investment. The manufacture of small cars especially stands out as a large engineering segment (along with upstream sectors like auto components) where India aspires to global leadership. Back in the 1980s, India's three tiny car companies produced shoddy thirty-year-old models and between them sold fewer than 50,000 cars in a year. A sardonic wisecrack at the time was that the only part of an Indian car that did not make a noise was the horn.

The turning point was a case of pure serendipity. The government had taken over Prime Minister Indira Gandhi's dead son Sanjay's scandal-ridden car project called Maruti and needed to do something with it. It set out to look for partners and settled on a relatively minor Japanese car maker, Suzuki, which specialized in the small cars that were and remain a good fit for the Indian market. Suzuki set up a plant in partnership with the government, and a bevy of Japanese auto parts suppliers were encouraged to follow in its footsteps. For obvious reasons, the project had an unusual level of political support, which translated into things like favored tax treatment. Meanwhile, other Japanese companies like Honda and Yamaha (and Suzuki too) came in to partner domestic businessmen and make new ranges of two-wheelers.

The key to change was not just the introduction of contemporary automobile technology but also the introduction of good production technology and work practices—everything from factory layout to Japanese shop-floor practices like "just-in-time" delivery of components, *kanban* (a signaling system to smooth the production flow), and *kaizen* (continuous productivity improvement). Indian component suppliers understood the importance of total quality management (TQM) and adopted it like a religion; quite a few went on to win the Deming Prize, the gold standard for recognition of quality processes.

Their innovations raised productivity levels continuously and helped to cut costs to the bone: by finding new ways of wiring a car to save five kilos of copper wire; reducing the layers of padding on the car's ceiling; compromising on flame-proof carpeting in the cheaper models, and so on. Suzuki (which eventually bought out the government's shareholding in Maruti Suzuki and listed it on India's stock market) improved its output per employee in India from fifty cars in a year to sixty, then to seventy-five, and now to more than ninety cars (about 12,000 employees for 1.1 million cars). Profit margins are relatively modest but good by industry standards (6.5 percent of sales), while employee cost is half that (3.2 percent). In the small-car business, where margins are low and where India has acquired a competitive strength, efficiency and extreme cost control are vital for profitability and growth.[9]

The introduction of contemporary cars came fortuitously at a time when India's nascent middle-class had begun to aspire to car and two-wheeler ownership, and had also acquired the means for realizing the dream. The creation of an ecosystem of efficient component suppliers and a dealer system that tapped latent demand led to rapid sales growth. Passenger vehicle sales have gone from fewer than 100,000 three decades ago to 2.6 million now.[10]

Hyundai, the Korean car company, saw Suzuki's success and became a follow-on investor. In 1996, it put up a factory in Tamil Nadu's Sriperumbudur for what the company hoped would be easy access to nearby Chennai port—exports were a key objective for the firm, and have been almost twice Maruti Suzuki's in volume. But, as with Maruti Suzuki, for Hyundai too the primary justification for a production base in India was the size and attractiveness of the domestic market, with a secondary advantage being markets around the Indian Ocean rim and territories beyond. In fact, Sriperumbudur has emerged as the hub for numerous automobile factories. Dubbed locally as the Detroit of India, it boasts the factories of Nissan and Renault, Ford and Hyundai, John Deere and Caterpillar, even BMW and the homegrown TVS, as well as component suppliers, including three tire producers.

What about all the inefficiencies of India's infrastructure, which have held back Indian manufacturing in general? Tamil Nadu has faced serious shortages of electricity, but Hyundai is protected by an agreement with the state government for uninterrupted power supply. The road to Chennai port is hopelessly clogged with traffic, but it is not a long distance and therefore is more an irritant than a serious cost burden. Hyundai has also had its share of industrial strife, but the company's local managers are more concerned about "harassment" by government inspectors, demands by politicians for jobs to favored candidates, and the massive traffic congestion on the way to the port. Hyundai too finds that employee costs are just 3 percent of the total—so one is tempted to suggest that the success story in small-car manufacture reflects, in part, the advantages of low labor cost. Discussing productivity, a Korean manager at the Sriperumbudur plant said: "The Korean worker is more productive, but the Indian worker's attitude is better." He might have added that the Indian worker is cheaper too.

Meanwhile, both Ford and General Motors (GM) have decided to make the country a car-manufacturing hub; in early 2015 Ford opened a new car plant at Sanand in Gujarat which, it hopes will grow to become its single largest production center in the world. Ford has also located a large back office for design work, employing some 8,000 people—doing the same work in the United States would take the costs up manifold. An international car manufacturer said localizing components lowered costs for a small car by over Rs 60,000. Differential wage costs are over and above this and would make a difference of at least another Rs 50,000 per car.[11]

The really big payoff will come if and when component suppliers in India, who supply the big international car companies for the local market, start competing for the global business of GM and Volkswagen, Ford and Fiat. The auto parts industry has kept going despite the global slowdown, taking exports from $4.2 billion in 2009–10 to $11.2 billion five years later—an annual growth rate of 22 percent (29 percent in rupees)[12] that is expected to be sustained as the global auto majors look more to Indian companies for sourcing components. Cost is an advantage, of course, but less important when compared to production centers like China or Mexico. If the big international car companies are persuaded by cost, quality, and efficiency considerations to source more components from India, Indian component manufacturers could become global giants by replacing suppliers in many higher-cost countries. The implications for manufacturing in India are enormous.

The key to all the changes over three decades lay in an anchor company entering the market, helped by supportive government policy, resulting in an ecosystem that has become India's successful small-car industry. The question is, why can't this success be replicated in other sectors?

The Limited Appeal of Chinese-Style Factories

One problem in the garments sector, namely, high absenteeism, would be solved if the Chinese practice of housing workers in dormitories next to factories could be adopted. That could even pave the way for large-scale factory work, Chinese-style. The system was attempted at Sriperumbudur, the industrial hub where (among many other units) Nokia ran its Indian handset assembly unit. But people preferred to stay at home and commute, even if that meant being bused to work over long distances.

It is no different for a large garments exporter in Bengaluru, who ships workers from long distances into the city in an effort to tap a cheaper pool of workers. But the turnover among its 29,000 employees is high. So is absenteeism, because women employees (the overwhelming majority) also have to deal with periodic crises at home, like a child falling ill. Given the operating constraints, the exporter said, he cannot outcompete Bangladesh and others at the low end of the product scale. But, he added, India is competitive in exporting garments that have a little design element or some unique feature, and therefore fetch a slightly higher price.

For Nokia, shipping workers from their homes meant running staff buses over 10,000 kilometers every day, for individual round-trips of more than 150 kilometers, to fetch new recruits (mostly those fresh out of school) who were paid a basic monthly wage of Rs 5000—about $100 at the time. Set in a neatly laid-out export processing zone in Sriperumbudur, a stone's throw from the Hyundai factory, Nokia once employed nearly 10,000 people. Associated companies like Foxconn were neighbors, employing another 20,000. The Finnish company (as it was at the time) had seen India's mobile phone industry grow to the second largest in the world, mostly for low-end phones. Setting up an assembly plant made sense, for servicing the local market and also for doing some exports. The factory turned out handsets at a rapid rate, and 700 million had been produced by 2013, with exports going to some 100 countries. It was one of Nokia's largest assembly centers, and the factory management said the local unit had a lower rejection rate than comparable facilities in China.[13]

The problem was that 75 percent of the value of the handset was still captured outside the country, because that is where the upstream manufacturing facilities were. The assembly work in the Sriperumbudur factory focused on repetitive low-end work by young women with small, nimble fingers. They were essentially in dead-end jobs; most would leave after a few years to get married and raise a family, which was fine as far as the company was concerned because older employees would have expected higher pay for the same work.

Nokia's decision to set up the facility in India had been seen as a breakthrough for the country, but the company had begun to consider Vietnam as a cheaper location for the assembly work. Then it got caught in a major tax dispute—indeed, more than one. One issue involved tariffs on the import of software embedded into an assembled handset (there was no such tax on complete handsets that came into the country). In 2014, when Nokia eventually decided to sell its global devices business to Microsoft, the tax demands on the Indian factory included tax that was said to have been evaded on royalty payments to the Finnish parent. The demand (including penalties and interest charged for late payment) was for an outsize Rs 210 billion, and prevented the unit from being a part of the deal with Microsoft.[14] In a business with razor-thin margins, such tax demands were the kiss of death. The plant eventually shut down.

Engineering Success

In recent years, many enterprising businessmen in India have shown imagination and flair in acquiring manufacturing firms, design shops, and used plants from Europe and elsewhere—and integrating these with operations at home to deliver better products or improve manufacturing processes. Eicher, TVS, Mahindra, Sona, and others have all used this approach to good effect. Eicher, which also makes trucks, struck gold when Managing Director Siddhartha Lal followed his personal interest and focused on a niche motorcycle market for heavy, retro bikes. The company has less than 3 percent of the 16-million market by volume, but sales have been growing at more than 50 percent annually, margins are double those of much bigger rivals, and the company's valuation reached $9 billion as its stock price soared from Rs 400 in 2009 to Rs 21,000 in 2015 before falling with the rest of the market. Another colorful story concerns Baba Kalyani, head of the Pune-based Bharat Forge, a company that supplies forgings to virtually every major automobile company in the world—including, it is claimed, half the front axles of all trucks operating in the United States.

In early 2012, Kalyani decided to diversify into defense equipment and looked at making artillery guns. He had already been making parts of guns, using his company's skills in metallurgy, forging, and machining. Now he wanted to make the full product. So he went to Cranfield University, an engineering center in the north of England that is a repository of artillery technology. The experts at Cranfield mentioned to Kalyani that he could get a ready-made gun plant that was up for sale in Switzerland.

Not one to let grass grow under his feet, Kalyani was on the next flight to Zurich, where the company, RUAG Defence, explained that it had been repairing and servicing guns for the US army in Iraq and Afghanistan. With those wars winding down, there was no business to be done and the plant was to be auctioned. Kalyani looked around the plant, said he was a buyer, and suggested that there need be no auction. RUAG quoted 2 million euros, and soon Kalyani's Pune-based engineers were in Switzerland, dismantling the plant to ship it home and reassemble it in a large, long shed.

Kalyani now had a plant, but he needed a gun. Following his network of contacts, he landed at Mfl, an Austrian gunmaker that had closed its plant for want of orders. They were willing to supply drawings and technology and, crucially, a gun prototype. In what was a forerunner of things to come, though, it took Kalyani more than a year to get the government's permission to import the gun. A total of half a billion rupees later, factory, drawings, and gun were all at the Pune plant—a package that would ordinarily have cost multiples of what the company paid.

Kalyani and his engineers were soon modifying and improving the gun, increasing its barrel length from forty-five times its 155 mm bore to fifty-two times for increased firing range (by comparison, the original Bofors guns, ordered in 1986, were thirty-nine times the bore). The barrel was now a monstrous piece of heavy metal, some twenty-six feet long. And the gun was ready for testing at the army's firing range at Balasore in Odisha. The problem was that the gun had only one possible customer, the government, and Kalyani soon realized what this meant. The government's ordnance factory at Pune was already making the guns, but not in the numbers and quality needed. Yet no one in the government would take up Kalyani's offer to produce a sample gun, free of cost, with no purchase commitment. Things changed when the Modi government came in, and Kalyani finally got a hearing.

Walk around the different sheds in the factory complex and the relative scarcity of blue-collar staff becomes clear. Most of the people you encounter are engineers. Ask Kalyani about it and you get a dismissive response about the productivity of blue-collar workers. Hence his reliance on qualified engineers. Returning to the guns, Kalyani says he has already developed four gun variants, one of them a lightweight howitzer of the kind the army wants for easy transportability by helicopter to battlefields in the mountains. He has reduced the gun's weight from its original 3.8 tons to just a ton by using aluminum and a soft-recoil system that needs less metal weight for absorbing the shock. (Imported gun variants use titanium, which is more expensive.) The army is ordering a large number, and Kalyani says he can offer enormous cost savings. But he cannot bid until his gun is tested and approved.

Sitting in his spacious office, as a delegation from Saab sits in the next room negotiating the details of a joint venture to produce shoulder-fired missiles, Kalyani explains that it is a natural progression for a company to move from steel to forgings to defense equipment; that was the sequence followed by Krupps in Germany. Kalyani too had started with steel before getting into forging and machining, developing expertise along the way in metallurgy. His long-term goal, he says, is to make jet engines. Just now, though, the challenge is to get the gun cleared, see it through field trials, and hopefully start manufacture.

Research Shows a Way

Bengaluru is home to many research shops, belonging to global firms such as Intel, DaimlerChrysler, SAP SE, and Shell. Typical of these is the research facility that GE opened in 2002 on a fifty-acre campus in the Bengaluru suburb of Whitefield, naming it after its last chairman, Jack Welch. This is GE's first research and development (R&D) center outside the United States.

A visitor in 2013 would have seen the facility's many buildings on the sprawling campus and its 4,500 employees (of whom 60 percent had advanced degrees) working on ambitious projects like lowering the cost of a robust electrocardiograph (ECG) machine to a fifth of a Chinese product—so that GE Medical Systems could expand its business in low-income countries like India. Other projects included lowering the cost of scanners and ultrasound machines to 40 percent of their current cost. Much of the work on GE's jet engines for the Boeing 787 and 737 had been done here, one objective being to get more thrust with a smaller size. Another project was to get wind turbines to function at lower wind speeds (which would raise India's wind energy potential). Researchers were also experimenting with glass blades for windmills and taller masts. Separately, a team was working on how to lighten the weight of railway engines, so that more freight could be hauled at lighter axle loads, while a "gee-whiz" project was to transfer power through the atmosphere (the possible applications are endless).

The man in charge at the time, Gopichand Katragadda, was a low-key electronics engineer with a ready smile who explained that the aim of their research in low-cost medical equipment was to make it feasible for what he called "a Tier-III hospital in a Tier-III town" in India to offer the same level of diagnosis and care as a leading hospital in a metropolis. Interestingly, none of the top team of twenty engineers took his first engineering degree at any of the prestigious IITs; Katragadda said they regularly recruited from the second-rung engineering institutes in the country, the better graduates of which are substantially cheaper while being almost as good as IIT graduates. Asked to compare his colleagues at the Jack Welch center with research workers at US facilities, he said, Indians are good at ideation but poor at some kinds of execution and documentation. He added that they tend to overcommit and then work extra hours to meet the commitments, and still slip on schedules. Essentially, he said, they work more than asked for.

Finding India's "Fit"

These stories point to some tentative but important conclusions. First and most important, India's workers are productive and proficient, but they are not always as productive as their counterparts in China or Korea. They are low-cost but not as low-cost as in Bangladesh or Cambodia. It is the combination of cost and productivity, ideally combined with a third advantage (like the availability of raw material or a large home market) that translates into a base for competitive manufacturing. If Foxconn, the Taiwanese maker of electronic components and products, has talked of investing billions of dollars in India, it is because of the large and growing domestic market for electronic products combined with India's strengths in design and entertainment software. Whatever makes a good "fit" for Indian manufacturing will have all or most of these elements, not just savings in costs.

The point is captured well in leather goods—an area of natural fit since the country has plenty of raw material. Dilip Kapur, the founder of Hidesign, a successful leather products company in Puducherry, not very far from Sriperumbudur, identified the market niche well when he told *The Economist* in 2011 that a worker in his factory managed to produce three handbags a day, compared to twelve in China. Despite everything he tried, he could not get productivity to go beyond nine handbags, so he had to change tack and focus on greater value addition through design inputs, in order to stay competitive. It is a lesson that applies equally to garment exports.

Second, the presence of large firms with contemporary production systems, work practices, and manufacturing efficiencies is essential—as the case of Maruti Suzuki and the other car companies proves. Such firms also drive efficiencies upstream, and with vendors, create a larger spread effect in both productivity and quality. This is an important missing piece when it comes to ready-made garments. However, the successes in small cars and other engineering products serve to make an additional point: looking to manufacturing as a solution to the employment problem is different from looking to manufacturing as an end in itself. Some kinds of manufacturing are indeed labor-intensive, but a good deal of successful manufacturing in India is not. However, even if car factories are getting more automated, they are the hub of a much larger employment system that involves upstream suppliers, downstream dealers, and service agents. Many of them would be considered part of the service sector.

Manufacturing = Jobs in Services

There are those who contend that manufacturing is not the solution for India's job problem, claiming that it lies in retailing, tourism, car repair, and other services. R. C. Bhargava is an unlikely candidate for such a view. But the chairman of Maruti Suzuki says, in response to a question on the greater automation that exists in newer car plants, that car factories should not be expected to solve India's employment problem. If job growth is to come, according to Bhargava, it will have to be in associated areas—manning petrol pumps or maintaining and repairing vehicles, which are service sector jobs and don't compare with high-paying factory work. Somewhat quixotically, Bhargava also points out that every third car in India is driven by a hired driver. If he is right, then 2.6 million passenger vehicles being sold in a year translates into more than 850,000 new jobs for drivers! For understandable reasons, though, issuing large numbers of driving licenses does not qualify in any government's book as a satisfactory employment policy.

Still, Bhargava is making a serious point because the ratio of non-factory jobs to factory jobs in the car industry is said to be 7:1. The head of another car company puts the figure at 16:1. Other manufacturers of engineering goods endorse the view that shop-floor employment in the engineering goods sector is unlikely to grow rapidly because of steadily increasing automation as well as gains in productivity. The real employment growth in the consumer durables industry, for instance, comes not on the shop floors that turn out refrigerators and air conditioners but outside the factory gates—in tasks like transporting, storing, selling, financing, and servicing. Jamshyd Godrej, chairman and managing director of Godrej & Boyce, the diversified engineering company, recalls a time when the majority of his company's employees worked in the factory. Today, he says, there are four or five times as many employees outside the factory as there are in it.

It is only in export-oriented production that the downstream service sector activity is minimized, since the products only have to be loaded onto a container. Success in quite a lot of manufacturing, therefore, leads to employment growth in services, not manufacturing. Not that it should matter, since incomes will be better in both than in agriculture.

An important consideration has to be identifying the sectors that will be competitive internationally, even after accounting for the inefficiencies of the country's operating environment—which introduces costs that do not exist in competing production centers. Moving cars a short distance to a port can be a challenge, as Hyundai has found. Moving a ton of freight one kilometer by road costs more than twice what it does in other countries: Rs 3, against Rs 1.30.[15] Power tariffs for industry tend to be higher, in order to cross-subsidize the underpriced or free electricity provided to farmers and domestic consumers. Ports are slow and shipping costs from India high—a twenty-ton container can cost twice as much as in China. These and other systemic deficiencies (remember the poor score on Ease of Doing Business) have complex causes and cannot be wished away quickly. Manufacturing success will come easier to those sectors where these disadvantages are overridden by the advantages.

Looking beyond Low Wages

While India has the opportunity to step into product segments that China is vacating because of rising labor costs, example after example shows that India will find it hard to compete purely on the basis of labor cost advantages. Nokia ran an efficient operation in Sriperumbudur, and the unit's defect rate was lower than China's. Yet, before the entire business was sold to Microsoft, the company was considering shifting its base to Vietnam.

In an array of industries, it may be more important to have producers who succeed on contemporary manufacturing practices—especially since segments with greater product variation offer better opportunities for Indian manufacturers than turning out cookie-cutter products like the zippers that China turns out in the zillions. Godrej, for instance, finds a greater part of his production going to export markets in lines like safes and safety devices than in refrigerators. Within refrigerators, his company has scored when it has innovated: using sensors to make a refrigerator that is not frost-free but acquires frost-free characteristics, for instance.

This, the Bharat Forge story and the success with small cars, among other examples, underlines the importance of what Baumol and his co-authors called "good capitalism"[16]—a healthy mix of big firms and entrepreneurial firms. Other than the obvious advantage on costs, even in labor-intensive activities like diamond cutting and garment manufacture, factors other than labor cost must be considered. In the diamond industry, it is the quick adoption by Surat's entrepreneurs of new processing technologies and equipment; in garments and leather goods it could be an extra element of design. In other words, a manufacturing policy that focuses on copying China and tries to score in labor-intensive sectors because Chinese wages are going up, while useful to a degree, may not be the primary strategy to adopt.

As for the light–heavy industry mix, forcing import substitution by setting up mother industries, like silicon fabrication units, with the help of large capital subsidies could end up as a repeat of the Nehruvian experiment with setting up heavy engineering industrial units. They will be unable to compete on level terms with imports and will saddle downstream users with high costs while also encouraging protectionist measures.

Strength in Services

Finally, it would be fatal if the focus on manufacturing, especially labor-intensive manufacturing that is vital to the employment question, were to come at the cost of neglecting one of India's natural areas of competitive strength, which is white-collar and technical services. Computer-aided design work in the engineering sector costs a fifth in India what it does in the United States. Engineers who are willing to work for the equivalent of $10,000–20,000 per year are more than useful when making satellites that require many thousands of man-hours of testing before being launched into space. That testing can be done cheaper in India than in almost any other country, and is one (but not the only) reason that India's space program is remarkably low cost. Unfortunately, the potential for creating a bigger commercial rocket-launching and satellite-building program that gets business from around the world is still largely unexploited.

The abundance of engineers and English-speaking graduates is also the reason the country's software services and BPO companies have been so successful. Once a network is created of large, medium, and small enterprises in a specific area of activity, the resulting ecosystem works out how to occupy all the niches in the value chain: from generating revenues of $10,000 per person-year in the low-value call-center business to $30,000 per person-year for writing code, and to $50,000 and more per person-year when providing business solutions. Tata Consultancy Services, the biggest in the business, had revenues per employee in 2014–15 of nearly $48,000. The net profit was more than $11,000 per employee.[17]

A more accident-prone but nevertheless successful ecosystem exists in pharmaceuticals, where India has gone from extreme technology dependence to developing the ability to adapt existing research and grab the generic drugs market in product categories where patents have expired. In research work too, leading international companies like Intel have found that it pays to use Indian workers. GE and Shell have set up key research and development centers in India. So has the software giant SAP, which has found that its Indian staff are as productive as those in California, at much lower cost. Sometimes, as Shell has found, the Indian research staff are not just cheaper but also as good or better when it comes to breakthrough research. Start-up companies in Bengaluru have made a mark in chip design, and some of them have been snapped up by bigger international companies: SmartPlay and four other companies have been bought by Aricent, SiCon Design Technologies by Altran, and Cosmic Circuits by Cadence Design Systems. Acquisition values have been climbing; seven-year-old SmartPlay with 1,200 employees has been valued at Rs 1.1 billion.[18] The role for the government here is to ensure the sustained supply of quality engineers in very large numbers, and smoothly functioning urban environments where they can live and work. The market will then find a way to use the resource and recognize the value created.

How should one conclude? Manufacturing that is and is not labor-intensive, and services with both low and high value addition—India does not have to choose; it needs to do all these well. Indeed, the more companies decide to compete on the basis of issues that go beyond cost savings, the better they will do. What the government needs to do is to provide them with an enabling environment.

The State and the Citizen

8

The Underperforming State

THE KOSI IS one of the most unstable of India's rivers. It is formed by tributaries that flow down from below Mount Everest on one side and the Kanchenjunga on the other, and in the peak monsoon season, its water volume can multiply as much as eighteenfold. Silt from hill slopes upstream is deposited on the riverbed, raising its level and causing the river to overflow its banks. The Kosi therefore has a giant alluvial fan. Over the centuries, it has changed course by up to 250 kilometers. To regulate the water flow and keep the river confined to its main channel, Nepal and India agreed in the 1950s to construct a 350-meter barrage across the river, on the Nepalese side of the border. The barrage was to be managed jointly by Indians and Nepalis. The main responsibility rested with the Bihar government, perhaps because most of the downstream plains were in Bihar.

Early in the new century, a senior Indian diplomat posted to Nepal decided to visit the Kosi barrage. What he saw shocked him. Two dredgers had been deployed to regularly dredge the river and clear it of silt—to keep the main river channel on course and trained through the barrage; but the dredgers were lying on their side, in disrepair and disuse. A nearby housing enclave for Indian officials who manned the barrage was mostly deserted because the people for whom it was built had gone back to live on the Indian side. The barrage's control room had a solitary junior engineer from Nepal.

Alarmed at the situation, the diplomat took up the matter with the Bihar government. He was assured of urgent corrective action, but nothing changed. Soon enough, the inevitable happened. The Kosi burst its banks, changed its course, destroyed homes and fields downstream, and left nearly 3 million people homeless.

The prime minister's office in Delhi investigated. It found that satellite maps of the river, which could have provided early warning of an impending breach, were not being supplied to the water resources ministry, reportedly because the ministry had stopped paying for them. Early warning could also have been provided by data on water flows available through the sensors installed at various points in the river. But the sensors had stopped functioning and no one had bothered to replace them. So the water ministry was blind about the state of the Kosi, a river that was predictable in its unpredictability (and, with reason, called the "sorrow of Bihar").

There was only one word to describe the situation. Snafu.

All Indians are familiar with such tales of the government failing spectacularly to do what it should. Another example came within months of the Kosi debacle, when ten suicide terrorists launched an attack on Mumbai from the sea. As Adrian Levy and Cathy Scott-Clark report in *The Siege*,[1] the Mumbai police had received twenty-six separate warnings over two years that a seaborne assault by the Pakistan-based Lashkar-e-Taiba was being planned simultaneously on the Oberoi Trident, the Taj Mahal Hotel, Leopold Café, and other places. But when Vishwas Patil was made the deputy commissioner of police in charge of south Mumbai, he checked with the coast guard and was told there were no funds for any high-speed boats to chase waterborne suspects who might show up.

That was not all. The city police had quick response teams, trained by the army and armed with AK-47 assault rifles—except that no bullets had been bought for three years and the teams had not done firing practice for over a year. The next line of defense, the "Striking Mobiles," had carbines and self-loading rifles, but often without ammunition. Their bulletproof jackets were defective in design. According to Levy and Scott-Clark, Patil had warned his superiors that the city's battle-readiness was in doubt.

Marx is often quoted for his comment that "all great, world-historical facts and personages occur, as it were, twice . . . the first time as tragedy, the second as farce."[2] And so it has been in Mumbai, where the follow-on to the tragedy was a farce. Six years after the 2008 attack, in which 164 people were killed and more than 300 injured, a good deal of the expensive new equipment that had been bought to improve city and coastal security was lying unused, while other essential equipment was yet to be ordered because of procedural delays. Snafu again!

And yet, for every Kosi and Mumbai, there is a remarkable success—like the Election Commission's record of organizing the world's largest general elections involving more than 800 million voters, 98 percent of whom have voter card IDs. The 2014 parliamentary elections used more than 1.5 million electronic voting machines and deployed nearly 10 million people to man more than 900,000 polling booths, in remote Himalayan hamlets as well as tiny islands in the Andaman chain—with zero room for error.[3]

Also impressive is the country's sending a satellite, *Mangalyaan*, into Martian orbit in 2013–14, at less than what it cost to make the Hollywood film *Gravity*,[4] and with success uniquely achieved at the first try. A third example is the quality of the organizational effort that went into facilitating the 2013 Maha Kumbh mela (a Hindu pilgrimage to bathe in a holy river once every four years), which brought 120 million people (up to 3 million at a time) congregating in the space of less than two months to Allahabad, to bathe at the holy confluence of the Yamuna, Ganga, and (the mythical) Saraswati rivers. The massive tented encampments built to house pilgrims sprang up in three months over an area of nearly 20 square kilometers, with water supply, sanitation, electricity, food stalls, garbage collection, and effective policing to manage pilgrim movement over 150 kilometers of makeshift roads and dozens of bridges across the rivers and connecting sandbanks—all the things that the country's urban planners and managers can't seem to provide on an everyday basis in the hundreds of rapidly growing towns and cities.[5]

The "Mission" Approach

There is a pattern to these successes and failures. The routine, everyday (including core) functions of the state are performed badly, like dredging a river or policing a city. Things usually work well, or at least better, when the system is in mission mode: election time, organizing a Kumbh mela or sending up a satellite into precise orbit. One solution therefore is to set up more "missions," which Rajiv Gandhi tried in the mid-1980s with a series of "technology missions." Some of these worked, like growing more oilseeds and reducing the need for importing cooking oils. Others did not—like cleaning the Ganga. Earlier, under Indira Gandhi in the 1970s, "Project Tiger" probably saved the Indian tiger from threatened extinction.[6]

It would seem that Narendra Modi has learned from these; he articulates objectives and goals in the form of projects: 100 Smart Cities, "Make in India," *Swachch Bharat* (Clean India), Digital India, and the like. But there is no shortage of "projects" that are executed badly and late, and go hopelessly over budget—like the highways program known as the Golden Quadrilateral and the North–South/East–West Corridor. Both started well because of good initial leadership, but it is hard to stay in such project mode for very long. The result down the road has been delays, cost overruns, and extended legal disputes.

In any case, many government functions cannot take the form of a "project." In the case of the polio eradication drive, started in 1995 and ending with 100 percent success in 2011, researchers have suggested that the mission approach to polio took attention away from routine immunization work—which therefore suffered. Or consider the state's core functions of delivering law and order and administering justice. India has far too few policemen to maintain law and order or investigate a crime—for which they are in any case poorly trained. The United Nations stipulates a minimum of 222 policemen for every 100,000 members of the population; many wealthy countries have more. The number in India is 130.[7] Inevitably, the numbers vary across states: Bihar has barely a third of the ratio in Karnataka. Overall, the country is short of more than a million policemen. But it is also a question of quality; Delhi has 75,000 policemen while New York makes do with 34,500.[8]

Then, some 36 percent of 1,017 high court judgeships are vacant[9] (as are more than 20 percent of posts in lower courts).[10] That is one reason for the massive backlog of cases in the courts: 31 million in all, of which 4 million are in the high courts.[11] It is not enough to merely fill the vacant slots—the number of judges and courts needs to be trebled. The Law Commission looked at international norms and recommended in 1987 that India should have fifty judges per million people.[12] The reality at the time was ten and a half; now it is fifteen. As one consequence, the chief justice of the Delhi High Court calculated in 2009, it would take 466 years to clear all the cases before the court. But once again, there is the question of quality: India has fewer judges per million people than most countries, and they also seem to be able to dispose of fewer cases per judge. Among other things, Indian judges routinely allow adjournments on flimsy grounds and provide too much time for oral arguments.

The corollary is that of more than 400,000 people in India's jails, two-thirds are awaiting trial; in Bihar, those awaiting trial constitute an astonishing 80 percent of the prison population.[13] The picture is even worse than a bare reading of the statistics suggests, because only a small minority of cases that are concluded result in convictions. So it is possible that more than half those spending time in jail should never have been there. Waking up to this monumental violation of basic human rights, the Supreme Court in September 2014 finally ordered the release of all those awaiting trial, who had already served time in jail that was equal to half the maximum jail term prescribed for the offense they were accused of. Last heard, state governments and jail authorities were trying to compile lists of those qualified for release.

The problem of understaffing is not confined to one or two sectors. The government has mandated a 30:1 student–teacher ratio,[14] but 600,000 teachers' positions in primary schools across the country are vacant.[15] One problem may lie with the quality of teacher training institutes (most of them privately run), since 90 percent of candidates for teaching positions in government schools are reported to fail the nationally conducted Teacher Eligibility Test[16]—provoking many states to demand that the test be dispensed with. If a mission approach is to be followed with regard to the core functions of government, the first mission has to be filling all the vacant positions in all key government departments, but what if suitable candidates don't exist?

Flailing, Sclerotic, or Passably Functional?

Lant Pritchett, once a World Bank executive in India and now a Harvard professor, has famously characterized India as a "flailing" state—intelligent and well-trained officials at the "head" can frame sensible policies, but the arms and legs lower down do not deliver proper execution and just flail around.[17] Businessmen and ordinary citizens would rather call the system sclerotic (that is, rigid and unresponsive) and incapable of delivering quick decisions or even of enunciating clear rules that can be followed. On top of that, framing and following standard operating procedure seems to go against the national grain. This accompanies the excessive use of discretionary power, and therefore arbitrariness—which creates room for extracting payoffs.

To many businessmen forced to deal with corrupt and arbitrary officialdom, and to ordinary citizens, the Indian state is essentially predatory. TRACE International, a nongovernmental organization (NGO) that helps companies comply with international anti-bribery laws, has reported that 77 percent of the bribes demanded in India were for avoiding harm rather than to gain an advantage. Of these, 51 percent were for the timely delivery of services to which the individual was already entitled.[18] Narendra Modi, during his 2014 election campaign, railed against "tax terrorism": the excessive and unreasonable demands that revenue collectors made on citizens and companies, sometimes because they were chasing unrealistic revenue targets set by finance ministers, and more basically because corruption among tax collectors has been among the highest (mirroring levels in the police system and the lower courts) in the country—all examples of "retail" corruption, so to speak.

"Wholesale" payoffs have stymied the procurement of defense hardware (more than 60 percent of the $15-billion annual purchase bill is spent on imports).[19] Many vendors have been blacklisted, sometimes leaving no qualified vendor in the field. Even otherwise, the process is glacial—and the often futile effort to prevent corruption only makes the process even slower and lengthier. Defense preparedness has suffered. Yet any official seeking to shortcut the purchase process feels he runs the risk of censure by the government's auditor and, worse, an inquiry by the central vigilance commissioner on a corruption charge.

Sloth combined with endless red tape, on the one hand, and extortion, on the other, does not make for a productive picture. But for all the failures of government machinery, one could argue that sustained effort is showing results on some key objectives—perhaps slowly and patchily but visibly all the same. A way to judge this would be to see how the country has scored on globally defined objectives, like the Millennium Development Goals set by the UN General Assembly. Eight key social and economic targets were to be achieved by 2015, along with some subsidiary goals, with progress to be measured using 1990 as the reference year.

On perhaps the most important objective, of halving the percentage of the population below the poverty line, India has comfortably overachieved. The target was to drop the headcount from 47.8 percent to 23.9 percent of the population; the likely achievement is 20.7 percent, or a drop of 56.7 percent (the world as a whole did well too).[20] Somewhat contrarily, though, the target of reducing the percentage of underweight children under three years of age stopped short, coming down from 52 percent to 33 percent, instead of halving to 26 percent.

On the stipulated education goals, there was progress but not enough. Net primary school enrollment had gone up from 77 percent in 1990 to only 88 percent in 2013–14, against the 100 percent target for 2015.[21] Retention of students till class five was also not a success story, while literacy among fifteen- to twenty-four-year-olds, at 93.4 percent, was significantly better than the 61 percent of 1991, but short of the 100 percent target. When it came to gender parity, it had been achieved in primary and secondary school enrollment. Female literacy among fifteen- to twenty-four-year-olds was over 90 percent of male literacy, up from 67 percent. As for women in non-agricultural wage employment, the percentage had nearly doubled from 12.7 percent to 23.1 percent, but was well short of the 50 percent target.

There was a similar story when it came to health: the situation improved over a quarter century, but not by enough, so that targets were missed. Infant mortality halved, from eighty (per 1,000 live births) to thirty-nine, but the target was a two-thirds reduction to twenty-seven. Child mortality (those under five years) did better, dropping from 126 per 1,000 live births to forty (surpassing the target of forty-two). And the proportion of one-year-olds immunized against measles doubled, from 42 percent to 89 percent, but the target was 100 percent.

This picture repeats itself on other fronts. Maternal mortality was reduced by 68 percent, but the target was a 75 percent reduction. And nearly a quarter of births are still not attended by skilled health personnel. However, the goals of arresting the spread of malaria, tuberculosis, and HIV/AIDS had been achieved.

Regarding household access to "an improved water source" and to sanitation, the figures were surprisingly good. On water, access improved in urban areas from 87.1 percent of households to 97.5 percent (the target was 93.6 percent), and in rural areas—somewhat incredibly—from 58.9 percent to 96.3 percent (well ahead of the target of 79.5 percent). In households without access to sanitation, the percentage halved from 24.1 percent to 12.1 percent in urban areas (bettering the target of 15.8 percent), and dropped in rural areas from 87.1 percent to 61.1 percent (this time well short of the target of 46.6 percent).

Taking all the goals together, it is sobering that a majority of targets have been missed by varying margins, though significant progress has been recorded on almost all the goals. Many developing countries have done as well or better, including poorer countries like neighboring Bangladesh.[22] The question is, shouldn't a country with the capabilities and the ambitions that India has, not to mention the inheritance of an administrative "steel frame" at Independence, seek to do substantially better on core development tasks?

Failing on the Basics

The answer has to be "yes." The problems are many—government budgets for health and education have been too small, and the money that is made available has not been spent well. There is plenty of evidence to show, for instance, that government teachers (who are well paid, and frequently the highest-paid people in a village) don't teach or even attend school because of the absence of effective supervision. Indeed, Abhijit V. Banerjee and Esther Duflo have come up with the remarkable finding that unqualified private "doctors" (that is, quacks) deliver better care than qualified government doctors, simply because government doctors have no interest in the welfare of their patients and often don't ask the basic questions, let alone touch the patient.[23] They also show, tellingly, that while absenteeism is a widespread problem in these service departments, an increase in the supply of trained staff results in still-higher absenteeism. While many experiments have been made to deal with the problem, no system has emerged that works to any degree of satisfaction.

Despairing of reforming an obdurate system, governments have been willing to rely ever more on private hospital services, giving tax breaks and paying for across-the-board medical insurance policies that supply these hospitals with customers. What is missing is a comparable willingness to expand public hospitals, which is where most poor people go. While most of the relevant statistics are out of date by about a decade, a 2012 McKinsey report[24] said the total number of hospital beds was 1.2 for every 1,000 people, of which 0.5 were in government hospitals.[25] Remarkably, India has close to the number of medical professionals (doctors, nurses, and midwives) that the World Health Organization specifies (2.3 per 1,000 population)[26] as the minimum required for reaching the Millennium Development Goals for health.[27]

The trend toward private provision of tertiary healthcare appears to be irreversible, but corporate health care is expensive. Public hospital beds are few, though it is expenditure associated with health episodes that pushes many families back into poverty. Almost any government hospital has at least twice the number of patients that it is equipped to handle; outpatient departments are like crowded railway stations, and emergency wards have patients on floors or on stretchers in corridors. In the regular wards, they frequently have to share beds, while the doctors and nursing staff are hopelessly overworked. If the tax write-off on medical insurance policies (mostly for the well-to-do) were to be diverted to set up public hospitals, it would be a push toward both equity and inclusion. It would reduce the crowding in public hospitals and thereby improve the quality of care—giving patients a real choice between private and public hospitals, instead of being forced to suffer the malpractice widespread in many corporate hospitals. Meanwhile, other countries that have turned to private healthcare, like South Korea, have ensured strict regulatory control,[28] which is notably absent in India.

The situation on the education front is different. Here, there is plenty of evidence from researchers that says private schools deliver better education at lower cost per student—because teachers are better supervised and are also paid much less than teachers in government schools. There is evidence, too, of parents preferring fee-charging private schools to free government schools. But governments have usually remained insistent on maintaining the dominance of the government school system. This would be fine if government schools offered a passable quality of education, but the NGO Pratham's well-known Annual Status of Education Reports (ASERs) have shown that they do not. The tenth ASER (which surveyed more than 15,000 schools in 577 districts) reported in 2014 that while school enrollment has consistently been over 96 percent, attendance averages only 71 percent—with wide variations. More important, the majority of schoolchildren in class five of government schools cannot cope with class two–level reading and arithmetic. Private schools do better, but the scores are not great—more than a third fail the test.

It is probable that private schools show better results because most of their students are children of better-educated parents and enjoy more privilege. But in a country where education is the primary vehicle for upward mobility, it is only to be expected that even poor parents would want the best education they can get for their children, though it means dipping into meager incomes to pay school fees. If this trend persists, free government schools will progressively lose students to private competition. The number of children aged six to fourteen who attend private schools in rural areas has gone up dramatically in eight short years, from 18.7 percent of the total in 2006 to 30.8 percent in 2014. The all-India figure is 43 percent; beyond class eight the majority are in private schools.[29] Private school enrollment is high in states with a poor education record as well as in states with the highest literacy, like Kerala. In educationally backward states like Uttar Pradesh, Punjab, and Haryana, private school enrollment is now half or more of the total; in Kerala, it is 62 percent. As incomes rise and affordability improves, this migration will accelerate.

It is not as though government schools have not improved; government budgets have poured money into providing not just basic facilities, like separate toilets for girls, clean drinking water, and more classrooms with blackboards, but also libraries and even computers. This drive has shown measurable results. But the focus has been on inputs, not output—one of many criticisms leveled against the Right to Education law that came into effect in 2010.

The second Manmohan Singh government decided finally to respond to the evidence presented by trends in parental choice and try out an experiment in government-funded private school education. Announcing a plan to set up a school in each of some 6,000 "blocks" in the country, it said that 2,500 of them would be tried out as public–private partnerships, or PPPs.[30] The PPP partner would have to acquire the land and erect the buildings. Half the students had to be from economically weaker sections, and the government would pay for them what it spent on a student in Kendriya Vidyalaya schools[31] (run primarily for the children of government employees across the country—admission to these is much sought after). There was a performance criterion: the school results in board exams would have to be better than the performance in the Kendriya Vidyalayas. In that sense, the PPP experiment was to be an improvement on the existing model of private "aided" schools whose costs were met by the government without any performance criterion and without focus on poor students.

This "buy, don't make" program was designed to test whether private-sector competence could deliver better results for the government money spent on education. Bids were invited and hundreds of PPP partners showed interest. Then the government changed in 2014 and the whole thing died a premature death. But the same idea is being revived in different guises—suggesting that its time may yet come. The Rajasthan government under Chief Minister Vasundhara Raje has introduced a scheme in which government schools will be handed over to private management and tested to see whether better education results. Another variant is to allow private agencies to run schools in government school buildings in the off-hours (afternoons and early evenings). This has been tried with quite a few of Mumbai city's municipal schools. The ones that offer Marathi-medium education have few takers, and school classrooms therefore lie empty. Committed NGOs like Muktangan and the Aakanksha Foundation have used the premises of these schools to deliver superior education through better pedagogy, but the problem here is one of scale. Overall change can come only when central and state governments recognize that there is a problem with government schools and experiment with options, using the scale that only government budgets can provide.

Meanwhile, Banerjee and Duflo's practical suggestion that students should not be slotted in classes by age but by their education level—a suggestion endorsed by Pratham—has, regrettably, met with no takers. The point is simple: if a child does not understand or keep pace with what is being taught, it is pointless moving him or her up to the next level each year because of age; no education is taking place.

Education, healthcare (including public health measures like immunization), law and order, the justice system—these are what any government would prioritize in its must-do list. It is progress on these issues that laid the groundwork for the remarkable economic success stories of East Asia, including China. All the rapid-growth Asia countries achieved dramatic improvements in the basic social parameters in two or three decades, while India makes do with numbers that should be embarrassing to every Indian, after close to seven decades of independence.

When successive governments fail in this manner on the most vital tasks, there is weight to the argument that an overburdened administration should focus on these and leave non-essential activities to private/

non-government players. Yet, such is mission creep, government bloat, ministerial and bureaucratic aggrandizement, and the combination of "misfeasance, malfeasance, and non-feasance" (to borrow coinage from the film *The Front Page*) that the only solution is to take an axe to the whole thing and force radical change. As an example picked at random to show the futility of so many government establishments, the country's employment exchanges have 40 million on their rolls, but manage 0.2 million placements in a year.[32] The overhead cost per placement is five times the annual pay that the average placement offers. Talk of unproductive activity!

It is a matter of regret that Narendra Modi, who was elected on the promise of "minimum government, maximum governance," has shown no taste for radical change or for minimizing government. He appointed a committee under Bimal Jalan, a former Reserve Bank governor, to recommend administrative reforms. Its recommendations have not been publicized, let alone implemented. Another committee, under former Himachal Pradesh chief minister Shanta Kumar, in its report recommended radical changes in the food management program, widely considered to be wasteful in its current form; that too has been shelved. Meanwhile, the government system continues to run loss-making airlines and hotels, three-wheeler units, and Mahanagar Telephone Nigam, whose sales revenue is less than 40 percent of expenditure. Fortunately, a loss-making watch manufacturing unit run by the government is being shut down, but that is a rare exception. Simply put, India's governments need to refocus and repurpose themselves.

9

Patchwork Experiments

PRESCRIBING SOLUTIONS FOR organizations as vast and impersonal as India's governments, at once amoeba-like as well as hydra-headed, seems to be beyond the capacity of even the experts. Forget "one size fits all" panaceas (like working out incentives and disincentives), every solution is seen to have a problem, and every situation can be played to advantage by the willful. In many ways, you simply have to go with what works—and what that is in the state of Tamil Nadu can be very different from the situation in other states like Bihar or Himachal Pradesh. A conscientious officer overseeing a project (however well or badly designed) can deliver results quite different from what an indifferent bureaucrat would. It is the will to make the system deliver that is more important than anything taught in courses in public administration—which senior administrative officials have started attending in large numbers, including those at the best universities overseas. Still, after all the caveats, some broad observations can be made.

India has made no system-wide attempt at reforming its administrative setup. Inherited two-thirds of a century ago from colonial rulers, government systems and processes have not changed enough to match the reach, scope, and ambitions of a contemporary developmental state, worlds removed though it is from the twin concerns of the colonial administrators—maintaining law and order and raising revenue. This is not to allege that everything is stuck in stone, only to say that change has been slow and inadequate. That there has been progress is evident; in even the remotest corner of the country, the state's presence can be felt and seen today in ways that was not the case three decades ago. But you also find dissatisfaction with the quality of service offered and a desperately felt need for improvement.

The Lanjigarh block of Kalahandi district is a remote tribal area in southern Odisha that became notorious in the 1980s when it reported starvation deaths. Visit the area now and you find that most villagers have job cards that entitle them to get work under the rural employment guarantee program. The majority also have cards that describe them as being below the poverty line (BPL), which allows them to get state-subsidized rice at a rupee a kilo (barely 5–6 percent of the market price). Roughly every tenth house in the hamlet would appear to have been rebuilt in the not-distant past, using noticeably better material, with the help of money from the Indira Awaas Yojana program, a government housing initative. The 80-kilometer stretch from the neighboring district capital of Rayagada to Lanjigarh is being broadened into a four-lane highway and surfaced with a smooth blacktop. When I was there the police were out in strength, combing the forested mountainsides for Maoist rebels. In short, the state was visible everywhere—something that was missing altogether in this remote tribal belt three decades ago, when reports of starvation deaths brought journalists like me flocking to the area.

Not everything that the state is supposed to provide is there, of course. For medical care, the villagers mostly go to the free hospital run by the private Vedanta group, which has an alumina factory in the area and is the center of much controversy because of a mining project;[1] a larger hospital is run by a religious charity not far away, at Bissamcuttack. The Vedanta school is also preferred over government schools in the area, but it is not free (a source of local complaint). Both healthcare and education services are evidently areas of failure for the Indian state, or why would people look to Vedanta for these services even as they seek to stop the company's mining project?

Delivering on such developmental tasks requires a mental focus and approach that is different from the traditional mentality of a civil service created in colonial times and classically structured in the manner defined by the German sociologist Max Weber—a meritocracy that adheres to rules and is hierarchical and impersonal. When you transplant that ideal into the hurly-burly of India's context and ask that multiple program targets be met, the cracks begin to show. The tools are never enough for the tasks at hand. Those recruited to elitist administrative services (mostly from the upper castes, until fairly recently) are worlds removed from the mostly poor, semi-literate people (predominantly lower caste or tribal) who don't know how to demand their due. It is only to be expected that the administrative system becomes aloof and paternalistic at best, and parasitic at worst—treating people as subjects to be shown "benign neglect" or exploited for personal gain, not as citizens with rights.

Service rules protect employees up and down the hierarchy, but there is no equivalent system for ensuring performance on the job. There is little incentive for anyone to penalize a junior colleague, and your own movement up the hierarchy is mostly assured. Over time, the civil service has also been subjected to increasingly frequent political interference in its routine functioning, creating a system in which bureaucrats become politically aligned and respond mostly to the powerful and influential or those willing to bribe. And when a lower-caste politician like Lalu Prasad Yadav gains power in Bihar, he seeks a deliberate weakening of the administration and state institutions (hitherto dominated by the upper castes) as a means of lower-caste empowerment—hence his mocking of state-administered development and his party's slogan "*Vikaas nahin, samaan chahiye*" (we need dignity, not development).[2]

Such a weakened and corrupted system has also become overloaded, being asked by an overarching state to do ever more. At the cutting edge, which is the district (of which there are nearly 700, typically with a population of close to 2 million each), the "collector" in charge of the administration is invariably an official in his or her twenties or early thirties who would be asked to monitor up to 200 different schemes in the district, mandated by the central and state governments. Simply reporting periodically on the progress made on so many fronts means enormous paperwork. In trying to do too much, the government has ended up achieving too little or doing things shoddily. It has to do less of some and more of others.

To the extent that the system is rigid and unresponsive, one way of improving delivery is to develop pressure from below. A related way is to delegate tasks down to the lowest level of administration and bring them closer to the people affected. India has experimented with both, but imperfectly. Developing and empowering local government (the third tier, after the central government and states) has been stymied in various ways because state governments and state legislators don't want to yield budgets and power to local panchayats (local government bodies from district down to village level). As for giving voice to the governed, there is plenty of criticism of how public hearings on programs and projects have been conducted. Unlike China, where local party officials are responsible for delivering on specified objectives, the Indian political machine at the grass roots has reduced itself to a spoils system, looking for ways to siphon money from government programs.

The one brilliant innovation for citizen empowerment was the Right to Information Act (RTI) passed in 2005, a triumph at the central government level for civil society activists who used their experience in Rajasthan with forcing district administrations to become transparent on projects and schemes, in terms of cost, schedule, and beneficiaries. But this is only one of many steps required; at no stage has there been a comprehensive overhaul of a manifestly underperforming system.

"New Public Management"

If one looks at developments elsewhere, Weber's administrative model began to be questioned in the 1980s, with the advent of what later came to be termed New Public Management. Fired in many ways by the Reagan–Thatcher ideas of rolling back the frontiers of the state and by the need to de-bureaucratize, governments underwent changes in structure, objectives, and performance. Thatcher's approach, as articulated later by theorists, was that the government's role was "to steer rather than to row."[3] It would create competition for public service delivery and empower communities to take on local tasks themselves. Government departments had to deliver on a mission, not just follow rules. The size of the UK government was reduced substantially, while Reagan's deregulation drive aimed at reducing regulations 5 percent annually for a decade from 1982 onward.[4]

New Public Management meant large-scale privatization, while much departmental work was outsourced to autonomous executive agencies that were charged with specific goals and offered performance incentives.[5] Also, anything that could be done by a small, local office would not be done by a larger, remote one—the principle of subsidiarity. Citizens would therefore see the government coming closer to them and become "customers" benefiting from, and with the right to demand, services. What was left of the core government would be a relatively small, compact body comprising mostly senior officials who could focus on evidence-based policy formulation and assess the effectiveness of implementation. The focus would be on results and accountability, not activity or inputs.

In recent years, New Public Management has been supplemented and in some ways overtaken by the drive to use technology to deliver greater speed, efficiency, transparency, and accountability, and to remove or sidestep government intermediaries who might be roadblocks. Similar changes have swept through governments in many countries, across the continents.

India has experimented in all these directions, but fitfully and half-heartedly, seeking to bypass rather than directly confront the reasons for red tape, delays, plain obstructionism, and sub-optimal decision making. Passport issuance has been partially outsourced to Tata Consultancy Services; the benefits of better service became evident soon after an initial hiccup. Technology has been deployed in the digitization of land records in some cities and states (giving citizens direct access to the records instead of having to depend on the whim of the local revenue official). Tax filing and refunds have also been digitized, reducing personal interface with tax officials and, with that, the scope for corruption. The most ambitious, and promising, program in this broad direction has been the issuing of unique identity numbers under the Aadhaar program, which has paved the way for replacing wasteful subsidies with cash payments[6] and could lead to more efficiencies down the road. The Modi government has sought to bring its technology initiatives under an umbrella term, Digital India, encompassing e-governance, broadband connectivity, public Internet access, e-delivery of services, and much more.

Still, the changes have not been across the board, and there has been little copying of best practice among the states. Also, public–private partnerships have been bedeviled by disputes—usually a death knell since any dispute in India takes years to resolve. The underlying problems, especially in the infrastructure sector, have been defective contracts, poor regulatory oversight, and compromised processes. The Planning Commission responded by developing Model Concession Agreements, but there was resistance because of alleged straitjacketing, and criticism by ministers who wanted elbow room to do things their way—not always with the best intentions.

Conscious of some of these issues, or anticipating them, the Manmohan Singh government appointed the second Administrative Reforms Commission, in 2005, with the seasoned politician Veerappa Moily as chairman. Four years later the commission submitted dozens of reports, covering thousands of pages. It is not clear whether anyone in the Singh government read any of it, because no action followed. In fact, the reports are a surprise in that they have many Thatcher–Reagan-style solutions to offer and are waiting to be picked up by a purposeful government.

This is not an unusual situation. One of the problems of memory-challenged governments is that no one has read the minutes of the last meeting or the previous expert report. Since no party in opposition adopts a shadow cabinet system—a practice followed by a number of countries, including Malaysia and New Zealand—that would familiarize its senior members with issues and options, all too many newly appointed ministers approach problems with the expertise of rank novices.

Of the reforms that have been introduced since 1991, a key idea has been to give the consumer choice—specifically, private-sector alternatives to the hitherto public-sector monopolies. Opening up sectors like telecommunications, aviation, and banking (all virtual state monopolies till the 1990s) has meant that customers have become accustomed to better standards of service, though the corollary of closing down or privatizing the failed public-sector organizations in these sectors has been off the table. The government-owned telecom companies have staff costs greater than revenue, and the government-owned airline has little hope of viability without radical surgery. The proposed new bankruptcy law might change matters for some of these companies—if the government is willing to face the unions in a political climate that still places a lot of faith in public-sector companies, however underperforming they may be. In the case of the more successful PPP projects, like airports and power distribution, there have been charges of artificially high capital costs and high tariffs. With the high costs, the airlines complain about excessive airport charges, but passengers recognize that the leading cities now have modern airports that figure in lists of the best-run airports in the world. In the case of electricity distribution, open access (which would allow consumers a choice of distribution companies) has been blocked in one way or another. All too often, the fear or suspicion is of regulatory capture by corporate entities that secure an infrastructure franchise. Such suspicions gain strength when the leaked draft of an audit report on Delhi's power distribution companies talks of overbilling to the extent of Rs 80 billion.

The stray experiments with new forms of governance can be taken into new fields. There is no particular reason that the railways should be an arm of the government, run by an ossified set of officials as part of the ministry of railways, when it can be made a viable service as a separate corporate entity with a proper commercial ethos (it would be publicly owned, at least for the foreseeable future). The postal service, stuck in old ways, has failed to give competition to private courier companies, whereas under dynamic management it could use its vast network (150,000 post offices, which compares with 110,000 bank branches in the country) to offer a variety of services, including basic financial services of the kind envisaged for the proposed payment banks[7]—provided the system is technologically upgraded. This would need managerial drive, not the current civil service leadership.

The railways and posts are two of the largest government agencies responsible for service delivery. With 1.8 million employees between them, they account for nearly 60 percent of the total 3.1 million employed in the central civilian government (security forces in uniform, civil and military, total another 2.1 million and are not included in these numbers). Privatizing the railways and posts would reduce the size of the non-uniformed central government to under a million. Tackling the armies of civil servants that oversee seventy-two centrally sponsored schemes and their implementation by the states would be a logical follow-through to the greater devolution of funds to states, announced by the Modi government, and should render surplus many thousands more government employees—available for redeployment in productive tasks. Modernizing the process by which the government arrives at decisions would reduce the massive preponderance of supporting staff (95 percent of the total) and reduce paperwork. The administration could then become lean, focused, and purposeful in a way that it is not today.

Different Strokes for Different Functions

Deciding which solution to apply to what problem means breaking down government activity into categories, to help understand the problem and then identify a possible solution. Analysts have put government functions into specific categories: high frequency but low value; low frequency with high value; and hybrid categories in between. Each requires a different kind of solution.

At one end you have high-frequency but low-value transactions with the public—like issuing driving licenses, passports, or below the poverty line (BPL) cards. As Pritchett has written, the process is made suitably complicated and time-consuming, so most people are inclined to go to a "tout" or intermediary who helps short-cut the process for a price. However, outsourcing, digitization, and greater transparency have made a difference, though there are still cases like a driver of a private taxi company in Delhi who was recently convicted for raping a passenger. Despite having a criminal history, the accused driver managed to get a taxi license on the strength of a "character certificate" from a police officer who did not exist.

The polar opposite of "high frequency, low value" is of course low-frequency, high-value transactions—like the purchase of major defense equipment or environmental clearance for large industrial and mining projects. Here, the payoffs could be large, including at the political level. If there are too many regulations and too much unregulated discretionary power, these cease to be low-frequency occurrences. The hope here has to be that the massive public outcry against rampant corruption and crony capitalism in 2012 and 2013, as well as the visible evidence of several powerful politicians going to jail on corruption charges, would make a difference to the approach that future governments adopt. Certainly, the Modi government has started on a better footing—but many governments have done that in their initial years.

Between the two corner categories of high- and low-frequency transactions, there flourishes a middle category: government functions that involve some application of mind and discretion, and which are not infrequent: like dealing with investment proposals or high-value tax returns. Here, too, digitization can reduce the human interface, while the use of technology can help improve transparency (for instance, approvals have to be given in a specific time frame that can be tracked, and any questions must be posed in writing, within that time frame). For the rest, there necessarily has to be a system that catches the rule breakers and the corrupt.

Institutional development is therefore vital. Acemoglu and Robinson merely stated the obvious when they argued that political and economic institutions make the difference between a system's success and failure.[8] That seems all too true of the Indian experience. The iron ore mining scams happened because there was (and still is) no effective regulator of mining activity—even after mines have been auctioned and private mining activity is supposed to begin. It is also true that regulators in other sectors (like telecommunications and electricity pricing) have been "captured" at various times by business interests or have been willing to bend to political pressure. Typically, correctives have been slow in coming.

The role of the media, of institutional watchdogs like the Lok Pal (or ombudsman) that was once planned, and of a credible and effective criminal investigation agency become important in improving the quality of governance. Voters play a vital role too; the growing evidence that electors in states are willing to return to office chief ministers who are seen to have performed well has acted as a powerful incentive for state-level leaders to deliver improved governance. One result in recent years has been the higher rates of economic growth notched up by even the most backward states, like Odisha and Bihar. The first currently has a fourth-term chief minister, the second a three-term one. Madhya Pradesh, which has done well on many fronts, including agriculture, has a third-term chief minister.

The Land Acquisition Law

The land law that the Manmohan Singh government piloted through Parliament, with much of the opposition voting in support (out of "casual populism" as Modi's finance minister Arun Jaitley later sought to explain), is a good example of India's penchant for imposing complex and time-consuming procedures on markets. In its long-overdue effort to make sure that those whose land is forcibly taken away for many projects (like a power station or a coal mine) get a fair deal, the law mandates that they must be paid two to four times the market price of land, as "solatium" (from the Latin word for solace) for being forcibly made to part with an asset and involuntary change of location and perhaps lifestyle. This was an understandable reaction to the accumulated history of pittances having been paid in past decades to vast numbers of the hapless dispossessed, and the distress caused by involuntary displacement. But did the law try to overcorrect?

By the time the new law came into being, in 2013, the market reality for land had changed. Land prices in India had multiplied some fivefold in most parts of the country in the space of a decade—in cities as well as villages. According to the economist Sanjoy Chakravorty, rural Punjab now had land prices that were higher than in any rural area of the United States barring New Jersey, and the average price of land in India was higher than in Germany, France, and Spain—though land productivity in India is much lower. But non-agricultural land commands higher prices than agricultural land (determining whether a piece of land is agricultural, residential, commercial, or industrial is an administrative decision, and a source of much corruption). Hence there is some logic to the stipulation in the land law that prices paid in cases of forcible acquisition must be in multiples of the price for agricultural land. However, the reality of the land market is that front-running (buying agricultural land on inside information prior to a government purchase to benefit from the uplift) is quite common, so prices are high at the start of an acquisition process. As a consequence of these different developments, forcible land acquisition could become unaffordable from the perspective of project viability in many cases—while the owners of land get unearned income that frequently translates into a windfall.

In a lucid study, Chakravorty has recounted a good deal of this and explored related issues.[9] He makes the important point that while the law assumes two players in a land acquisition, that is, the buyer and the seller, there is a third stakeholder, the public, which would find the costs of everything from power to irrigation and transport climbing even as those on one side of the triangle (those asked to part with their land) get windfall gains.

The Modi government moved quickly (perhaps too quickly) to limit the scope of the new law and to ease some of its procedural rigors, especially the elaborate stipulations for getting the consent of those who would lose their land (with many intermediaries involved in the laid-out process)—a quite separate but in some ways even more important problem than the one of price. By one assessment, it would take a minimum of four years to go through a land acquisition process—much too long from the perspective of anyone wanting to set up a project. But the Congress and the rest of the opposition pitched tents for battle on the issue. With the government in a minority in the Upper House of Parliament, it has been blocked even as the opposition onslaught cast it in the role of being anti-poor and anti-farmer. The central land law may remain unchanged in the same way that counterproductive labor laws have proved impossible to change for more than three decades. That will not be good news for either farmers (whose children need non-agricultural jobs) or for the country as a whole, which needs infrastructure and industry.

Anti-Market Mindset

The land acquisition law may or may not have been good politics (it did not save the Congress from a disastrous performance in the 2014 elections), but it is one more example of the problems created when governments follow good intentions while being innocent of market or practical realities. It is still not written into any political party's ideological DNA that market forces have a logic that must invariably be respected, even as they are regulated.

This anti-market mindset is an important part of the story of why India has underperformed. Many problems of governance, including overreach by governments, have been born out of the politician's ever-ready willingness to interfere with the functioning of markets, supposedly in pursuit of a larger good. But price controls over products fed the black economy, and industrial controls corrupted the administrative and political system. Import controls created a flourishing smuggling business and led to the birth of uncompetitive industries, while public-sector enterprises functioning in sub-optimal operating environments typically delivered returns that were lower than the cost of capital. With economic reform, many of the controls have gone into the history books. But the continuing overreach by governments and the long years of experience that businessmen acquired in influencing government decisions have created a culture of cronyism that surfaced in the selling of the telecom spectrum and allocation of coal mines without any market principles being followed. The subsidy regime, with its problems of misallocation and leakages, not to mention high overheads, is another example of a desirable objective being ruined by poor delivery, and also by a reluctance to look for alternatives. As the Planning Commission found in 2005, it cost Rs 3.65 to deliver a rupee's worth of benefit in the form of subsidized food, while more than half the grain reached the wrong people.

For all the piecemeal reform that has been done since 1991, the state socialism that was Indira Gandhi's economic legacy retains a broad political purchase that a politician will tackle at his peril. In 2016, the biggest if not the dominant players in the key sectors of finance, transport, and energy are government-owned enterprises. In these and in other sectors, when competition has been allowed, the public sector has come off secondbest. But the logic of this outcome is not understood or followed through.

The business of administration remains largely unreformed because no politician wants to take on organized groups, like trade unions. As the political scientist Mancur Olson argued seminally half a century ago, special interest groups cause economies to ossify as they wrest for themselves benefits at the cost of the majority.[10] To succeed, all such groups need is to be organized and focused on capturing benefits (government schoolteachers might be a good example). In India, trade unions have acted as a strong pressure group to protect laws that serve the interests of those already employed, at the cost of the vast armies of the unemployed and underemployed. Producer firms have lobbied for high tariff walls, thus reducing competition—the price being paid by consumers. Employees in state-owned organizations have struck work repeatedly to protest the sale of shares to the public, for fear that this might expose them to the discipline of the stock market.

Strong autocratic systems can find ways to deal with such issues, but electoral pressures in democracies often come in the way of governments tackling interest groups. The result is that the reform and restructuring of government organizations, in particular the introduction of performance-based reward–punishment systems, has become next to impossible even as government employees, armed with constitutional protections, assume lifetime employment as the inviolable norm. Such reform as is attempted is therefore usually designed to leave existing administrative structures alone and to create new institutions to take on new roles.

India is not about to get a Thatcher or Reagan, both of them leaders who were willing to challenge entrenched interest groups. Modi has talked of finding a third way, one that is neither the sustained inaction of his predecessor nor the radical structural reform that might stir hornets' nests. This may amount to practicing the "art of the possible," but it will slow administrative change and limit what can be achieved in terms of improving governance.

At the end of the day, India's government leaders have been opportunistic rather than conviction reformers, sidestepping interest groups rather than tackling them. They have experimented with what works and what does not, but on the margin. They have tried out different organizational structures and new technologies—but not strong disincentive systems. There has been an abiding faith in passing laws without asking how well they might be implemented, and a persistent willingness to distort markets. The end result is uneven, because no one has tried systemic change on the basis of a holistic understanding of the problem. Patchy experiments have produced patchy results and have left loads of room for improvement.

10

Corruption

HOPE AFTER THE HEISTS?

AT VARIOUS TIMES in the turbulent years from 2011 to 2013, there were two former central government cabinet ministers[1] in jail, as well as four former state chief ministers.[2] Criminal investigations had been ordered into the unexplained wealth of two other former chief ministers,[3] while in 2014 a sitting chief minister[4] had to step down on being sent to jail following conviction by a trial court on a corruption charge. All of them are now out of jail, waiting for court/appeal hearings, while in one case conviction has been overturned on appeal. Meanwhile, three former chief ministers of Maharashtra were indicted in an inquiry report on a building scam in Mumbai. And four central ministers[5] had been forced to resign, after their names cropped up in the context of various scandals. The total tally of thirteen arrests, resignations, and arraignments of top-level politicians was something the like of which India had not seen till then, and perhaps had never thought it would see. But then, no one had dreamed that scams would be executed in broad daylight, with the press and the whole country watching.

Cut to Sanchar Bhavan, home of the department of telecommunications. On January 10, 2008, at 3.30 P.M., businessman Mahendra Nahata was sweating profusely as he waited along with many other recognizable business faces for the door to a room to open. Nahata was one of those hoping to bag a telecom license and scarce radio spectrum for his mobile telephone company. Less than two hours earlier, at 1.47 P.M., the ministry had put out a press release saying that "letters of intent" would be issued to all those who had applied for licenses by an arbitrarily chosen cut-off date. The great Indian telecom scrum was about to begin.[6]

At 2.45 P.M., the department put out another press release, on the process to be followed. Applicants would have to assemble by 3.30 P.M. in the Committee Room on the second floor of Sanchar Bhavan (telecommunications department building) to collect their letters of intent. Armed guards were posted at the door to ensure that each applicant sent in only one representative. Fifteen applicants assembled at the appointed time, armed with bankers' checks, bank guarantees, and the relevant papers—preparations that ordinarily would have taken days. It was clear that the favored few had been tipped off well before the last-minute flurry of press releases or had used their sleuths to track what was coming.

Once you got your letter of intent, you had to rush to a reception room on the ground floor, past television crews recording the drama, and hand in a completed application. Whoever did that first would be assured of radio spectrum, which mobile companies use to carry voice and data signals. Without the spectrum, the letter of intent was meaningless.

Nahata's application was found to be defective. Agitated, he got into a shouting match with officials and a scuffle with other applicants, until he was physically escorted out of the room. Venugopal Dhoot, who ran the Videocon group, and his parliamentarian brother Rajkumar Dhoot, were there too. People charged down staircases from the second floor to the ground floor, some used relay teams—anything to gain those extra seconds on the competition. In about forty-five minutes, eight companies walked off with 122 licenses for different telecom "circles" and the precious spectrum. They paid only a fraction of what the spectrum would have commanded in an open market, which is what explained the mad rush to be there first.

There was an immediate uproar. Companies that had been waiting for months after submitting their applications were kept out, while latecomers qualified under the bizarre rules. But the scale of the scandal dawned on the public only months later, when two companies that had acquired spectrum cheap decided to cash in, getting valuations that ran into tens of billions of rupees when they sold shares in companies that had no assets other than the spectrum. The government's chief auditor decided to take a look, and put the potential loss of revenue from underpriced spectrum at up to Rs 1.76 trillion. The swirl of scandal began to lick at the toes of the then finance minister and even the prime minister. Finally, it all caught up with Andimuthu Raja, the telecom minister and the master of the January circus, who had to resign and go to jail along with some of his officials; they are out on bail and face trial.

The question remained: how had things come to such a pass that, almost anywhere you looked, in both central and state governments, there was the reek of scandal? Heists that were so in-your-face that they provoked mass protests in cities became one of the overriding issues in the 2014 general elections. If it wasn't the underpriced sale of scarce resources, it was bribery in defense deals. If it wasn't real-estate skulduggery, it was one-sided renegotiation of contracts with obliging governments. If it wasn't large-scale "leakages" in virtually every government spending program, it was rampant crony capitalism.

Four "What" Questions

This chapter addresses the following questions: What are the principal types of corruption today in India, and what are their causes? What is the scale of corruption, and is it growing? What is the relationship between economic development and corruption? Finally, what are the possible solutions?

If the scandals of the last few years are analyzed and categorized, they present a surprisingly simple set of issues and causes. Table 10.1 lists more than a dozen scandals of recent years and illustrates something fairly straightforward: the opportunity for large-scale scams was created primarily by mispricing scarce assets of various kinds, creating arbitrage opportunities so large that they were gilt-edged invitations to make a quick billion (or at least a million). In some of the other cases, there were poor controls on spending. In others, the demand for a product or service was rendered illegal by being banned, but the demand for the product/service did not go away. There were also cases of regulatory failure and of plain bribery. But the main lesson in the table flies off the page: don't meddle with product prices and distort markets because you create room for intermediaries to grant favors, usually in return for a quid pro quo, for price arbitrage in one form or another, and for sharing the profits. The second lesson is this: even as you allow markets to function freely, you need better regulation and supervision.

Despite long years of economic aberrations on its account, the Indian politician's favorite instrument of intervention is price control, or dual pricing for markets that are segmented on some basis, or some other way of twisting the market. The fact that markets have turned healthy and led to higher production and better efficiencies in almost all cases when price distortions were removed (the list includes pharmaceutical products, bathing soaps, cars, cement, steel, tires, and paper) has not registered with, or convinced, most of the political class that this is the way to go. The Manmohan Singh government approved up to 90 percent foodgrain subsidy for two-thirds of the population; the Aam Aadmi Party's state government in Delhi believes in providing free water and heavily subsidized electricity for segments of the population;

Table 10.1 Scandals of Recent Years: The Principal Enabling Cause Is Price Distortion

Scandal	Type	Problem
Spectrum sale	Scarce resource	Underpriced
Coal mine allocation	Scarce resource	Underpriced
Adarsh building	Real-estate grab	Underpriced
Italian helicopters	Large government contract	Scope for payoffs
Illegal iron ore mining	Resource grab	Regulatory failure, cronyism
Bihar fodder	Bogus purchases	Poor financial controls
Illegal sand mining	Scarce resource	Ban drove market underground
Commonwealth Games	Government contracts	Dishonest administrators
Cooking gas gray market	Supply leakages	Price arbitrage
Foodgrain public distribution system	Supply leakages	Price arbitrage
Fake muster rolls	Government contracts	Poor controls
Railway Board appointment	Selling of "wet" posts	Bribery and kickbacks
Robert Vadra	Land speculation	Non-transparent market, rules of land use

Source: Author's research.

and while in opposition the BJP spoke against adjusting fuel prices to reflect cost, it paradoxically removed controls on diesel pricing soon after coming to power. The political logic for price controls is that poor people need subsidies. And the political reality is that the promise of such subsidies wins votes, even though most of the subsidies are captured by the middle class. But if corruption remains as hydra-headed as ever, price distortions will be the biggest (but not the only) cause.

What is the scale of distortion or corruption? There have been many assessments over the years and the numbers vary massively—partly because people have used different definitions. Some have looked at the quantum of bribery, others at money laundering, and yet others at tax evasion. On the first of these, two Delhi-based economists, Laveesh Bhandari and Bibek Debroy, have estimated "the private earnings of public officials" at 1.26 percent of GDP (or Rs 921 billion crore in 2010–11).[7] On tax evasion, the Wanchoo

Committee on direct taxes estimated in 1971 that non-salary income which escaped tax in 1968–69 was 0.5 percent of GDP (Rs 1.8 billion at the time; the 2015 equivalent in relation to GDP would be Rs 70 billion).[8] And in the early 1980s, the National Institute of Public Finance and Policy did a study for the finance ministry, which came to the alarming conclusion that non-corporate income that evaded tax in 1980–81 was between 68 percent and 139 percent of assessed income.[9]

The same study totaled up black (unaccounted for) income, which it estimated "conservatively" at 18–21 percent of GDP. The World Bank in a multi-country study concluded in 2010 that India's "shadow economy" was between 20.7 percent and 23.2 percent of GDP in the period 1999–2007. While substantial, this was said to be lower than the world average of 31 percent to 34 percent. Some individual estimates quoted in a government White Paper have been higher, ranging from 35 percent to 51 percent of GDP.[10]

Few reports have raised eyebrows as much as one from the Washington-based Global Financial Integrity, which put the capital flight from India (mostly through under-invoicing of exports and over-invoicing of imports) in 2012 at $94.7 billion (Rs 4.27 trillion in 2012), or about 5 percent of GDP.[11] A quite different figure came from an IMF study that put capital flight from India at $20–30 billion (or $1–2 billion annually) during 1971–86; this was later revised to more than $3 billion annually ($88 billion for the 1971–97 period). As can be imagined, such numbers are more in the nature of guesstimates than hard calculations. As the White Paper observed in 2012, the IMF figure was equal to a fifth of the total overseas debt taken on by India during the same period.

These numbers should be seen in juxtaposition with the figures put out by the Swiss National Bank, which show that Indian money in Swiss banks totaled a paltry 1.8 billion Swiss francs (Rs 126 billion) in 2012, down sharply from Rs 234 billion in 2006.[12] Those figures tested credulity, since 1668 Indian accounts at just one bank branch in Geneva in 2007 were shown to have had as much as $4.1 billion (about Rs 180 billion at the time).[13] The bank (HSBC) was reported saying that such accounts (only some of which violated country laws on foreign exchange and taxation) had since seen a 70 percent drop, following a tightening of norms.[14] Reports of Swiss banks becoming more transparent (voluntarily or under pressure) may have resulted in a good bit of money being moved elsewhere.

The numbers given out in most studies are usually gross outflows; no estimate is made of the money that comes back to India—by part-financing the imports of high-tariff items, for instance, which could be under-invoiced to evade duties. The opportunity to evade duty, by making undisclosed payments offshore for a part of the import value, would be an incentive to take the money out in the first place. Also, about half the total foreign direct investment flowing into India ($200 billion) has come through Mauritius and Singapore, both tax havens; a good chunk of that could be Indian money coming back. Ditto with investment in the Indian stock and debt markets through what are called Participatory Notes, which allow the investor to operate through a foreign institutional investor and avoid registering with the stock market regulator—thereby getting confidentiality with regard to identity. Participatory Notes in early 2015 amounted to about $45 billion.[15] Some of that would be genuine money from investors, like hedge funds, but a lot of it is likely to be dodgy.

Meanwhile, Kotak Securities raised some intriguing possibilities by pointing out in an analyst's report that the official trade numbers did not tally with the numbers put together from the balance sheets of large companies. Later, a prominent business house, Essar, was issued a show-cause notice in 2015 for (it was alleged) inflating by 90 percent the cost of imported capital goods for a power plant, by routing it through an intermediary company created by the group in the United Arab Emirates, and siphoning off Rs 26 billion.[16] Whether the charge was substantiated or not, it brought to mind Global Financial Integrity's report that more than 10 percent of India's foreign trade is mis-invoiced.

What the "right" numbers are might be difficult to assess, since estimates vary so widely. What is obvious is that the sums are large. The Modi government responded to the problem of money held illegally overseas by enacting a draconian law that harked back to the rigors of the Foreign Exchange Regulations Act of the mid-1970s, a law that had manifestly failed to check foreign exchange violations and therefore had been replaced by a milder law. The effect of the law was that thousands of people shifted their formal residence outside the country rather than bring their money back. Meanwhile, a scheme to encourage disclosures of wealth held abroad delivered little. More practical solutions to illegal transactions are reasonable tax and policy regimes, and open economies. In most people's books this would include low taxes on incomes and products, low tariffs, fewer controls on imports, some freedom for cross-border capital flows, and no price distortions in markets. In essence, the incentive to evade tax or escape a country altogether should be so low that it would not be worth the game or the risk of being caught. That is the logic of why the economic reform program, kicked off in 1991, was expected to reduce the scope for corruption.

In some ways, it did—black-marketing and smuggling virtually disappeared from many key markets, the exceptions being items where subsidies and dual markets still operated. On the one hand, a more liberal policy regime meant that many shortages disappeared—from scooters to telephone connections—thereby eliminating flourishing gray markets. On the other, the Planning Commission estimated that 57 percent of the foodgrain supplied through the public distribution system at heavy subsidies did not reach the intended beneficiaries—a scale of diversion that suggested organized activity. The room for discretion, and therefore arbitrary action, remained across a broad front, even as there was always room for enforcing regulations (such as those to protect the environment) lightly or rigidly, and for bribes on large government contracts—as in defense deals. As the economy grew, the sums involved got larger, as therefore did temptation—especially when the financing of political parties and elections remained largely beyond the scope of any real scrutiny. All political parties have refused to subject themselves to the transparency required by the law on the right to information. The Congress has protested that it is not obliged to provide its income and expenditure figures to even the Election Commission, but has done so under protest. The Association for Democratic Reforms (ADR) reported in August 2015 that for five national parties that submitted their accounts for 2013–14 to the Election Commission (including Congress but excluding BJP, which delayed filing), 79.68 percent of income came from anonymous sources—from those who bought "coupons" issued by the parties and from donations below Rs 20,000 each, for which the donor's identity does not have to be disclosed.[17]

It is a related matter that India is among the most difficult countries in which to do business. Naturally, there would be corruption—if nothing else, then to speed up the clearance processes or simply to get the job done (those manning government offices with a public interface function usually have fixed rates of "commissions" for doing their job—such as registering property transactions, or sanctioning an electricity connection).

Corruption, Economic Growth, and Democracy

The debate about the relationship between rapid growth and corruption is not new. Do the two go together, and if so which is the cause and which the effect? Does corruption facilitate growth? Conversely, does rapid growth bring with it more corruption? Manmohan Singh teased the subject by saying in late 2011 that economic growth created new opportunities for corruption. Raghuram Rajan found another way of saying it a little earlier when he argued that "strong growth tests economic institutions" in their capacity to cope, and India's were found lacking.[18] This is not unusual; corruption has been a familiar feature of many societies during phases of rapid growth, some examples being China, Russia, and Indonesia. South Korea and Taiwan too were known to be corrupt during their years of rapid ascendancy, as was the United States. But, interestingly enough, none of them (except the United States) were democracies at the time. The result of corruption in an open society like India has not been encouraging. Economic growth in India began to falter just when corruption charges mushroomed. More correctly, the resulting uproar and the correctives that were applied stopped business-as-usual.

So while it is conceivable that some forms of corruption (like speed money, or "commissions" to officials) can facilitate growth, the public reaction and institutional response to widespread corruption, especially in an open democracy, can derail not just growth but a whole system. After a typically delayed outcry about the illegal mining of iron ore in Karnataka and Goa, the courts and governments stepped in, and mining activity was stopped pending a cleanup; the inevitable consequence was that iron ore production in the country dropped by about 34 percent in two years, from 217 million tons to barely 143 million, and steel plants were forced to cut production for want of raw material.[19] One reason the industrial production curve flattened for many quarters was that mining output had fallen.

Likewise, the travails of the usually buoyant telecom sector were a direct consequence of the multi-stage drama following the spectrum allocation controversy—with court cases, audit reports, media frenzy, and parliamentary committee inquiries, not to speak of the ceaseless lobbying and counter-lobbying. After the Supreme Court canceled the licences issued by A. Raja, three international companies (Telenor, Etisalat, and Sistema) that had invested a mammoth $4.5 billion in their Indian businesses had to announce huge write-offs.[20] Meanwhile, those who played fast and loose with the system over environment clearances for projects, building permits, coal mine allocations, and the illegal mining of sand all suffered when environmental rules were enforced or the builder–politician nexus was tested. These and other examples support the broad thesis—advocated by, among others, the World Bank—that corruption leads to misallocation of resources, undermines the legitimacy of the government, raises the cost of (and uncertainty surrounding) projects, results in the creation of arbitrary rules, and facilitates the extraction of surplus "rent" by a powerful few. When the backlash comes, as it eventually did in India, the wheels stop turning.

This may have been a part of what happened with environmental regulation. If you ask India's angry businessmen whom they blame most of all for applying the brakes on economic growth, they are likely to point somewhat simplistically to Jairam Ramesh, who as the environment minister in 2009–11 held up, rejected, or canceled environmental clearances for several large, high-profile industrial, power generation, and mining projects.[21] When he was moved to the portfolio of rural development, he (in the eyes of businessmen) did even worse by piloting the new law on land acquisition, which businessmen said was so complicated that no land could be acquired any longer to set up industry. Ramesh became the lightning rod for an acrimonious debate on whether to treat environmental rules seriously (his critics would say arbitrarily) or simply flout them. What is usually ignored in the name-calling is that many of Ramesh's predecessors had used the environmental approval process for projects as an opportunity for extracting payoffs. Ramesh had decided to take the law seriously. The remedy in some eyes was worse than the disease (more on this in Chapter 12).

Cold analysis would suggest that India as a maturing polity was learning from the scandals and controversies. The old ways of doing business were simply not feasible any longer. Civil society activists, courts, and constitutional watchdogs had both become more watchful and active, so corruption or the sidestepping of laws could no longer be easily swept under the carpet. Tragically, though, the correctives that were applied threw the baby out with the bathwater. The Supreme Court canceled all 122 telecom licenses across the board and (as already noted) banned iron ore mining across two states; even the legal mines had to stop working. Coal mine allocations were canceled. The power plants that they were to supply with coal had in some cases been built, and they lay idle. The country waited for a Hegelian outcome: thesis and anti-thesis leading to synthesis, which came in the form of open auction of the mines. The auction saw unreal bids that offered to supply free coal to power plants. The government thought this was a great success.

The policy paralysis that was said to afflict the United Progressive Alliance (UPA) government in its second term (2009–14) was a consequence, at least in part, of the proliferating corruption charges and their corrosive consequences. The prime minister complained that no government could function in an environment in which policy decisions, made in real time with imperfect knowledge, were subjected to criminal investigation launched with the benefit of hindsight. Bureaucrats were said to be avoiding making decisions for fear of being hauled out of retirement later and sent to jail or facing criminal charges (as has happened to some). And those who traveled along the country's highways—a focus of infrastructure investment—could see the terrain dotted with stalled projects that were the subjects of dispute between private contractors and the highway authority. Dispute resolution dragged out over years in the courts, which themselves were not free from taint. It reached a point when the highway authority could not get anyone to bid for 24,000 kilometers of road-building projects.

And yet, vast areas of activity continued to exist in which scandals were an everyday reality, some of them waiting to blow up in the country's face. In September 2013, the television news channel Headlines Today (since rebadged as India Today) telecast secretly recorded clips of half a dozen Haryana legislative assembly members, or MLAs (all belonging to the then ruling Congress), negotiating with reporters who posed as farmers wanting their land converted from agricultural to commercial use; such conversion could multiply the value of the land at least tenfold. In conversation after taped conversation, the MLAs mentioned a price for helping to get permission for change of land use—a minimum of Rs 10 million per acre, sometimes Rs 12.5 million. During the eight years (till then) of the Bhupinder Hooda government's rule in the state, land use had been changed for a record 21,000 acres[22]—with, it may be assumed, enormous amounts of money changing hands. As an interesting side story, these cases included a few acres reclassified speedily for Robert Vadra, Sonia Gandhi's son-in-law, who, as it happens, paid (the pre-conversion price) for the land after the conversion had been done, thus giving him an overnight windfall gain with no capital deployed till then. It is telling that the TV exposé on legislators facilitating large-scale land speculation caused no political ripple, while much attention was devoted to Mr. Vadra.

Samuel Huntington said, "A country's ratio of political to economic opportunities affects the nature of corruption. If the former outweigh the latter, then people will enter politics in order to make money, and this will lead to a greater extent of corruption."[23] It is certainly the case, as we will see in Chapter 14, that being a politician in India usually comes with a dramatic increase in personal wealth—which most other careers cannot promise.[24] It is said that the only thing that beats entering politics is becoming a "godman," (self-styled gurus or holy men who dot the country's landscape and who seem to acquire vast assets very quickly). But even a godman cannot compete with the opportunities that abound in the most opaquely governed sectors, like real estate, during periods of market buoyancy.

Corruption—Big and Small

At the bottom of the ladder, as Katherine Boo shows graphically through her award-winning book on life in a Mumbai slum, bribery is the only weapon with which the poor negotiate their way through a world in which the cards are stacked against them.[25] A politician who intercedes to gain you a teaching job in a government school, a surgeon in a free government hospital who is to undertake a desperately needed heart surgery, a bank official in charge of giving a loan, a policeman who has to be persuaded to examine a false charge sheet, a guard who has to let you through a gate—all of them have to be paid. The poor have no other way to get them to pay attention or to do their job. As Boo notes, "For the poor of a country where corruption thieved a great deal of opportunity, corruption was one of the genuine opportunities that remained."

It is always surprising that petty corruption, so widespread as to be almost ubiquitous, has rarely figured as an issue in electoral contests, the one time when voters have a real say. Perhaps that is because voters feel, as Boo suggests, that corruption is actually an equalizer; or perhaps because no party or candidate can credibly offer deliverance. Whatever the reason, it is big (not small) corruption that has rocked the country and influenced electoral results. Indeed, recent experience suggests that in a democracy, big corruption may oil the wheels for a while, but eventually it undermines the system and extracts a heavy price.

More Indian governments have been brought down by scandal than by anything else. Indira Gandhi's political decline, after the high point of a victorious war to break up Pakistan and create Bangladesh in 1971, began in part because of scandals over import licenses and her younger son's racket of a car project, which was funded by quasi-government money and yet produced no cars; it did not help when she tried to dismiss mounting criticism by saying that corruption was a "global phenomenon." Rajiv Gandhi as prime minister came under siege midway through his term after a payoff scandal erupted in connection with the purchase of Bofors field artillery. And Manmohan Singh's second term was ruined by scandals emanating mostly from his first term.

In the so-called developmental states, like Taiwan and South Korea, where the state has played an active role in pushing economic growth, including determining the nature and direction of growth, and the role of private players, there often is corruption but it is not disruptive of growth or the political process. Autocratic but non-developmental states would of course deliver very different results, as in the case of Zaire.[26] Weak states have a more corrosive corruption that undermines the legitimacy of the system, discredits the government, and disrupts growth. China's case is instructive, if nothing else because comparisons are often made between it and India. Andrew Wedeman concedes that corruption in China has been anarchic and predatory, unlike what prevailed in the developmental states of East Asia, where businesses financed rightist political parties that in turn gave them pro-growth policies.[27] But he argues, as an explanation of the paradox of rapid growth coexisting with large-scale corruption in the Chinese system, that serious corruption did not crop up in China until the mid-1990s, by which time the economy had already acquired enormous momentum.

Compared to India, a difference might have been that corruption in China was mostly tied to new value being created, not feeding off the existing stock of capital; officials merely took a part of new profits. The economist Jagdish Bhagwati says that a crucial difference between India and China is the type of corruption they have. "India's is classic 'rent-seeking,'" where people jostle to grab a cut of existing wealth. "The Chinese have what I call profit-sharing corruption": the Communist Party puts a straw into the milkshake, so "they have an interest in having the milkshake grow larger."[28]

Whether the milkshake "grows" or not, most of the authoritarian developmental states dealt with only two variables: development and corruption. India throws in a third—democracy, which comes with a free press. As already seen, that changes the dynamic, but not necessarily in predictable ways. Does it act as a check on corruption or does it inure politicians to criticism in minimally urbanized places that have too small a middle class and often no effective mass media—and therefore no effective public opinion? Do identity-based political parties naturally veer toward pork barrel politics, because voters will vote for their caste or community, and thereby ignore corruption as an issue?

One could look to India for answers, to a variety of South American countries, or to some African ones; in many of them, either democracy got derailed or the economy did. In some, a kleptocracy took over. In quite a few democracy and a free press continued to survive because the vote did not change anything and the press was ineffective. India has seen a combination of all these outcomes at the center and in the states, but it may now be on its way to a partial overhaul of the system.

The Gilded Age

Comparisons have been made between present-day India and the United States of the last third of the nineteenth century. The late nineteenth century was the United States' period of most rapid growth, with the twin engines of industrialization and urbanization fired up simultaneously. While the United States had experienced rampant corruption even in the first half of the nineteenth century, it was the subsequent decades of rapid growth that saw the simultaneous rise of corrupt political bosses and of the "robber barons." These latter had led the charge when it came to extending economic frontiers westward and industrializing what until the US Civil War of the 1860s had been a mainly rural economy. Whether it was railroads or steel, banking or oil, men with names like Vanderbilt and Carnegie, Morgan and Astor, Mellon and Rockefeller became synonymous with sudden wealth, so much so that Mark Twain referred to the period as "the gilded age." Not the golden age, but a period when there was a lot of gilt being put on a harsh reality that included rampant corruption and crony capitalism. One commentator recalled that a railroad tycoon bought up the whole of the Pennsylvania legislature because he wanted clearances for running a railroad through the state.

Some writers have begun to call the recent period India's own gilded age. Jayant Sinha (now a minister of state for finance) and the political scientist Ashutosh Varshney, in an article in the *Financial Times* in early 2011, listed the similarities: a roughly equivalent rate of urbanization (30 percent and on its way to 50 percent), the rise of industrial capitalism in a noisy and participatory democracy, the sprouting of millionaires who used comparable methods (grabbing resources, influencing regulators, keeping out foreign competition), and the birth of political bosses in cities and party machines.[29] New York's Tammany Hall politics certainly finds reflection in how, for instance, the city of Mumbai is run. But such comparisons are also misleading, because when you point to the obvious similarities (sudden rags-to-riches stories, corrupt party bosses, crony capitalism, extraction of monopoly profits, cornering of resources, etc.), the danger is that you ignore the substantial differences, as Varshney himself said later. America's problem was an unbridled capitalism, though its politicians also had the power to grant favors, based, for example, on barriers to entry. India has too many stultifying rules of a kind that did not trouble the United States. America's west was opening up, whereas India with a population density eight times the global average (twenty times in states like West Bengal and Kerala) suffers an acute pressure on land—and land has been the reason for a great deal of political corruption.

The gilded age in the United States ended with a boom–bust cycle of the kind India too has recently experienced. The overconstruction of railroads led to a collapse of some railroad companies and the failure of many banks. A recession that began in 1893 lasted three or four years. Unemployment increased and there was a rash of strikes as well as worker violence. As we know too well, crisis can beget reform and that is what followed in the United States. A variety of new laws came into effect: anti-trust legislation to curb the power of the big companies, new banking laws, laws against unfair labor practices, social legislation to give women the right to vote (they were believed to be less corruptible), laws that gave the state greater control over natural resources, and of course the introduction of prohibition, which was seen among other things as cutting the power base of corrupt party bosses. A muckraking press, feeding a growing middle class of readers spread nationwide, exposed scandal after scandal, prompting a good bit of the change and giving birth to (for instance) the Food and Drug Administration. The first two decades of the twentieth century have thus come to be known in the United States as the Progressive Era.

As in the United States, so in India. The forces that have worked toward the transition from a problematic phase to a reform era are the same: growing urbanization that increases interaction between diverse groups of people and helps to create Jürgen Habermas's "public sphere";[30] growing literacy that allows people to read, understand issues, and express themselves, creating an effective public opinion; and the rise of the middle class, which Habermas thought created an arena of common concerns. It is no surprise therefore that the general discontent with the political system boiled over in urbanized Delhi, where a new party campaigning on an anti-corruption platform, and led by a former tax official, was able to mobilize hitherto "non-political" volunteers and capture the imagination of many voters—all within a year of its birth.[31]

Corruption and the Stages of Growth

An interesting hypothesis put forward is that societies often become more corrupt as they start on the growth curve, but clean up their act once prosperity reaches a level at which the majority in a society decide that tackling corruption is important. The countries that have the best scores (least corrupt) in the Corruption Perceptions Index compiled by Transparency International happen to be the wealthiest ones. Countries in Scandinavia (with scores of 86 or better on a scale of 0 to 100) and other parts of Western Europe, plus outposts like Singapore (84) and New Zealand (91), are recorded as the least corrupt in the world. In Latin America, which has both rich and poor countries, Chile (the richest country on the continent) has the best low corruption score (73), while Paraguay, Honduras, and Nicaragua have the worst (going down as low as 24). The BRICS countries (Brazil, Russia, India, China, and South Africa) offer a mixed picture. Brazil (with a corruption score of 43) is richer than China (40 in 2013, and only 36 in 2014), which until the latest year used to have a better score than its poorer neighbor India. Russia, which is closer to Brazil on per capita income, scores only 27 and is the outlier, possibly because of its oligarchy-driven system, while South Africa, which has gained a reputation for political venality even as its economic performance dips, has seen its corruption score drop over almost a decade from 51 to 44. In India's case, its corruption score improved over the years, from a miserable 27 in 2002 to 35 in 2007. The score then dropped during the years of scandal, to 31 in 2011, but has moved up since to 38 in 2014—a score that places it in league with noticeably better-off countries like Peru and Thailand.

Despite visible variations in the pattern, the hypothesis put forward by Vivek H. Dehejia of Carleton University is that corruption follows a trajectory somewhat similar to the trend that the economist Simon Kuznets postulated for inequality.[32] It increases in an economy up to a certain stage of development, then levels off and eventually comes down as incomes rise beyond a certain threshold. The Kuznets thesis on income inequality has come under question in recent years because some of the most advanced countries have seen inequality of income and wealth rise sharply. But in the case of corruption, it is undeniable that the best corruption scores are for the richest countries and the worst are mostly for the poorest—Somalia, Afghanistan, Sudan (all below 15). Indonesia in its worst days had a corruption score of 19 or less, but it has since improved to 34. Bangladesh, emerging as a success story that in many ways outshines India, has seen its score jump from 12 in 2003 to 25 in 2014. The only poor country with a score better than 60 is Bhutan, and there is no rich country with a score worse than 40 (Italy and Greece are at 43). The moral of the numbers: wealth and low levels of corruption go together. But which is the cause and which the effect? Or are they mutually reinforcing?

We need to understand the social context, in terms of the forces and processes that are unleashed as development takes place and incomes rise. One is urbanization, which for India is expected to accelerate in the next three decades. Urban voters in India are more likely to vote issues and less likely to vote their identity than their rural counterparts; in Delhi, for instance, state elections in a predominantly urban state feature issues like women's safety and corruption, clean air and reliable power supply, proper public transport and better medical care, whereas most voters in a poor, predominantly rural state like Bihar tend to vote along the lines of caste and religious community. The party that swept the Delhi state elections in early 2015 promised free wi-fi, but also free water and subsidized electricity—testifying to the abiding attraction of government freebies. Still, it was different from identity politics.

A second and related development is of course the growth of the middle class, as Habermas noted. By most accounts, India's middle class and neo-middle class are reaching a size, especially in urban areas, that could bring about a sea change in the nature and responsiveness of administration. Also, some 40 percent of parliamentary constituencies now have a significant urban voter segment, and the middle class in cities and towns has given birth to a more vocal public sphere, through a noisier media and an active civil society. The political class ignores these trends at its peril. As the thoughtful parliamentarian B. J. Panda of the Biju Janata Dal, a regional political party in Odisha state, has argued when talking of the gilded age and the passage to the Progressive Era, India's own Progressive Era is still some way off. But Narendra Modi swept into power in 2014 on the twin promises of good governance and development—promises that found resonance particularly with the young.

Without waiting for the long-term play of social and economic forces, are there shorter-term solutions to corruption? The answer is of course yes, and technology provides some of them—especially when it comes to the widespread problem of petty corruption, which throws grit into the government–citizen interface. The corruption isn't really "petty," because the government spends many billions on a variety of income transfer schemes—food subsidy, fertilizer subsidy, old-age pension, widows' pension, kerosene and cooking gas subsidy, free meals for schoolchildren, and free medical insurance. It is widely recognized that much of the money in some of these schemes is misdirected or lost in transit, so to speak, or subject to such heavy overheads that the intended beneficiary gets only a minuscule part of the money the government spends. Rajiv Gandhi famously put the figure at 15 percent. West Bengal's food minister Jyotipriyo Mullick claimed in late 2014 that he had eliminated 19 million bogus ration cards—in a state that according to the 2011 Census had all of 20 million households! The potential saving in expenditure: Rs 30 billion. Bogus cards don't get created by accident, and leakages are usually designed to feed the bottom rungs of different political machines. Kerosene leakage and its diversion to adulterate petrol and diesel cannot really be an "unorganized" business; it needs political protection. So there are substantial vested interests involved.

The great hope on the technology front is said to be the Aadhaar program (see a detailed discussion of the project in Chapter 11). In theory, this has the merit of enabling cash transfers to replace existing programs that involve costly duplication of distribution systems, avoiding the distortion of product and factor markets and reducing overheads, thereby saving the government a ton of money at a time when the fiscal deficit is bloated. It also helps to tackle partially the problem of mis-targeting through wrong selection of beneficiaries. Meanwhile, other solutions enabled by information technology (IT)—for delivering ration cards, driving licences, and passports; paying taxes; and getting easy access to property records, for instance—are making processes simpler, quicker, and more transparent, thus making a noticeable difference to the government–citizen interface. The computerization of railway reservations made a dramatic difference to the ease of booking a seat or berth for a journey and also cut out rampant corruption involving "touts" or middlemen. However, driving licenses are even now issued not only to those who pass a test, as Abhijit Banerjee and Esther Duflo show.[33]

India is at a halfway point. Corruption had caught the system in a maelstrom, enmeshing what was a rapidly growing economy and testing the political class, challenging it to devise new rules for the system. Until the results of the Delhi state elections in December of 2013, and then the Lok Sabha polls of 2014, both of which swept out incumbent rulers who faced corruption charges, the political class did not seem to recognize that the old way of doing business was no longer sustainable. But recent electoral success has gone to those who could claim a clean record without being seriously challenged. While they would be naive who believe that all corruption will end, the risk–reward equation has changed, and it could change some more. Has a tipping point been reached? Perhaps not yet. But even allowing for the birth and power of homegrown oligarchs, the system is moving in the broad direction of positive change and not descending into a Russian-style kleptocracy that overrides all institutional checks. After four years of almost endless scandal (2010–14), that is something to be grateful for.

Stronger Institutions

One reason for hope is that new life has been breathed into institutions like the courts, the Election Commission, and the Comptroller and Auditor General (CAG) office, added to which is the vital new legislation on the right to information (RTI), which has brought a new level of transparency to government functioning. Meanwhile, the courts' willingness to admit public interest litigation has played a key role in enabling concerned citizens to challenge government decisions. It was public interest litigation that led to court orders forcing the Delhi government to clean up the city's air by mandating the use of compressed natural gas (rather than diesel or petrol) in all public vehicles, including taxis.

The greater enthusiasm that the Election Commission and the CAG have brought to bear on their functioning has been another transformational development. Starting with T. N. Seshan as chief election commissioner in the 1990s, the Election Commission has taken its mandate more seriously than before. It has checked once-widespread practices like the capture of polling booths to enable stuffing of votes into ballot boxes, and now tries to watch election spending with a hawk's eye.[34] It has been less than successful in monitoring such expenses, and the task remains a daunting challenge. Meanwhile, the constitutional body that has hit the headlines more than any other in recent years is the CAG, the government's auditor. Whether it is the spectrum scam, the coal mining scandal, the misuse of public money in the conduct of the Commonwealth Games of 2010, or for that matter the contentious issues of gas pricing and favors to a private gas producer,[35] it is the CAG that has set the cat among the pigeons.[36]

The arc of containment put in place by these institutions has been extended by the growing power of two other sets of players. Non-government organizations (NGOs) of all shapes and sizes, usually manned by activists who have the patience and commitment to sift through masses of data to expose government claims, have influenced and altered public debate on issues ranging all the way from land acquisition to civil liberties, and from public health to cases of crony capitalism. One example is the half dozen professors at the elite Indian Institute of Management at Ahmedabad who got together in 1999 to form the Association for Democratic Reforms (ADR). They had returned to India from US universities like Harvard and Stanford, and decided (along with a couple of other Ahmedabad-based founders) that something had to be done to improve the standards in India's politics. Helped by an active Election Commission, sympathetic judges who handed down favorable verdicts, and new disclosure norms for candidates standing for elections, the association began to document the asset ownership of politicians, the number who had a criminal record, and so on. Soon, the Central Information Commission, in response to a petition under the RTI, handed down a landmark ruling in 2008 that the accounts of political parties were open to public scrutiny.

Parties also had to disclose the identity of anyone who donated more than Rs 20,000. Even closer scrutiny was to follow, but the political parties soon began resisting it. One of the negatives of the Modi administration is that it has been less than enthusiastic about RTI; indeed, it took a year to appoint a chief information commissioner (the chief RTI executive).

As the movement launched by ADR gained momentum, with some 1,200 other NGOs joining to monitor the conduct of elections, the Supreme Court struck down a discriminatory provision in the law that elected representatives would not automatically lose their seats in a legislature if convicted of a criminal offense provided they filed an appeal in three months. The pincer attack from the Election Commission and the Supreme Court, combined with media reports that draw on information from the ADR's website, may well prompt political parties to become more careful about the candidates to whom they give party tickets—though many with criminal records still manage to get party tickets, and most candidates are able to conceal the truth about the money spent on campaigning.

The ADR analyzed the tax returns and donation reports of the six national political parties for 2012–13. It found that they had reported total income of a paltry Rs 9.91 billion, with only 10 percent of the money coming from donations of more than Rs 20,000. Even more incredibly, the ADR reviewed the election expenses of those elected to Parliament in 2014 and found that a third had declared expenses that were less than half the permitted expenditure limit (Rs 7 million per constituency in the more populous states and Rs 5.4 million in smaller ones). The average expenditure reported on campaigning was a scarcely believable Rs 4 million. No one doubts that the candidates spent many multiples of the declared sums.

The media have become an important factor, helped by greater reach because of growing literacy (well over 100 million copies of newspapers are sold daily), and the rapid penetration achieved by private cable and satellite television into more than half the 250 million homes in the country. While the aggressive culture of television news anchors is widely decried by commentators, it is also true that more substantive debates seem to take place in TV studios than in a semi-dysfunctional Parliament. It is a reflection of how much of the public space has been taken over by the media and by activists that the government at one stage was forced to negotiate the contents of a proposed Lok Pal (ombudsman) bill with a group of activists gathered under the "India against Corruption" banner, with the army truck driver turned social reformer Anna Hazare (who went on a fast over the issue) as their leader.

The arc of containment would have been extended in its reach if the law on a Lok Pal (or ombudsman) which had already been approved by Parliament had been given effect to by the government; a Lok Pal is yet to be appointed. More action is needed, as by giving effect to the 2014 law to protect whistle-blowers. Also, the highly compromised Central Bureau of Investigation needs operational autonomy when it comes to investigation and prosecution, and also perhaps a cleaning of its stables. These changes have been demanded for years but stonewalled by the major political parties. Since 2011, the pressure for change and then change itself have become more visible. But it is still an open question whether all of the required action will come, and whether political funding will be reformed or parties will find new ways of evading disclosure. There should be no illusions; those in the Opposition who argue for transparency in government—and for autonomy for the public service media and also for investigating and prosecutorial institutions—change attitudes and positions as soon as they assume government office. *Plus ça change, plus c'est la même chose*.[37]

If technology-aided solutions are helping to tackle petty corruption, and if the arc of containment becomes more effective on big-ticket corruption, a key issue to tackle is administrative reform, broadly defined. *Prabhat Khabar*, the campaigning Hindi newspaper published from Ranchi in eastern India, has listed the standard rates for bribes for different kinds of government contracts. Similar rates emerged later for Maharashtra irrigation contracts—pointing to how the problem has been institutionalized in many government departments, at the center and in the states, and therefore how difficult it will be to bring about change.

Still, something can be done to reduce or simplify the plethora of rules, regulations, and controls—and the armies of inspectors for checking whether the rules are being followed. There are "wet" posts and "dry" posts, terms that denote the scope for bribe-taking by officials, notably in the most corrupt departments—believed to be tax collection, the police, the public works department, and others that hand out large contracts (like highways)—and a bidding system is in place for grabbing the wet ones. The Modi government, having promised a scandal-free government, has moved to break the bureaucratic stranglehold on decisions so that there are fewer gateways where government gatekeepers can extract their pound of flesh. Modi has also focused on making India an easier place in which to do business, and to send down the message to ministers that political contributions to the party will not be linked to the dispensation of favors by the government. And court decisions have meant that resource-grabbing is going to be next to impossible in the future, since most resources (ores, radio spectrum, land, etc.) are now given out on auction or subjected to market discipline in one form or another.

Whether change extends to big-ticket defense and other government contracts that have been associated with kickbacks is still an open question. There has been a lengthening list of defense purchase contracts that have hit landmines because of suspected or confirmed payoffs: HDW submarines and Bofors howitzers in the 1980s, followed by Westland Helicopters, South Africa's Denel guns, light howitzers from Singapore Technologies, and a VVIP helicopter squadron from Italy. The majority of new defense purchases is now bilaterally negotiated, without competitive bidding, and done either with Russia (Sukhois and MiGs, frigates, and an aircraft carrier) or with the United States (the government accepts prices negotiated by the Pentagon, for both ships and planes). The decision to buy Rafale fighter aircraft from Dassault has also moved from being a competitive bid to direct negotiation.

But the political class is not yet willing to restructure the administration for delivering better results, has yet to turn away from price controls and other distortions of the market, and has yet to switch to legitimate means of political fundraising. So it is hard to say that a new, corruption-free India is about to be born. To adapt Churchill, we are not near the end of the fight against corruption; we are not even near the end of the beginning; but we are probably at the end of the period of doing nothing about the problem.

11

A Way to End Poverty?

IT HAS BEEN a signal failure for India that two-thirds of a century after gaining political freedom, about a quarter of the country is still desperately poor. That figure used to extend to more than half the population. The improvement, while substantial, has been slow. India therefore accounts for the largest number of the world's poor—a distinction that the world's seventh-largest economy must surely want to shed. Has the time come for the country to attempt what Indira Gandhi promised in an election slogan in 1971: *garibi hatao* (abolish poverty)? This chapter addresses that issue, not by looking at policies that deliver faster economic growth and more employment-intensive manufacturing that can provide a sustainable solution (which they will eventually), but by accepting that the poor have waited long enough and need shorter-term answers. It therefore seeks to weave its way through the many contestations that surround the questions of who and how many are poor, and what is the best way to address poverty, to arrive at what is feasible and what is not.

The state of Bihar, a byword for poverty even in a land that has been a byword for poverty, is a good place to begin the search for answers. On the campaign trail in the state during the 2009 Lok Sabha elections, Chief Minister Nitish Kumar routinely asked the large crowds who came to listen to him: Would you like subsidized products from the government or would you prefer cash? At election rallies in small towns like Banka, Begusarai, and Bhagalpur, the crowd responded with the same answer: they wanted cash. Perhaps that was because they weren't getting much foodgrain, the main item in the government's public distribution system. Bihar was the state where, at the time, grain leakage or "diversion" had been found to be the highest—75 percent.[1]

Meanwhile, it doesn't get poorer than in Odisha's Kalahandi district, which earned national notoriety in the 1980s for having reported starvation deaths. Many of the tribal women even today have just a single piece of cloth wrapped around their bodies, along with what might pass for a towel; many of the men are bare-bodied. More than a quarter century after the starvation death controversy, the state government program that has the maximum visible impact is the provision of massively subsidized rice, at the throwaway price of a rupee a kilo. A day's wage for unskilled or semi-skilled work (Rs 80 to Rs 125) could more than pay for a family's requirement of its staple for a month.

So which should it be when it comes to a social welfare program for the poor: grain that is virtually free or cash transfers as income support? That choice has been fiercely debated since 2009, when the second Manmohan Singh government appointed Nandan Nilekani, a co-founder and former chief executive officer (CEO) of Infosys Technologies, to set up a project called Aadhaar (meaning foundation) that would give each resident of the country a unique twelve-digit identity number, backed by biometric details—fingerprints and iris pattern recognition.

Many things have been claimed for Aadhaar: that the numbers, once issued to every resident, would help tackle the misdirection of government benefit programs by reducing or eliminating duplication, waste, and other problems, and thereby saving the government vast sums of money. McKinsey estimated in 2012 that a successful Aadhaar program would save the government about Rs 1 trillion annually.[2] Later, Montek Singh Ahluwalia as deputy chairman of the Planning Commission speculated that a 20 percent saving on subsidy payments of Rs 3 trillion, achieved by using Aadhaar, would save the government Rs 600 billion annually (0.5 percent of GDP at the time). Critics argued that the program was unproven and its claimed benefits overstated. Civil society activists are instinctively suspicious of technology-driven solutions and were skeptical if not hostile to the idea, in part because of concerns over privacy. For good measure, the Supreme Court decreed that getting an Aadhaar number (which is voluntary, not mandatory) cannot therefore be made a precondition for getting government benefits. Still, the initial uses to which Aadhaar has been put have shown that its proponents were right in their assessments—it would indeed help save the government vast sums of money.

The Scale of Poverty

The debate over Aadhaar is part of the larger question: how best should the government help India's poor—estimated in 2011–12, on the basis of two different committee reports, at 270 million and 363 million, out of a national population at the time of about 1,225 million? The approach followed so far has been to provide subsidies in kind and free services. There are also cash benefits in the form of old-age pensions, medical insurance premiums, and student subventions. More recently, the government has offered guaranteed employment in rural areas, or cash in lieu of this.

Almost all these programs have been designed to be ameliorative, not curative; they tackle the effects of poverty, like inadequate food intake, but not its underlying causes. Indeed, through the years of initially slow growth, then moderate and eventually more rapid growth, the total number of the poor had mostly hovered between 300 million and 400 million,[3] even though as a percentage of a growing population it had dropped by more than half, from 54.9 percent in 1973–74 to 21.9 percent in 2011–12, according to the methodology adopted by the Suresh Tendulkar Committee.[4] What could be said for the years of rapid growth was that the numbers graduating out of poverty expanded. The Tendulkar Committee's approach led to the conclusion that some 137 million people moved out of poverty between 2004–05 and 2011–12, of which 86 million graduated out in just the last two years. The subsequent Rangarajan Committee[5] estimated a poverty headcount fall of 92 million in the two years to 2011–12.

There has been criticism of the Tendulkar and Rangarajan numbers, but it is hard to dispute that the fall in poverty headcount numbers as a percentage of the total population has accelerated. These were the years of rapid economic growth when incomes went up, including incomes for landless farmworkers; indeed, the acceleration of agricultural growth during this period may have been the main contributor to the reduced spread of poverty. Nevertheless, a very large number remain poor, and amelioration therefore has remained a social necessity as well as a political imperative.

The Cost of Subsidies

The size of the bill for what the government calls the "major subsidies" has fluctuated, peaking at around 3 percent of GDP. This has dropped back for 2014–15 to about 1.7 percent as diesel fuel stopped being subsidized. In 2015–16, as international oil prices have fallen, subsidies have been reduced or virtually eliminated also on kerosene, cooking gas, and fertilizer. Indeed, taxes on petroleum products have been raised. The real problem with the subsidies, though, is not the size of the bill (now quite modest) but that the bulk of the benefit does not reach the poor. The subsidy on fertilizers, for instance, is routed through the distributors of fertilizers; their primary customers are medium and large farmers, who are not poor. The annual bill has been comparatively static in recent years and was Rs 730 billion for 2015–16, or barely half of 1 percent of GDP.

The subsidy on cooking gas (Rs 464 billion in 2013–14 but virtually nothing two years later) went substantially to the non-poor who use gas as fuel; the poor use biomass like fuelwood and cow-dung cake or, in some cases, kerosene. A good deal of the subsidized cooking gas was diverted to restaurants and eateries that are supposed to pay a commercial price. In 2013, after the government limited the number of gas cylinders per consumer and began paying the equivalent of the price subsidy directly into bank accounts, the leakage began to be plugged: some 30 million bogus gas connections (20 percent of the total) were uncovered in fairly quick time.[6] That alone, as a recurring number, was more than the cost of the Aadhaar program; if Aadhaar were to be used on a broader scale, it would pay for itself many times over. For instance, subsidized kerosene is widely used to adulterate diesel (priced nearly four times as high). The estimates of misdirected kerosene (whose subsidized supply is supposed to benefit 160 million households) vary from 40 percent[7] to much higher numbers.

India's policymaking establishment has had a long love affair with such distortions in product markets, in the belief that market segmentation for benefiting the poor or for other preferred objectives is not only desirable but also feasible and (implicitly) cost-free. In sugar, the practice was that a subsidized quantity would be distributed through the public distribution system, while sugar millers were expected to make up the loss through profits on open market sales. The program cost nothing for the government. The result, though, was the same as in grain and kerosene or cooking gas: leakages from the subsidized segment of the market into the open market.

When it comes to foodgrains, where the subsidies are between 50 percent and 90 percent of cost, the Planning Commission estimated that more than half the grain issued through the public distribution system did not reach its intended beneficiaries; other estimates have placed the misallocation at 75 percent, while defenders of the system have put it at 35 percent.[8] In 2015, the Shanta Kumar Committee estimated the diversion of subsidized grain at 46.7 percent in 2011–12.[9] In this as well as in the adulteration of diesel with kerosene, local politicians get involved, thereby creating a political interest in the status quo.

The public distribution system buys 70 million tons or more of grain in a year, leaving about the same amount for private trade (the rest of the output is retained by farmers for their own use). The state's procurement agencies are notoriously wasteful: a staff loader (hired to "load" sacks of grain) at the Food Corporation of India (FCI) got as much as Rs 79,500 per month in 2014 (the same as middle-level government officials), because of an incentive-based payment system. Naturally, there was widespread malpractice in the form of using proxy workers.[10] FCI and other agencies are tasked by the government with maintaining a buffer stock for years when there is a poor harvest. In practice, grain procurement has usually outpaced what is needed for subsidized distribution (about 50 million tons), so that stocks have steadily mounted. Occasionally, the government gets rid of some of the stock by allowing export—in steadily larger quantities, though often at prices lower than the internal procurement price. At its peak in 2013, stocks reached 80 million tons—thereby locking up capital, raising the risk of storage losses, and adding to cost. More and more people recognize that there must be a better way of delivering food security. But committee reports on how to reform the whole system to get better bang for the buck are routinely buried—the latest to meet this fate being the Shanta Kumar Committee report, at the hands of the Modi government. The issue of replacing subsidized grain with cash payouts remains a political touch-me-not.

Nutrition: More Than Calories

The irony is that increasing the supply of grain through the public distribution system does not seem to have a direct or proportional link to improved nutrition levels. The system's foodgrain throughput nearly trebled in fairly short order, with procurement going from about 20 million tons in the mid-1990s to 40 million by the turn of the century and then more than 50 million tons from 2008, while distribution climbed from 15 million tons to more than 40 million tons in the same period.[11] Even this last figure was only a fifth of the quantity of foodgrains people actually consumed. So India's nutrition numbers remained problematic—some indicators improved but others did not. The National Family Health Survey (carried out every 6 to 10 years) reported little change in the nutrition status of children, for instance. The International Food Policy Research Institute's Global Hunger Index (which incorporates child mortality rate and the prevalence of underweight children and of the undernourished) did show improvement over time: over fourteen years to 2014, India progressed from "extremely alarming" to "alarming" to "serious." But it reported malnutrition levels for India that were worse than in much of sub-Saharan Africa.

In fact, overall calorie consumption per head has been falling, provoking one well-known economist to compare the contemporary food situation in

India with that during the Second World War,[12] a period that included the Bengal famine that led to 3 million starvation deaths in a province with a population of 60 million. More careful economists[13] have argued that the declining level of calorie consumption per head in the country is linked to changing lifestyles, with a similar trend having been observed in other countries with growing incomes. Indeed, they say flatly that "there is no tight link between the numbers of calories consumed and nutritional or health status."

Yet such a link is the bedrock belief of those who pushed ahead with the food security law that was passed by Parliament in 2013 after intense public debate. This has become a part of the holy chalice of the Congress Party's achievements, but the truth is that it reduced the grain entitlement of those below the official poverty line from 7 kg per head per month to 5 kg. Advocates of a "right to food" had argued in favor of supplying 7 kg of subsidized grain per head per month to three-quarters of the 1.25 billion population. This would have meant procuring and distributing nearly 80 million tons of grain, at a potential cost to the government of more than 1 percent of GDP. If there was the usual level of waste and misdirected supply, the need for both grain and money would be much higher. This was manifest overreach, since no one could reasonably argue that three-quarters of Indians were underfed and needed large food subsidies. Eventually, the law as finally enacted prescribed 5 kg for (in effect) two-thirds of the population, reducing the required throughput of grain to a more manageable 50 million tons. While this would be less demanding on the delivery system, the dubious trade-off was between expanded coverage on the one hand and reduced entitlement for the poor on the other.

Meanwhile, Arvind Virmani, a former chief economic adviser in the finance ministry, has argued that India's nutrition problem is linked more to poor sanitation and the prevalence of waterborne diseases than to foodgrain supply—an argument that Deaton and Drèze endorse, even as they underline the importance also of a balanced diet. Deaton later expanded on this[14] to emphasize the importance of clean water and good sanitation practices.

Such arguments point in a direction away from further expansion of the foodgrain distribution system and toward the replacement of subsidies with income support through a cash transfer system (which the food security law provides for, in passing). But civil society activists have contended that the supply of subsidized grain works much better than the Planning Commission has suggested. In support of this contention, the two states usually cited are Tamil Nadu and Chhattisgarh, where the leakage is less than 10 percent. If these states can do it, goes the argument, so can others. But in Chhattisgarh, which introduced an expanded public distribution system in 2013, only 6 percent of all households were listed by the state as being above the poverty line (such families get a smaller subsidy). Worse, a total of 7.03 million households had been issued ration cards, though the state has only 5.6 million households. When the scandal came to light a year later, in 2014, 1.4 million ration cards were canceled or declared ineligible.[15]

Over-registration of families reckoned to be below the poverty line (BPL) has been a problem in almost all the states, not just Chhattisgarh. The incentive for a state government to game the system is obvious and such over-reporting of the poor is to be expected. In Karnataka, 75 percent of all families were listed as being BPL, though the poverty headcount for the state was only 21–22 percent of the population in 2011–12.[16] In the state's Hassan district, the BPL tally was an unreal 95 percent of rural families.[17] Besides, any government program needs an effective administration if the scheme is to work well. Typically, the poorer states have weaker administrative structures and systems. The result is that the public distribution system works least well in especially poor states like Bihar.

Guaranteeing Employment

The debate on programs that distort markets has acquired a new edge in recent years because of the ambitious rural employment guarantee scheme, the Mahatma Gandhi National Rural Employment Guarantee Act (MGNREGA), launched in 2006 by the Manmohan Singh government and intended to guarantee work to anyone who asked for it. Those who applied for job cards under the scheme (the initial eligibility was one adult per family)—which involves hard manual labor for a modest wage—numbered an astonishing 120 million in a country with 170 million rural families. This might suggest that the scheme met a massively felt need, but only 50 million got work under the program in any year. In addition, the average number of days worked by these 50 million was closer to forty in a year, not anywhere near the stipulated maximum of 100. Still, like the food distribution system, this has been one of the largest such programs initiated anywhere in the world. The total employment created was the equivalent of 40 million person-years (assuming 300 days of work making a person-year) over a six-year period, 2006–12. The figure peaked at 9.5 million person-years in the drought year of 2009–10, and dropped off by 2011–12 to 7 million person-years.[18] Wages accounted for around two-thirds of the annual program budget of about Rs 400 billion, which was reduced in 2013–14 to Rs 330 billion;

for 2015–16, the provision was slightly more than Rs 340 billion. These sums delivered fewer man-days, pro rata, than earlier because the stipulated wage per day went up with inflation. In effect, the coverage of the program had been shrinking even during UPA rule and (despite official denials) continued to shrink under the Modi government.

As was inevitable, a program rolled out rapidly on a massive scale (expanding from the initial 200 districts in 2006 to all rural areas in just two years) was initially bedeviled by many problems: fake muster rolls, delayed payments to those who got and did work, no proper assets created through work programs, low awareness of the program, particularly in the poorer areas and states, and so on. Many of these operational problems were gradually addressed through sustained effort. Among the spin-off benefits was the fact that 80–100 million new bank accounts were opened, after it was decided as a precautionary step that payments would be routed through banks and post offices.

The scheme is widely believed to have resulted in higher rural wages and reduced migration of workers from high-migration areas—someone who is guaranteed the minimum wage under the program might refuse to work at a more distant location unless paid significantly more. Anecdotal evidence suggested a scarcity of workers at harvesttime in the granary state of Punjab because of reduced in-migration from poverty-ridden Bihar. If true, this national wage effect has been achieved by spending only about 0.25 percent of GDP (less in the later years) on wages. But caution is advised when coming to conclusions; the period of these labor trends was one of accelerated growth in agricultural output, sustained high inflation (especially in food products), much higher grain procurement prices, rising wage rates across the board, and diversification to more labor-intensive crops. So there were many factors at work that would have contributed to higher wages. Wages have tended to settle in the subsequent years of slower economic growth, lower inflation, and less-than-bumper harvests.

The main advantage of the program is that it is self-selecting. Those who want work have to register and then show up at work sites; only the genuinely needy will seek to do hard manual labor for a relatively meager wage. So the program's benefit as an insurance against seasonal unemployment at the bottom of the pyramid is beyond question—provided fake muster rolls and other operational issues are completely eliminated. The question is whether superior alternatives exist. Since a third of the outlay is on non-wage costs, as in the material used during construction work, would cash transfers in the form of a minimum income supplement deliver 50 percent more coverage and leave people free to seek work elsewhere (this option would not create public assets, which the employment program is supposed to do)? And would comparable attention to the promotion of labor-intensive manufacturing create as much or more sustainable work that pays better and is not dependent on state handouts?

Direct Benefit Transfer

The second of those questions has been dealt with in Chapter 6, but the option of cash payouts deserves to be explored, especially since much of the ecosystem for enabling such payouts has been, or is being, created. Some 950 million Aadhaar numbers had been issued by the end of 2015. At the enrollment rate of 25 million a month, there should be near-universal enrollment by the end of 2016. Second, the number of smartphones (whose price has dropped to barely $60, or about Rs 4,000) is expanding exponentially and, it has been estimated, could reach 500 million by 2019. Third, banking coverage has become near-universal, following the Jan-Dhan program that Narendra Modi announced in 2014. What has been called a "JAM" tripod (Jan-Dhan, Aadhaar, and mobile transfers) is something on which a direct benefit transfer (or DBT) program could rest.

Meanwhile, the National Payments Corporation of India is working on an "app" (technology application) that will enable person-to-person transactions. Anyone with an Aadhaar number would then be able to use a remittance received as a cash transfer from the government (accounts could be cloud-based) to pay for routine purchases at the local grocer's (who could be a business correspondent, or BC). Some 100,000 BCs have already been appointed; more will sign up if and when they are offered a small commission (say, 2 percent) on every transaction they facilitate. If the Aadhaar-linked account were to be cloud-based, it would even obviate the need for everyone to have a conventional bank account. It helps that the Reserve Bank has announced a policy for allowing payment banks—whose creation would put another cog in place. Eventually, a dense institutional network would facilitate billions of transactions, and perhaps obviate the need for credit cards—especially if smartphones are developed (perhaps in 2016) to also offer biometric readers for additional authentication of the person doing a transaction. However futuristic all this might sound, almost all of it will soon be technically feasible.

The system can be activated only if cash payments are routed electronically to those who have Aadhaar numbers, and this too has begun. Some 130 million accounts now receive cash payments instead of the subsidy on cooking gas; 80 million accounts get electronic payments of wages earned under the rural employment program. As and when kerosene subsidies are replaced with cash payments, 160 million families would be covered. These are overlapping numbers, but Aadhaar can get rid of the problem of duplication, and therefore of subsidized goods being diverted to unintended beneficiaries. The savings (and efficiency gains) would be enormous.

Large-scale income transfer programs have been tried out in some other countries, especially in Latin America—though all of them get dwarfed by the scale of the Aadhaar project. The two best-known examples are those in Mexico (Oportunidades) and Brazil (Bolsa Familia, or family stipend). Both cover roughly a quarter of the population, which in both countries is much smaller than India's. In Brazil, the annual payout to a family is the equivalent of about $500. On a per capita basis, that works out to only a tiny percentage of Brazil's annual per capita income of over $12,100. The program's total cost is said to be just 0.36 percent of GDP.[19] The fraction of household income that the payment represents is said to be just 0.5 percent.

The money therefore provides financial relief to poor families but falls well short of what would be required to lift them out of poverty. Even for the poorest 5 percent of the population, the money transfers are said to account for less than 10 percent of their total income. But such limited transfers have helped to reduce inequality as well as the poverty gap. It also turns out that the recipient families spend most of the money on food (belying concerns expressed in India that such cash transfers might be misspent on alcohol). And it is not cash in return for nothing. The transfers are conditional: children of recipients must be sent to school and make regular visits to health clinics. School attendance as well as attention to health are said to have improved as a result, but sometimes very poor families have been left out because of the schooling condition or the family's remote location. In India, where the quality of government schools and public hospitals is poor, improvement on the counts of education and rural health is doubtful. There is also the obvious danger of making families dependent on fiscal transfers, and (depending on their quantum) reducing the incentive to work—especially among women, whose participation in the identified workforce is already low at about 25 percent.

However, while the primary claim on behalf of an Aadhaar-based cash transfer program (better targeting through avoiding of duplication) has been established, mis-identification of the kind that has bedeviled the process for deciding who is poor (or below the poverty line) remains a challenge. In Bolsa Familia, the inclusion error according to one study was as high as 49 percent, and the exclusion error even higher, at 59 percent.[20] Others have said these numbers are far too high. Depending on which estimates you accept, the scheme reached between two and four out of every five potential beneficiaries. These are sobering numbers. If a limited cash transfer program in a much wealthier and more developed society than India's, on a much smaller scale than India would adopt, has significant mis-identification problems, should India proceed with caution—feeling the stones on the bottom of the river, as it were?

The Means to End Poverty

In the event that such transfers do prove feasible, would the cost savings enable a more ambitious objective, of trying to end extreme poverty completely? What would it cost to bring everyone above the poverty line through an income supplement payout? If one goes by the Rangarajan report, the income cutoff for determining who is poor in 2011–12 for a five-member family was a monthly income of Rs 4860 in rural areas and Rs 7035 in urban areas (translated into per head per day, this means Rs 32 in rural areas and Rs 47 in urban areas). Translated into dollars at purchasing power parity (PPP), the Rangarajan Committee calculated that it came to $2.14 per head per day in rural areas and $2.44 in urban areas. Both numbers were therefore better than the higher of the two international poverty benchmarks set by the World Bank, of $1.25 and $2 per head per day income. On this basis, India in 2011–12 had 363 million who were poor; of these, 260.5 million were in rural areas and 102.5 in urban areas.

The total income that these 363 million would have had to earn, in order to rise above Rangarajan's poverty benchmark, would have been Rs 3.04 trillion in rural areas and Rs 1.75 trillion in urban areas, during 2011–12, making for an all-India total of Rs 4.79 trillion. If we accept official survey figures[21] which show that the average poverty gap (that is, the gap between the poverty line and the average income of those below the line) is about 25 percent, the money required to bring everyone above the poverty line would be a quarter of Rs 4.79 trillion, or about Rs 1.20 trillion in 2011–12—a very affordable 1.43 percent of GDP in that year.

Covering the average shortfall is not enough, any more than you can cross a body of water by calculating its average depth. There will be quite a few whose income falls short of the minimum by more than 25 percent. The state would therefore have had to make up more like a 50 percent shortfall, so that all, or virtually all, families rose above the poverty line. For a five-member family, the income support in 2011–12 would have been Rs 2,430 per month in a rural area and Rs 3,518 per month in an urban area. This would have cost around Rs 2.4 trillion, or 2.86 percent of the GDP in that year.[22] That would have strained the government's budget but may not have been unaffordable, given the bill for "major subsidies" in the past. Such payments would of course have to be indexed to inflation, so the bill would grow each year, but perhaps shrink in relation to GDP since the assumption is that more people emerge out of poverty each year.

The real world intrudes on such hope-inducing calculations. First, it is next to impossible to clearly identify the 363 million who are poor; statewide surveys of BPL families have resulted in massive over-reporting, as we have seen. One option would be to accept that many non-destitute recipients will be included. As an alternative, one could adopt a method of exclusion, by identifying those who can safely be left out of a cash transfer scheme. Everyone else would then be covered, including a number of non-poor. The scale of the cash transfers, the number of beneficiaries, and the total money involved would then expand substantially. The cost could go well beyond 2.86 percent of GDP.

Following the exclusion approach, one could exclude all the 35 million payers of income tax (who by definition have an annual taxable income of more than Rs 20,000 per month). Farmers who own larger lots of land could also be excluded. If the cutoff were set at ownership of five acres, a further 20 million would be excluded. These are mutually exclusive categories (farmers don't have to pay income tax), so 55 million households would straightaway be marked for exclusion. Along the same lines, one could exclude all car owners (4.7 percent of 250 million households, according to the 2011 Census) and powered two-wheelers (21 percent). Another excluded category could conceivably be those owning houses with three rooms or more (27.6 percent), or houses built with specific materials—such as concrete roofs (29.1 percent). These would be overlapping categories, but each category would have grown since 2011; 1 percent of all households buy cars in a year, and another 6 percent buy two-wheelers. These are all categories that can be easily identified. One could justifiably and feasibly hope to exclude half the 250 million households from coverage under a cash transfer scheme, and more over time. Even so, this would be much more than the number of the officially poor; including them all in monthly income support payouts would raise the bill sharply.

One way to control the bill would be to have two levels of payment, one at 50 percent of poverty line income, and the other (covering a larger number) at 25 percent. This has the additional merit of graduating people out of such payments as their incomes rise. A reasonable assessment of the cost might then be 4 percent of GDP (in 2015–16, that would have meant Rs 5.6 trillion). Finding that much money would certainly be difficult (central and state governments together collect 18 percent of national income as taxes, and spend 25 percent of national income, thereby running up a combined fiscal deficit of 7 percent of GDP, among the highest in the world), but not impossible. Remember that the "major subsidies" used to be 3 percent of GDP. Also, governments provide an array of underpriced products and services, like higher education. Whatever money is saved by a careful scrutiny of such subsidies, especially that portion of "non-merit" subsidies that goes to the non-poor, and from cutting down on overheads, would make a cash transfer program more affordable. But it is just as well to recognize that finding the money to finance payouts that total 4 percent of GDP poses an obstacle.

Real-World Complexities

The further problem is that what works on a drawing board may not work out in the messy world of political contestation. First, only some of the subsidies are given by the central government; many state governments have expanded the central scheme of subsidized grain supply by either increasing the list of food items and/or lowering the price at which they are sold. The promise of free electricity to farmers, to take another example, is a favorite among state-level politicians as an election-time promise—one reason that electricity distribution organizations are invariably bankrupt. All efforts at pricing reform, including incentives from the central government for cleaning up and charging rational electricity tariffs, have been frustrated.

Even if a grand bargain were to be conceived—offering cash payments in return for the acceptance of commercial tariffs and prices—there is the real danger of politicians promising both cash transfers and product price subsidies. So long as voters respond to such promises and give their votes to those making populist promises, there will be no shortage of vote-hungry politicians willing to match demand for subsidies with supply.

And yet, the situation is not without its checks and balances. At the state level, there is the "hard constraint" that governments cannot spend beyond their means (the center has the theoretical option of creating more money). Indeed, the encouraging reality is that most state governments have been running surpluses on their revenue account—which means that consumption expenditure is fully financed out of current revenues. The overall deficit on state budgets is within 2.5 percent of GDP and should fall with greater devolution of tax revenue, while debt levels have been sustainable. Nor can states simply give away tax revenue; the pressure to build roads, provide reliable power, and improve education continues to rise. Some chief ministers have been repeatedly re-elected on the basis of performance, and this has become a powerful example for others.

The fiscal deficit problem has been harder to crack in New Delhi. The central law on fiscal responsibility, enacted in 2003, mandated an overall central deficit of no more than 3 percent by March 2008, along with zero deficit on the revenue account (in other words, deficits should be incurred only to finance capital investment). In practice, the central government's fiscal deficit has been well above this level after 2008. The business of getting to the prescribed 3 percent limit has been like running in the Red Queen's race[23]—finance ministers keep running to stay in the same place. It is hard to see the target being achieved in the foreseeable future.

However, it is also true that finance ministers are now judged more clearly on the deficit question; a large deficit is seen by the financial community within and outside the country as a symptom of poor macroeconomic management. The pressure to deliver on fiscal responsibility and also on poverty alleviation could well lead to a gradual, possibly partial, switch to cash transfers in preference to supply in kind—if the cash transfers are demonstrated in practice to be an improvement on the latter. This then becomes a multi-stage process in an extended time frame.

There is an underlying issue to be kept in mind, one that goes beyond the relative attractions of different forms of inclusion and the choice between subsidies and cash transfers. This is the operational reality that emerging market economies are characterized by limited government capacity and excessive demands being made on the state, out of proportion to its capacity to deliver. In that context, a cash transfer system is less taxing to the system, being easier to administer. But even if that is the option chosen, poverty can be tackled to some level of satisfaction only if there is improvement in governance standards and greater accountability, so that (at the very least) the enumeration of those to be excluded or included is done properly. Further, performance levels have to improve when it comes to the delivery of public healthcare as well as basic education, the absence of which blights lives and limits opportunities such that lifelong poverty becomes inescapable even if there are generous cash transfers. As Pranab Bardhan has emphasized, the inequality of opportunity should not be ignored in the focus on the inequality of end result (that is, income).[24] This is the parallel challenge that has to be met, in order to achieve inclusion through government programs. Without that, cash transfers will have only limited utility.

Can India expect an ambitious assault on poverty through liberal cash transfers? On careful consideration, it does appear to be a bridge too far—despite the preparatory groundwork on the JAM tripod. The political reality in 2016 is that the Congress is committed to the food security program that it authored when in office. The Modi government has been painted as anti-poor because of its bid to amend the land acquisition law. Its response has been to go on the defensive and become politically risk-averse. Will it be willing, in such a context, to take up the food subsidy issue and to replace it with cash transfers? The answer is, probably not. That being the case, all that can be attempted is a limited cash transfer program as the best that is feasible for the time being, even as other policies address inequalities of opportunity and employment growth.

Emerging Realities

12

Aam Aadmi *and a Universe of Realities*

SUPINDER SINGH USED to work as a messenger in the *Tribune* newspaper's head office at Chandigarh. He got the job when his father, a chief proofreader at the *Tribune*, died on the job in 1999; the trust that runs the newspaper offered young Supinder (then twenty-one) a job on compassionate grounds. Today, the short, thickset Supinder, with fashionably close-cropped hair and trimmed beard, and an oversized *kada* or bracelet made of solid silver on his wrist, drives around town in a Toyota SUV. The former messenger boy has also started a commodity trading company, in partnership with a friend; they trade on the Multi Commodity Exchange. Supinder says they make Rs 50,000 (in 2013, about $1,000) a day.

It is a world away from running errands in a newspaper office. To explain the transition, Supinder jumps into his SUV and drives us through his nearby village of Jandpur, not far from Chandigarh, around which a real estate developer called Bajwa is building a housing project. Large chunks of farmland have been bought and sold. Supinder's family owned ten hectares, putting them at the boundary line between the official classifications of medium and large farmers. They were not poor. But farming paid only so much, and a salaried income was useful. That's before the explosion in land prices around urban centers.

With Chandigarh overflowing into the satellite town of Mohali in Punjab, land prices in surrounding areas have gone through the roof. Supinder grabbed the opportunity to sell about 1.5 of his 10 hectares for Rs 120 million, reinvested Rs 110 million to buy 8 hectares of cheaper land in a more rural district, and then leased that out at an annual lease rent of Rs 60,000 per hectare. The remaining Rs 10 million he has invested in his commodity trading firm and in his expansive home, which sports a portico with yellow Corinthian pillars and bright blue trimmings. He is now cash-rich and there is no need anymore to work for someone else.

Tales of sudden riches and conspicuous consumption (Supinder is a minor legend in his old *Tribune* office) are not uncommon in such suburban centers across the country—whether Jandpur outside Mohali/Chandigarh, Gurgaon and Noida outside Delhi, Hebbal which lies between Bengaluru and its new airport, or Hinjawadi outside Pune—where land prices have exploded around expanding cities hungry for more land. When DLF, the country's largest real estate developer, began hawking residential plots of land in the Delhi suburb of Gurgaon in the mid-1980s, the price was no more than Rs 500 per square yard. By 1992, that figure had multiplied sixfold to Rs 3000, and then peaked at an astronomical Rs 200,000 per square yard by 2012 before the market settled in the downturn that followed. DLF's own stock valuation went on a roller-coaster ride, peaking at a stratospheric Rs 1.8 trillion in 2008 (about $40 billion at the time), before crashing to a tenth of that value in the debt crisis that later engulfed the company.

Land price inflation has helped primarily those who invested early enough in urban areas and their new suburbs, but many farmers have profited too. People who had managed a modest living through agriculture have become rupee-millionaires many times over by selling out to real estate developers. Some have frittered away the sudden wealth on lavish weddings or expensive toys like sports utility vehicles, or simply paid off old debt. Smarter ones like Supinder have reinvested in cheaper land in the interior and moved into businesses like real estate—becoming the new, flashy rich in what for many like them has become a land of prosperity.

Admittedly, in a country of 1,250 million people, the almost lurid stories of farmland turning into expensive real estate relate to a tiny minority, but they are an important part of a kaleidoscope that contains within it tales of a myriad of lives: vignettes from *Les Miserables*, Horatio Alger stories of the rise of impoverished boys to middle-class security, scenes from *Oliver Twist* contrasting with others from *The Great Gatsby*, countless revivals of *Do Bigha Zamin* jostling with others from *Behind the Beautiful Forevers*, and reality bytes taken from *Peepli Live* as well as from Gordon Gekko in *Wall Street*. To make sense of it all, one has to identify the broad patterns. Analysis is complicated because the statistics do not always point in the same direction; indeed, some numbers are plainly contradictory. Still, one can discern the broad directions of change.

This chapter looks at recent trends in employment, income levels, expenditure patterns, and asset ownership to understand what Indians have achieved in terms of their personal financial situation. India is a universe of realities housed in one country, but it has been a growing economy with rising incomes. In the World Bank's classification, it ceased some years ago to be a low-income economy, having graduated to a lower-middle-income status. For 2013, the Bank's dividing line between the two was an annual per capita income of $1,045 (nominal dollars); India's had reached $1,500. Graduating further to the upper-middle-income category would mean attaining a per capita income of $4,125, which is a long way away.

As in most countries, India has people at all levels of income, but there are more extremes here than is usual. While it has the largest number of poor people in the world, it also has the fifteenth-largest number of dollar millionaires (164,000 in 2013).[1] The question is, how many people in India are rich, how many poor, and how many middle class? Crucially, when politicians talk of the *aam aadmi* (common man), who exactly is this person and what is his standard of living? This chapter seeks to provide the answers. But first, a survey of contemporary realities.

The Rural Picture

For vast numbers in the countryside, the story of recent times would seem to have been grim as mushrooming towns and cities failed to absorb enough of a rapidly growing workforce. In three decades, from 1980–81 to 2010–11, the average size of the country's farm holdings shrank by 37 percent, from 1.84 hectares to 1.16 hectares.[2] The area under cultivation remained virtually unchanged in these thirty years, but the land was divided into more (therefore smaller) holdings, with the total number of holdings going up from 88.9 million to 137.7 million.

The entire increase in the number of farm holdings was accounted for by the growth of farms smaller than 2 hectares, which went up in those thirty years from 66.2 million to 117 million. The number of farms bigger than 2 hectares shrank from 22.7 million to 20.7 million, of which those larger than 4 hectares were just 5.9 million (Table 12.1). But whereas more than six out of every seven farms were now of a size that allowed only subsistence farming and very limited incomes, well over half the cultivated land still belonged to semi-medium, medium, and large farms (those larger than 2 hectares).

This subdivision and marginalization of land holdings is to be expected when the rural population has grown in thirty years from 524 million to 833 million.[3] Somewhat unusually, Supinder Singh is still a large farmer because he is the only son of his father, who in turn was the only son of his

Table 12.1 Farm Holdings (Million) and Area (Million Hectares), 2010–11

Category	Size	Number	%	Area	%
Marginal	<1.0 hectare	92.3	67.0	35.4	22.3
Small	1.0–2.0	24.7	17.9	35.1	22.1
Semi-medium	2.0–4.0	13.8	10.0	37.5	23.6
Medium	4.0–10.0	5.9	4.3	33.7	21.2
Large	>10.0	1.0	0.7	17.4	10.9
Total		137.7	100.0	159.1	100.0

Source: Government of India, Agriculture Census, 2010–11

father. In the ordinary course, the family's land would have been subdivided eight or ten times through three generations, and everyone in Supinder's generation would have been operating "small" or, at best, "semi-medium" farms.

As farm holdings have become smaller and uneconomic, the inevitable has happened: millions of cultivators have sold their land or leased it out, moving down a step in the social and economic hierarchy to become agricultural laborers or giving up agriculture to take non-farm jobs—especially when there is a transition from one generation to the next. In the decade to 2011, while the rural population grew from 743 million to 833 million, or by 12 percent, the number of cultivators actually dropped in number, from 127 million to 119 million. At the same time, the number of agricultural laborers went up sharply, by an astonishing 36 percent, from 106 million to 144 million. The message was stark: shrinking farm holdings, fewer stakeholders, a growing rural proletariat, and some movement of people from village to town.

In the midst of this asset crisis, the Census showed that there was an employment crisis as well. Those who found work for more than six months in a year, called "main" workers, numbered 362 million in 2011 (up from 313 million a decade earlier), and accounted for three-quarters of the total worker population of 483 million. The remaining one-fourth worked for six months or less, some of them for less than even three months in a year. The absolute number of these "marginal" workers had gone up in a decade from 89 million to 119 million. In short, the number of "marginal" workers went up by a third, while the number of "main" workers went up by less than a sixth. Simply put, the work available did not grow as fast as the numbers who needed it.

That would explain why 120 million people (a quarter of the total workforce) applied for, and obtained, job cards under MGNREGA. However, only about 50 million actually got work under the program in any year, and the average number of days of work provided under the program was less than fifty in all but one year (against a stipulated maximum of 100 days). Still, for a "marginal" worker employed for less than half the year, this program would have translated into a not insignificant addition to income, especially in the lean agricultural months.

The shift from "main" (or mostly employed) to "marginal" (or mostly unemployed) workers was particularly striking in some of the poorer eastern states. In Bihar, for instance, the number of marginal workers went up from a quarter of the total in 2001 to nearly 40 percent in 2011. In equally poor Jharkhand, the increase was from 36 percent to an overwhelming 48 percent. The better-off western states, like Gujarat and Maharashtra, were a study in contrast: the percentage of marginal workers fell to 18 percent and 12 percent, respectively—even though these states attracted significant numbers of migrant workers from places like Bihar. Divergence at the state level had become an integral part of the evolving story.

The large numbers of "marginal" workers do not match the official unemployment numbers, based on National Sample surveys and Labour Bureau surveys. The latter records unemployment at no more than 4.7 percent in rural areas and 5.5 percent in urban areas.[4] It is as well to note that no socio-economic picture of India is uniformly drawn. Some of the data point in quite different directions—the problem could be with the numbers, the definitions used, or the contradictions of India's reality. Whatever the reasons, what you get from looking at many different numbers is a complex mosaic of images.

Importantly, the poverty numbers released by the Planning Commission, on the basis of the National Sample Survey's numbers on household consumption levels, tell a hopeful story. Those below the poverty line in 1993–94, on the basis of a benchmark set much later by the economist Suresh Tendulkar, were reckoned at 45.3 percent of the population. This dropped to 37.2 percent in 2004–05. However, the absolute number of officially poor people in the growing population base remained virtually unchanged during those eleven years, at a little over 400 million. That changed in the years of rapid economic growth, as the number of poor dropped from 407 million in 2004–05 to 269 million in 2011–12.[5] In percentage terms, the shadow of poverty shrank in those seven short years, 2004–05 to 2011–12, from covering 37.2 percent of the population to 21.9 percent. This was the most dramatic such decline since absolute poverty began to be tracked from the early 1970s. The faster growth in per capita income during this most recent period (about 7 percent annually, compared to earlier periods that recorded less than 4 percent) is an obvious explanation for the good news.

The decline in poverty numbers would have been impossible if the good news had been confined to towns and cities and had left villages untouched. In fact, there was plenty of good news in the countryside too—because agricultural growth accelerated to a handsome average of 4.2 percent annually between 2004–05 and 2011–12, up from 2.7 percent in the preceding eleven years. States like Gujarat and Madhya Pradesh enjoyed twice the national rate of agricultural growth, which of course means that other states did worse than the average. But note that the overall agricultural growth rate of 4.2 percent compares with the growth rate of the rural population of less than 1.5 percent.

Faster output growth was accompanied by sharply higher government procurement prices for grain. In wheat, the price moved from Rs 510 per quintal in 2004–05 to Rs 1120 in 2010–11, that is, an increase of 120 percent, or almost twice the overall price inflation during this period. Not only were farmers producing more per head, but they were getting much better prices for their produce. Rural wages went up even faster than grain prices, and rural demand for a variety of consumer products ballooned.

This period also saw a significant diversification to higher-value and/or more labor-intensive crops like vegetables—whose growth (along with fruits) averaged 6 percent for a decade, taking up per capita availability by 50 percent. Milk production grew annually by 4.5 percent, while the production of lentils grew 56 percent in a decade and of oilseeds by 62 percent. Maize production went up 80 percent and potato output doubled. But cotton beat everything—with output growing from 9.5 million bales in 2000–01 to 35.2 million in 2011–12.[6] The staples of wheat and rice now constituted barely half the income generated through agriculture.

Odd as it may sound for a country with embarrassing malnutrition statistics, India became something of an agricultural power in select markets. It emerged as the largest exporter of rice, and the combined shipment of rice and wheat exceeded 20 million tons in 2013–14—despite which the country still had a mountain of grain stocks. Fish exports doubled in five years. An even more interesting development was that demand from consumers for many of these items was increasing faster than production, causing a price spurt in fruits, vegetables, and the like that fed into higher inflation rates.

This agricultural growth story provides a striking counterpoint to the numbers on the spread of unviable farm holdings and the growth of the rural proletariat. Agricultural wages stagnated during the years of low agricultural growth (also a period of relatively low inflation), and shot up when growth accelerated and farmers got better prices. The daily rates for plowing, for instance, were relatively steady between 1998 and 2005—climbing modestly, according to Labour Bureau data, from Rs 58.01 in April 1998 to Rs 74.05 seven years later, before nearly trebling to Rs 214.31 in the next seven years, in April 2012—an annual rate of increase that was far ahead of the high rate of inflation that had come to be. Although there were variations, the pattern was broadly similar in the wages for sowing, cane crushing, and for carpenters and masons—the first seven-year period saw static wages, the second seven-year period saw wages close to trebling in most cases.[7]

If the two seven-year periods are taken together, wage rates nearly quadrupled, while the consumer price index for rural workers just about doubled. Real wages therefore went up substantially—mostly in the second seven-year period. Over the full fourteen-year period till 2011–12, rural workers as a whole did manage to better their condition. This is hard to square with the numbers that tell us "marginal" workers were increasing in number faster than "main" workers. If there was not enough work to go around for everyone, why were wage rates rising so sharply?

The contentious question has been about the role played by MGNREGA in the transition from static rural wages to the rapid wage increases post-2005. Although anecdotes from farmers and even businessmen (like the owners of sugar mills) in many states ascribe the sharp wage increases to the introduction and expansion of MGNREGA, this is hard to reconcile with the numbers and the timing.

The money paid out as wages in MGNREGA make-work programs in a year was about Rs 250 billion (the rest of the outlay was spent on construction materials). Even if all the wages recorded as having been paid reached the intended beneficiaries (which they manifestly did not), the figure was barely a quarter of 1 percent of GDP, while the man-days of work generated was less than 1 percent of total rural employment. It is hard to see this level of intervention making a substantial difference to rural wages across the board or provoking a spurt in wage levels that, as it happens, started before MGNREGA began its all-India rollout in April 2008. However, there would have been an impact in specific pockets during the lean agricultural seasons—when they would have prevented wages from crashing. But bear in mind that the reported wage rates for most kinds of farming activity, and even for unskilled work, were usually ahead of the wages on offer under MGNREGA; for skilled work (like digging wells) the differential increased.

The growing population pressure on land might have led to regressive patterns of asset control, and the work available might have been increasingly inadequate (as the Census figures show), but in the same period when these negative trends were established, wage and income levels went up substantially. It might be that a combination of higher farm productivity and better product prices more than made up for the negative trends in asset ownership. Even if there wasn't enough work for everyone round the year, farmers had to pay more because food costs for workers had gone up sharply. MGNREGA would have played a role too, large or small. The rate of increase in wage rates tapered off as soon as food inflation subsided. Also, in states like Kerala, wages increased to a level that made a good deal of farming unviable, leading to a reduction in the potential for farm work. Finally, around growing cities and towns, surging land prices created a spread effect, with land prices going up in more remote locations too—often provoking smaller landholders to cash out.

Meanwhile, in the Cities . . .

The 2011 Census said that in the towns and cities, 13.7 million households (or a little over one-sixth of 78.9 million urban homes) lived in slums. But you would have to revise your mental picture of what a slum is, because half the homes in slums were said to have more than one room, and almost as many had tap water. Access to electricity and cooking gas was near-universal, while 70 percent of the "slum" homes had a TV set. The biggest surprise was that two-thirds had a toilet within the premises. Yet fewer than half the slum dwellers owned a bank account.

As might be expected in a city, the quality of life was better than the more downbeat picture in villages. About 70 percent of all urban homes were made of material like burned brick and concrete, with cement/mosaic floors. Also, 65 percent had two rooms or more, with 70 percent of families enjoying homeownership. Further, 70–80 percent of households had tap water and a kitchen, along with a bathroom and water closet, while about 90 percent had electricity. As much as 45 percent owned a vehicle; 10 percent owned cars, while more than three-quarters owned a TV set. These numbers improved between 2011 and 2015; the ownership of vehicles and TV sets went up substantially, as did gas connections, while telephone use must have gone up to near-universal level. It seems safe to conclude that well over half of urban India already enjoys a middle-class lifestyle or belongs to an "aspiring neo-middle class," while another substantial cohort is the "vulnerable non-poor." These and other categories are explored later in the chapter.

Higher up the ladder, in the corporate world, what came to be dubbed the "LPG" (liberalization, privatization, globalization) story led to new opportunities, rising salaries, and dramatic increases in wealth, creating a heady urban excitement that was far removed from the gritty reality of slum life and even more so from the complex story lines in hundreds of thousands of villages. This was tempered in the most recent years by the change in economic tempo and a sapping of self-confidence that was one of the reasons for voters deciding on a change of government in the 2014 elections. And yet significant numbers saw their economic situation improve dramatically.

Engineers who joined the pathbreaking information technology sector did well for themselves, but surprisingly (given the rapid growth of the sector) failed to keep pace with the growth in per capita incomes across the economy.[8] One of the largest companies in the sector paid an annual sum of Rs 42,000 in 1992 to a fresh engineer; two decades later, that figure had climbed seven and a half times, to Rs 3,15,000. But growth of nominal per capita income (growth plus inflation) during the two decades had been nearly tenfold, so the tech sector had failed to keep pace.

On the campuses of the leading management institutes, the story was better. A large international company producing consumer goods, which has regularly recruited at management institute campuses, offered MBA (master of business administration) graduates Rs 1,05,000 per year in the early 1990s. Two decades later, it was offering Rs 2 million—a jump of nineteen times, or twice the increase in per capita incomes during the intervening period. A broader picture emerged from the elite Indian Institute of Management at Calcutta, where the average annual salary during campus placements in 1990 was Rs 53,000. Less than a decade later, in 1999, that figure had shot up to Rs 526,000. By 2010, the figure had further trebled, to Rs 1.53 million—or a twenty-ninefold increase in twenty years, which translated into a threefold improvement on the growth in per capita incomes.

If the times were good at the first step on the corporate ladder, life was great on the highest rung. Chief executives of the 100 largest firms earned an average pay of Rs 17.5 million, and a median figure of Rs 11.3 million, in 2002. Ten years later, the average figure had jumped to Rs 118 million, and the median to Rs 87.7 million. During a decade when per capita income roughly trebled, median CEO pay for the largest companies had grown nearly eightfold. Kalanidhi Maran, TV czar and failed airline owner, topped the list with Rs 600 million in 2013–14; his wife Kavery drew a similar paycheck.

Where Does the Money Go?

Figuring out where people put their money involves dealing with yet more numbers; trawling through them helps one understand the economics of individual households. Bloated CEO pay (especially notable in companies where the person who held the controlling interest was also the CEO) does not tell the broader story of how the fortunate sections—especially those owning assets—did during the boom years. The price bubbles that built up during that period meant that the prices of shares, land, and gold soared beyond the most upbeat forecasts—with land and housing stock being the largest asset class by far. Property prices increased fivefold in four of the five main cities during the 2001–11 decade, and threefold in the fifth (Bengaluru).[9] Gold (a significant item, since its purchases accounted for about a tenth of household savings in most years) multiplied fivefold in price in as many years before dropping back by a third. The Bombay Stock Exchange's Sensitive Index (or Sensex) for thirty leading shares went from 3,300 in January 2003 to 29,000 in January 2015 before dipping.

Many prominent companies and groups saw dramatic surges in their value over the entire post-reform period. In March 1992, the listed Reliance group companies run by the Ambani family, for instance, were worth Rs 77.64 billion—a figure that seems positively modest when compared to the combined value of the companies controlled by the brothers Mukesh and Anil Ambani (who parted ways in 2005) in early 2015: Rs 3.5 trillion. The value of Tata companies rose twenty-fivefold in a little over two decades, from Rs 312.95 billion to more than Rs 8 trillion—60 percent of it accounted for by the software services firm Tata Consultancy Services, which had by then become India's most valuable company as well as its largest corporate employer. Wipro was even more impressive as it went from Rs 2.31 billion to Rs 1.45 trillion, while a first-generation entrepreneur like Subhash Chandra founded the Zee Entertainment network and went from barely half a billion to Rs 370 billion. (Note that most of the value created on the stock market was not by manufacturing firms.)

The value of all listed companies was only 12 percent of GDP in 1990. Once the reforms process got under way, market capitalization ranged between 20 percent and 40 percent of GDP before surging post-2004. By December 2014, the market capitalization of all listed companies was 70 percent of GDP, totaling Rs 98.4 trillion[10]—of which about a quarter was held by overseas portfolio investors and half by people or entities classified as the "promoters" of companies, which included government and foreign entities. A little more than 20 percent of shares was held by retail investors. Most people investing in company stock had therefore done very well for themselves. The government helped by making dividend income tax-free in the hands of shareholders (instead, companies paid a tax on the dividend distributed out of profits) and by abolishing capital gains tax on listed shares held for more than a year.

Despite the attractions of the stock market and how much money it has made for the relatively small number of people who had invested in it, the overwhelming majority of Indians put their money in everything other than stocks and shares. The two share depositories have 23.4 million accounts, but multiple account registration is common because accounts are opened in different combinations of names for the same family members; the number of individual investors therefore will be very much smaller. One estimate of the non-duplicated total is about 10 million accounts (which compares with 35 million who pay income tax).

Among other forms of financial savings, bank deposits account for Rs 87 trillion, life insurance companies Rs 19.6 trillion, mutual funds Rs 10.8 trillion, and provident funds (a form of long-term saving) Rs 8 trillion.[11] Not all the money is held by individuals: of the Rs 10.8 trillion in mutual funds, individuals hold barely half (Rs 5.58 trillion); the rest is held by companies, banks, and foreign institutional investors.

These are figures for the total financial assets owned. Indian households have been adding about Rs 10.5 trillion annually to their financial wealth, but they also take on about 30 percent of that sum in additional liabilities.[12] So the net addition to wealth in a year has been slightly more than Rs 7 trillion during this period, or about 12 percent of average household income.

In most years, though, Indians put more money into non-financial than financial savings. The country has been assessed to have a gold hoard of 20,000 tons,[13] valued currently at more than Rs 50 trillion. Real estate is an even more important form of saving, being the principal asset of most households—but the current value of all marketable holdings is virtually impossible to guesstimate. The short point is that while stock market excitement has been a staple for the business press, Indians put less of their money into equities than the global average of about a one-third share.

On the liabilities side, about 1.5 million households (0.6 percent of the total) take a housing loan each year; the accumulated total of outstanding housing loans has been estimated at Rs 9 trillion.[14] The average housing loan in 1990–91 was for Rs 75,000; with inflation and growth of incomes, this had increased to Rs 2.3 million—a multiple of more than thirty. Further, the average age of a home loan customer had dropped from forty-five to between thirty-five and thirty-eight.[15] Homes had become costlier because of rising real estate prices, but more people could afford them at a younger age.

Despite the steady broad-basing of asset ownership, it remains heavily skewed toward a few, as might be expected. According to Credit Suisse's 2014 study on global wealth, 733 million adults had marketable assets of less than $10,000 each (a little over Rs 600,000 at the time). Another 40 million had wealth going up to $100,000 (Rs 6 million). Only the remaining 2.8 million had more.[16] Of this niche group, 182,000 had wealth of over a million dollars, of whom 27,105 had more than $5 million each.[17]

And yet India was by no means the most unequal of societies when it came to wealth. India's Gini coefficient for wealth (a measure of inequality on an ascending scale from 0 to 100), at 81.4 percent, was lower than the global average of 91.1 percent, and lower also than the Gini numbers for Africa, North America, Europe, and Asia-Pacific. Only Latin America (slightly) and China (significantly) did better.

When the financial newspaper *Business Standard* published India's first listing of the country's rupee billionaires (based on holdings in publicly listed companies), in 1999, 100 people who made the grade had a combined wealth of Rs 83.8 billion. Of the 100, only four were classified as dollar billionaires. By 2010, though, there were 657 rupee billionaires and forty-six dollar billionaires; that latter number rose to fifty-five in 2014. By then, the richest in the list had greater individual wealth than all top 100 together had in 1999. The increase in incomes and wealth naturally created a new class of uber-consumers who bought luxury cars (whose annual sales grew from around 3,000 in 2002 to more than 30,000 in 2014, and were forecast somewhat optimistically to grow to 100,000 by 2020). Also in demand were high-end homes that cost between Rs 100 million and Rs 250 million (and more) in the tonier enclaves—competing with wealthy Singapore and Dubai, if not yet New York and London.[18]

A Bulge below the Top

The far more significant development than the surging number of dollar millionaires was the broadening of the consuming class in the upper half of the pyramid. While the "1 percent of 1 percent" (to borrow a term from the Occupy Wall Street movement of 2011) grabbed headlines, the broader trend of rising salary levels and all-around surge in land and share prices was the more substantial story. It defined the growing wealth and comfort of what must be called the "middle-class rich" (the rich are too small to be a numerically significant class by themselves). There is of course no one definition of the middle class. The term has been used loosely over the years, without a clear or commonly shared idea of what one is talking about. Some have said the purchase of a motorcycle or scooter defines a person as middle class, others have looked at the sizes of homes and the conveniences in them, and yet others have looked at income levels. How does India stack up on some of these yardsticks?

Across Indian society as a whole, in the decade to 2011,[19] the number of households with TV sets went up from 61 million to 116 million (out of about 250 million), and of those owning two- and four-wheelers from 27 million to 63 million. Those "availing banking services" went up from 68 million to 145 million, while those using cooking gas went up from 34 million to 70 million. In each case, the number had nearly doubled or more than doubled in a decade. Then the pace accelerated. In the four years since 2011, the use of cooking gas grew another 70 percent, to reach 120 million homes.[20] So perhaps did vehicle ownership as 14–16 million passenger vehicles (including motorcycles and scooters) were sold annually. Cable and satellite TV connections reached 144 million households. Banking access was made near-universal (though many accounts remained non-operational), and more than 600 million people had mobile phones (some of them had more than one phone, while many among the 900 million subscriber identification module [SIM] card connections were not in use). In broad terms, 40–50 percent of households now had the basic conveniences and owned a vehicle—a higher percentage in urban areas, lower in rural.

It is in the nature of a growing economy that the middle class will account for a steadily larger share of the population, so its number is likely to grow faster than that of the population as a whole. Hence many product and service markets catering to this class are destined to outpace overall GDP growth rates. For instance, the International Air Transport Association forecast in 2014 that in the next twenty years India would move from being the ninth-largest aviation market (domestic and international combined) to the third largest; the country's domestic aviation would see perhaps the fastest growth among all countries.

At the same time, the poor (urban and rural taken together) have remained the largest cohort. The 2011 Census recorded that out of 250 million households, 100 million still lived in homes with one room or less, 115 million homes had mud floors, and 91 million had walls and roofs made of grass, thatch, bamboo, or unburned brick. This told us that the bottom 40 percent and more (landless laborers in the fields, migrant workers in urban areas, marginal farmers, unskilled workers everywhere) were still either not part of the Indian story, or only marginally so. Some of them would no longer officially qualify as being poor (wage rates had risen, after all), but they were eking out a bare living on the edge of survivability.

And So, Four Classes of Indians

India has a definition of what constitutes poverty—rather, many definitions, devised by expert committees over more than forty years. But as already noted, there is no universally accepted definition of who or what constitutes the middle class—in India or elsewhere. One definition of the middle class is in relation to the rest of society—for instance, those who occupy the mid-rungs of the consumption ladder, say, between the 20th and 80th percentiles. The more common method, however, is to look at the absolute levels of income or consumption, above a qualifying minimum—but this minimum has varied. Abhijit Banerjee and Esther Duflo adopted in 2007 a range between $2 and $10 per day, at purchasing power parity (PPP; $2 being the higher of the two poverty benchmarks used by the World Bank).[21] At the higher end of various estimates, Lant Pritchett of Harvard's Kennedy School suggested a starting point for the middle class of $15.[22]

More recently, the Pew Research Center has used the World Bank's database and treated Banerjee–Duflo's $2–$10 range as low income. Instead, it has taken the $10–$20 bracket as middle income and $20–50 as upper-middle income.[23] Surjit S. Bhalla postulated in 2007 an income range of $10–100 for defining the middle class.[24] He took the bottom of the range as equivalent to a population-adjusted poverty line in developed countries in 2006 and fixed the higher figure arbitrarily (he says) at ten times the lower number. In a 2012 report on the middle class in Latin America released by two World Bank economists, the income range used was Pew's $10–50.[25] Before that, Homi Kharas of the Brookings Institution used the $10–100 range. Kharas argued in a 2010 paper for the Organization for Economic Cooperation and Development (OECD) that a person in the "global middle class" would have a minimum expenditure of $10 per head per day in PPP terms, going up to a maximum of $100. Kharas gave the logic of his numbers by saying that the "global middle class" at the bottom of the income range would exclude those considered poor in the poorest advanced countries (like Portugal), and at the upper end exclude the rich in the richest advanced country (Luxembourg).[26]

For our immediate purpose we need to focus on the lower cutoff for being middle-income; the commonly used figure (apparently blessed by the World Bank and others) is $10 per day, PPP. By this yardstick, how many would be properly middle class in India? The World Bank in 2014 gave a PPP dollar–rupee conversion rate for 2011 of Rs 15.11.[27] So a middle class person's consumption level would be Rs 151.10 per day, and a five-member household's monthly consumption expenditure would be Rs 22,665. Adjusting for inflation till 2014, the minimum monthly consumption for a "global" middle-class family would have been around Rs 28,500. As against this, the national income figures for 2014–15 say that the average five-member Indian household's monthly consumption level was slightly shy of Rs 25,000,[28] which falls short of the $10 benchmark.

Such an "average" household does not occupy the middle slot in an income ranking of households. Because of skewed expenditure–distribution patterns, such a household probably occupies the 70th percentile (or the seventieth rung on a ladder with 100 rungs).[29] It follows that India's "global" middle class is smaller than 30 percent of the population. In the absence of reliable and precise data, one has to stay in the world of guesstimates. A reasonable one would be that something like 27 percent of households—about 340 million people—qualified for inclusion in 2014–15 under the definition of "global" middle class. This being the top 27 percent of households, it would include the rich.

At the other end of the income ladder, we have the Rangarajan Committee's definition of the poor. This was a five-member household that lived, in 2011–12, on less than Rs 4,860 per month in a rural area and Rs 7,035 in an urban one, giving an all-India average of Rs 5,530. Adjusting for inflation over three years, these numbers for 2014–15 would have been around Rs 6,000 and Rs 9,000, with an all-India average of about Rs 7,000. The PPP dollar equivalent was $2.44 per day in 2011–12, or about a quarter of the minimum level for the middle class. Rangarajan said that 29.5 percent of the population, or 363 million people, were below this level in 2011–12. As incomes and expenditures have grown in the years since then, both the percentage and the absolute number of poor would have continued to fall. It would not be unreasonable to assume that around 27 percent of the population would have been poor in 2014–15.

We now have a broad idea of who are the poor (the bottom 27 percent of the population) and who constitute the middle class-cum-rich (the top 27 percent). What about the remaining 46 percent in the middle, and the question of defining the *aam aadmi*, or common man? We have already noted that the five-member household that spent Rs 25,000 per month in 2014–15 probably occupied a position at or near the 70th percentile in an expenditure ranking. The true *aam aadmi* is the one who occupies the 50th percentile, that is, the median position. Using the available data on consumption and distribution patterns, it can be said that a five-member household on the 50th rung would have had monthly consumption expenditure in the ballpark range of Rs 15,000 in 2014–15; the figure would be higher in urban areas and lower in rural ones. On PPP conversion, this would be $6.62 per head, per day.

These strictly ballpark—and yet plausible—numbers should be treated with circumspection, since they are only informed guesstimates. It is also worth noting that costs in Mumbai will be different from those in, say, Patna, though both are classified as urban centers. There will be even greater variations between urban and rural areas. Still, a monthly expenditure of Rs 15,000 can be used as a working figure for defining the *aam aadmi* household. Those above this benchmark would belong to the neo-middle class, while those below it but above the poverty line could be called the vulnerable non-poor.

The easiest way to picture the first category would be to look at the owners of two-wheelers, especially in the urban areas. The next-lower rung, the vulnerable non-poor, would be those who have emerged out of poverty but are not yet high enough above the water level to be free from the fear of falling back in, if the fates are unkind—think a poor harvest, a recession that leads to lack of work, or a catastrophical medical episode. It would not be unrealistic (also convenient and symmetrical!) to assume that these two groups are of equal size. In the broadest terms, therefore, a classification of India's population for 2014–15 would look like that in Table 12.2.

Table 12.2 Possible Class Breakup in India, 2014–15

Category	Number of People *(in millions)*	Expenditure Cutoff *(Rs per month/family)*
Middle-Class Rich	340	> 28,500
Aspiring Neo-middle Class	285	15,000–28,500
Vulnerable Non-poor	285	7,000–15,000
Poor	340	< 7,000

Source: Author's own work.

An aam aadmi*'s household budget*

Any numbers that are arrived at as broad guesstimates (as done in the preceding paragraphs) need a reality check. For instance, what would be the economic picture of the *aam aadmi* who belongs to a family at or near the 50th percentile, and therefore at the dividing line between the neo-middle class and the vulnerable non-poor—with a monthly household consumption expenditure of Rs 15,000? (In an urban setting, the expenditure level would be higher, perhaps Rs 18,000.) In order to assess what food would cost, the retail chain Easy Day (managed at the time in partnership with Wal-Mart) was requested to put together a food basket that would meet the nutritional norms prescribed by the National Institute of Nutrition, norms 25–30 percent better than the calorie intake used for defining poverty-level consumption. The costs were presented by the chain in a detailed table and would drop by about 15 or 20 percent if rice and flour were obtained from government-subsidized shops. On that basis, and going by the calorie needs of a husband–wife couple and the smaller requirements per head for three children, the daily cost of food would have been about Rs 140 in April 2013—or Rs 4,200 per month. Eighteen months later, on the basis of food inflation rates, that sum would have ballooned by an outer limit of 20 percent, to about Rs 5,000.

After food comes shelter: a two-room place would rent for Rs 5,000 per month in any of the "urban villages" of the kind that dot Delhi. As for utility bills, 40 percent of domestic consumers in Delhi have monthly electricity consumption at the lowest tariff level of 200 units (Kwh) or less, according to one of the city's power distribution companies. Our *aam aadmi* or common man's household would consume slightly more than that, say, eight units of electricity daily; its monthly electricity bill would then be about Rs 1,000. For that, it could enjoy the benefits of using a small refrigerator, a TV set, a couple of fans and lights, and occasionally an electric iron. Add the cost of a cooking gas cylinder (Rs 600 every month). Finally, education for two schoolgoing children in a low-cost private school (better than a free government school) would have cost Rs 2500.

The practice at this income level would be for the breadwinner to commute on his bicycle or walk to work (as more than half the city's commuters do). If he had to commute by public bus or Metro, add up to Rs 1500 for transport costs (the monthly pass on the Delhi Metro for a 30-km commute is Rs 750). Throw in Rs 2500 for sundry living costs (including a cable TV connection and a mobile phone), and the monthly spending by such an *aamaadmi* household in an urban setting totals up to Rs 18,000 or thereabouts.

It is a tight budget that has no cushion and provides for no savings, but it takes care of the minimum modern conveniences: electricity and cooking gas, cable TV and mobile phone, piped water supply (which more than half the city enjoys), and a bicycle or an old motorcycle. Slightly lower down the income ladder, a family would have to make sacrifices on living space and settle for a single room, fewer gadgets, or a free government school with its inferior education standards. A somewhat higher income would allow it to feel economically more secure, and that family would almost certainly own a motorcycle or scooter. That would be more easily affordable if the woman in the house also went to work, perhaps part-time; but only one-sixth of urban women join the workforce.

An *aam aadmi* urban household at Rs 18,000 per month (about $900 in PPP conversion, give or take a bit) is not poor in the government's or any international dictionary, since the consumption figure per head would be $6 per head per day. Rather, such a household would belong to what is officially termed the lower-income group (LIG), a notch above someone in the economically weaker section (EWS). This is a measure of the distance India has traveled from the days when the median Indian family lived on less than $1.25 per head per day. It is also a measure of the distance that it has failed to travel so far.

13

Politics

A FOURTH MASTER NARRATIVE

Indian politics has witnessed three master narratives in the twentieth century: secular nationalism, Hindu nationalism, and caste-based social justice. . . . On the whole, economics is subservient to the master categories of religion and caste.

Sadiq Ahmed and Ashutosh Varshney[1]

WHEN THE LEADERS of the Congress Party met at a Chintan Shivir (retreat) in Jaipur in January 2013, the party formally started the process of preparing for elections to the Lok Sabha (lower house of India's Parliament) due fifteen months later. Speaking at the Shivir, party president Sonia Gandhi did something unusual—she spoke of gaining the support, not just of the party's conventionally constituted base of the *aam aadmi*, or common man, but also of a new, more aspirational class. She said that India was increasingly peopled by a younger, more impatient, and better-educated generation. Economic growth over the past decade, she added, had been impressive. This had had a major impact on reducing poverty. The party's Jaipur Declaration later said that the "Congress acknowledges the fact that there is a rising educated and aspirational middle class, especially in urban areas. We will continue to create new opportunities for them and a climate conducive to their advancement."[2]

These comments were notable, coming as they did from a politician and a political party whose lack of conviction in the ability of market-oriented economic reforms and unalloyed growth to extend benefits to the poor had become a commonplace. Was it possible that Sonia Gandhi's recognition of the political importance of the rising classes was in response to Narendra Modi, then the Gujarat chief minister and BJP's rising sun, talking a month earlier of a "neo-middle class"? The BJP's manifesto for the Gujarat Assembly elections, released in December 2012, had highlighted such a classification. And Modi had explained then that the term referred to those who had risen above the poverty line but were not yet a part of the middle class. A year later, in its 2014 manifesto for the Lok Sabha elections, the BJP continued with the theme and pledged to "meet the aspirations" of this "neo-middle class," saying they needed "proactive hand-holding." In the new government's first Budget in 2014, Finance Minister Arun Jaitley declared: "Those living below the poverty line are anxious to free themselves from the curse of poverty. Those who have got an opportunity to emerge from the difficult challenges have become aspirational. They now want to be a part of the neo-middle class."

Earlier, in the summer of 2011, some communists too had been in an introspective mood when surveying the wreckage that was the Left Front combine in West Bengal, following state elections that swept it out of office after thirty-four years. A. B. Bardhan, general secretary of the Communist Party of India, said that the Left would have to reckon with the fact that while it had "lost its influence in the old middle class, it had not yet found a way to talk to the new."[3]

The basis of the emerging political reality of a "neo-middle class" and of a "vulnerable non-poor" has been spelled out in the previous chapter. To recap briefly, India had developed its economy to a point where the proper middle class (families with monthly consumption expenditure in 2014–15 of Rs 28,500 and more—equivalent to an international benchmark of $10 per head per day, converted using PPP) numbered perhaps 340 million, or 27 percent of the population, while another 285 million or thereabouts belonged to an emerging category that conformed to Narendra Modi's "neo-middle class." These numbers are not precise, but they give an idea of the emerging reality.

The neo-middle class comprised people yet to get into an income bracket that would afford them economic security in terms of a savings bank balance, or a truly middle-class consumption pattern. Nor did they have a characteristic usually associated with the middle class—a proper education (only 21.1 percent of college-age youngsters were enrolled for a university degree or post-school diploma courses; the share of the entire adult population with at least one college degree was of course much smaller).[4] The point, though, was that the middle class and neo-middle class were now about half the total population, or approaching that landmark.

Below the neo-middle class was a category that should be called the "vulnerable non-poor," comprising people who had emerged from dire poverty but remained vulnerable to financial shocks that could push them back into poverty and were barely able to meet minimum consumption needs. This group attracted the eye of even those politicians whose instinct until then had been to focus on people at the bottom of the pyramid, the poor—who were slightly more than a quarter of the population.

The emergence of powerful new voting categories was particularly evident in urban areas—though these accounted for less than a third of the total population. In a self-consciously middle-class urbanized entity like Gurgaon (population about 2.5 million), neighboring Delhi, the credit rating agency CRISIL estimated that 30 percent of households owned cars, 41 percent owned two-wheelers, and 77 percent owned TV sets. Here, the middle class and neo-middle class were in a clear majority.[5] Some other urban areas were comparable. In Delhi, according to data collected for the 2011 Census, 20.7 percent owned cars and 38.9 percent owned two-wheelers, while in Chandigarh the numbers were 25.7 percent and 46.7 percent. In the small coastal state of Goa, the figures were even more impressive: 24.6 percent of households had cars and 56.9 percent owned two-wheelers.

There would be some overlap in these two ownership categories, of course. But since the all-India ownership of cars, as reported by the 2011 Census, was 4.7 percent, and of two-wheelers 21 percent, it was clear (and to be expected) that those with powered personal transport were essentially in towns and cities. Further, with the majority of the 5 million university graduates or diploma-holders who were being turned out each year concentrated in urban areas, there could be little doubt that the new majority in urban India was from the middle and aspiring classes. From a political perspective, more than a third of all Lok Sabha constituencies are urban, or have a significant urban component; so a government could stand or fall depending on the level of its support from these two categories, or the lack of it.

A substantial chunk of the middle class proper had been historically apolitical, usually not bothering to vote in elections, in which its members saw themselves as marginal players, able to influence the outcome only in exceptional circumstances (as in the 1977 elections, when the overriding issue was ending Indira Gandhi's draconian "Emergency" rule with its press censorship and suspension of civil liberties). Politicians too recognized that this group's numbers were small, and hitherto ignored them while appealing to the more numerous poor. Now it was time for politicians to take note of the fact that a quarter century of fairly rapid economic growth had trebled per capita income and changed the demographic, economic, and therefore political reality. India's politics would have to change too.

Thirty-three years after Indira Gandhi had fought and won the 1971 Lok Sabha elections on the promise of *garibi hatao* (abolish poverty), the Congress

Party had moved from talking of the *garib* and switched to the *aam aadmi* (common man). That was the first shift of focus from those at the bottom of the pyramid to a population cohort a step or two higher up the income and consumption slope. There is no word as yet in the political lexicon to describe the second shift of focus, by 2014, to what is loosely called the aspiring classes, but doubtless one will be coined.

Nancy Birdsall, founding president of the Centre for Global Development in Washington, DC, had forecast that the middle and aspiring categories in India would be 625 million strong by 2020. It was a reasonable enough assessment, but probably late by a few years. Homi Kharas was more on the mark when he postulated that by 2015 half the population would have crossed a $5 per day line; our numbers in the previous chapter have shown that half the population had indeed crossed this mark if you take a mix of rural and urban areas, in 2015. Kharas's long-term forecast, that by 2025 half the population would surpass the $10 per day line and become part of the middle class proper, may well fructify.[6] This much was clear: even without waiting for the seismic change implicit in half the population becoming properly middle class, Indian politics had added a new focal point. Political success, and power, would now depend not just on appealing to the poor and vulnerable non-poor, who still constituted half the electorate, but also on reflecting the aspirations of the more upwardly mobile segments of the population.

Positioning and Reality

But change in India is slow and partial, never complete, marked often by two steps forward and then a step back—precisely because a politician has to deal with a universe of realities, as even the BJP was to discover. For the Congress, meanwhile, old habits died hard, too. In the year and more after its Chintan Shivir (retreat) in Jaipur, the party continued to focus on what it could do for the *aam aadmi* even as it aimed its programs and promises closer to the base of the pyramid. Rahul Gandhi, who had been elevated as the party vice president, made symbolic visits to the poorest Dalit (the erstwhile Untouchables) homes, campaigned in poverty-stricken tribal areas against the setting up of extraction industries that would affect forest cover, and joined farmers protesting the forcible acquisition of their land by the government for urban housing and industrial projects. The thrust of the party's "rights-based" approach to policy formulation was the same—to underline the need for inclusion, with no one left out of the tent.

So when in the summer of 2015 Rahul Gandhi launched his comeback bid in Indian politics, he positioned himself where he was most comfortable, as the standard-bearer of the "farmer and labourer" (*kisan aur mazdoor*). He picked on the amendments that the Modi government wanted to make to the land acquisition law so that it would not block investment in industry and infrastructure projects, and launched an assault on what he called a "suit-boot" government that was changing laws to repay businessmen who had backed it in the elections. It was posturing or positioning, depending on how sympathetic you wanted to be to Mr. Gandhi (if anyone had been in cahoots with businessmen, it was the previous Congress-led government).

Still, the Modi government was sufficiently unnerved to step gingerly on economic reform measures that might upset large categories of voters—like industrial workers. In an interview timed for the first anniversary of his government, in May 2015, Modi declared in answer to a question on the land law that he stood with *gaon, garib aur kisan* (the village, the poor, and the farmers). By 2016, Modi shifted his focus even closer to the base of the pyramid and emphasized policies for the neglected countryside, racked as it was by stories of farmers committing suicide in the wake of successive monsoon failures. All mention of the neo-middle class had disappeared from his speeches.

Still, the changing arithmetic of elections was there for all to see. Urban voters, enthused by the rapid economic growth of the years leading up to the 2009 elections, and seeing that they themselves were noticeably better off than five years earlier, had voted the ruling Congress-led United Progressive Alliance (UPA) back to power. But, for the same reasons that the Congress Party won many of the towns and cities in 2009—in the process bagging more than 200 Lok Sabha seats for the first time since 1984—it lost those very towns and cities in 2014 because of the alienation of the urban voter on account of higher inflation, slower growth, the resulting scarcity of jobs, and waves of scandal. Even if politics were to slip back into the old rhetoric, the middle and aspiring classes could and did make a difference.

The sequence of events tells its own story. When Mumbai was attacked by Pakistan-backed terrorists in the winter of 2008, the non-voting classes came out onto the streets, held candlelight vigils, and declared "Never again." That mobilization was missing, however, when the Lok Sabha elections came around six months later; well-heeled south Mumbai once again saw a low voter turnout. But as public anger rose over corruption scandals and outsize skeletons began tumbling out of government cupboards, the need for cleaning up politics became the new battle cry. Anna Hazare, a former army truck driver who had turned social reformer and environmental activist in his

Maharashtra village of Ralegan Siddhi, and then extended his appeal across the state with periodic calls to sack corrupt ministers, reached Delhi to lead an anti-corruption rally and to demand a law to set up an ombudsman who would be empowered to handle corruption cases. A second show, asking for broadly the same thing, was organized soon by a yoga exponent with a massive following, Baba Ramdev. This time a more varied crowd, less upper crust than before, was out in the streets, capturing the media space and forcing the government to introduce in Parliament a bill to set up an ombudsman (Lok Pal). This was an idea that had been debated for decades without achieving practical shape, but though the bill was now passed by the Lok Sabha, it was deliberately blocked in the Rajya Sabha and sent off to a committee—where it lay buried for a while.

Soon afterward, when a young Delhi woman was raped and brutalized in a moving bus, resulting eventually in her death, the city was traumatized; students and youth from the now more readily mobilized middle class were at the barricades yet again, braving police water cannon and lathis (bamboo staves). People learned to mobilize using mobile phones and social media. Reports and images of the "Arab Spring," which had bloomed in Egypt's Tahrir Square a couple of years before, were doubtless in many minds. The media, especially the plethora of television news channels—many of them only a few years old—gave voice to the anger over very middle-class issues like corruption, law and order, and the lack of government responsiveness. The political class was caught flat-footed and went into hiding, not knowing how to deal with this new phenomenon. A new master narrative was being created.

The young woman whose tragic rape and death shocked the country and brought large numbers out into the streets of cities, was herself a representative of India's new emerging class. Her parents had migrated from a village in eastern Uttar Pradesh (UP) and her father worked at the modest job of a loader (hauling baggage on and off conveyor belts) at Delhi airport. The daughter was bright but could not raise the money for the medical education that she had set her heart on. Undaunted, she went to Dehradun, 250 kilometers from Delhi, to enroll in a relatively expensive course that taught her physiotherapy—to finance which her father sold his land in their ancestral village. Nearing the end of her course, she was about to become an intern and would have soon been adding significantly to the family's income. Along the way, she acquired a taste for trendy clothes, cosmetics, and footwear; she had attained for herself a fair degree of personal freedom from her parents to live her own life; she streaked her hair, liked to visit shopping malls, and became friends with a young man with whom she developed a close relationship. But they had decided not to marry—after all, they belonged to different castes.

The family's story captured in microcosm the change in urban India. There was significant upward mobility in the space of one generation, acquired principally through education; there was the promise of greater spending power and the acquisition of some aspects of what one might call modernity, or at least a departure from traditional practices. Any Western academic would find it hard to describe the family as middle class. The head of the household was blue collar, the family lived in a single-room home with no significant financial assets or modern conveniences. Yet this was a new, young India that went to public rallies, rode the city's Metro, aspired to better careers and incomes, and expected its politicians to deliver. In towns and cities across the country, these were not people who might automatically vote their caste, as their counterparts in villages still did for the most part; in Delhi, no one cared what your caste was when the pressing concerns were the basics of urban life: safe public transport, assured electricity supply and piped water, clean air, the freedom to not have to pay a bribe in every interface with a government functionary—all of these in addition to the economic issues that traditionally were prominent at election time: inflation and jobs.

One of Anna Hazare's cohorts was Arvind Kejriwal, an engineer from one of the elite Indian Institutes of Technology (IITs) who had taken a job in Tata Steel before sitting for the civil service exam and becoming a tax official, only to give that up and get into civil society activism (winning Asia's Nobel, the Magsaysay Award). Kejriwal now decided to make the shift from activism to electoral politics, forming a new party that he called the Aam Aadmi Party (or AAP). The party's election symbol, a broom, suggested it wanted to sweep clean. When the Delhi state elections were held toward the end of 2013, AAP surprised even its supporters by winning 40 percent of the seats in Parliament and eventually formed a minority government with Kejriwal as the chief minister. In fresh elections held a year later, the party won an astonishing sixty-seven out of seventy seats.

Although the Kejriwal-led government was to prove disappointing to many of its supporters, and the party's legislators became embroiled in a variety of controversies (the allegations ranged from fudging educational records and real estate fraud to wife-beating), its ascent had been a political earthquake and forced both the BJP and the Congress Party to wake up to the need for a new brand of manifestly middle- and aspiring-class politics. The urban and neo-middle class vote had arrived and would not be pushed aside.

Enter Narendra Modi

The politician who moved with the greatest ease and success into the new space that had been created by economic growth, urbanization, and demographic change was of course Narendra Modi. His catchwords and phrases during the campaign for the 2014 Lok Sabha elections were "development" and "good governance" (*su-raaj*). The promise was that he could do for India what he had done for Gujarat in his twelve years as chief minister: high rates of growth in agriculture, 80 percent growth in milk production, more than a fivefold increase in cotton output, round-the-clock electricity supply, quadrupling the number of universities, attracting investment in industry, and so on. "Today the whole world is talking about Gujarat's progress," he said with typical bombast.[7]

Ever the master orator, with facts and figures at his fingertips, and a showman underestimated by critics who had dubbed him an "event manager," Modi became the focus of prime-time television news coverage wherever he went. A taste for clever coinages became part of the message and the persona, like P2-G2 ("pro-people, good governance"). Emerging quickly as the central figure in the campaign, he skillfully played on the mood of frustration in an electorate alienated by tales of corruption, an economic slowdown, and the aggravations of the simplest citizen–government interface. And he promised to make things better.

Conveying a message through the choice of locale, Modi launched himself with a speech at the Shri Ram College of Commerce, a premier college attached to Delhi University. (Rahul Gandhi had been invited too but had declined.) Delivered many months before his party chose him as its candidate for prime minister, the speech was televised to nationwide audiences and immediately put Modi front and center of the elections that were still more than a year away. "Today, the eyes of the entire world are on India," he said. "Why? Because they think that India is a large bazaar. The whole world thinks they can dump all their things in our markets. They think they can sell easily in India. It is time that we decide that we will lead the world in manufacturing and make the world our bazaar and dump our goods in their markets" [applause].

Since he was addressing college students, (and half of India is under twenty-five), he talked of a visit to Taiwan before he had become chief minister, when his interpreter asked if India was still a land of snake charmers. Said Modi: "The poor fellow knew only those things. . . . I said, 'Our ancestors used to be snake charmers. Our generation is not that good. We have lost our abilities. These days we are mouse charmers.' And, my friends, today our youth moves the whole world by keeping their hands on the computer mouse [applause]. This is the power of our youth."[8] Both young and old voted for the messenger of change and hope, his appeal enhanced by the resurgent nationalism in his speeches.

Trickle-Down Politics

Even if Indian politics is to be driven more than before by middle-class and neo-middle-class interests, it is debatable how new this is as a phenomenon. The century-plus history of Indian politics is that it has rarely been done from the bottom up or been revolutionary in nature. The Congress Party began as an initiative by the national elite in the late nineteenth century but could not afford to stay that way because of the logic of numbers in a colonial entity that aspired to freedom through mass mobilization, and then to democratic governance as an independent republic. The history of the Congress Party, therefore, was of a slow ceding of ground by the dominant middle and upper classes to broader social groupings and interests. Those who felt the emerging mainstream did not represent them—Muslims on the one hand, lower castes on the other—went their separate ways then and later, with the formation of the Muslim League and the Justice Party.

Even when the Congress Party under Mahatma Gandhi's leadership became a mass movement in the 1920s and sought to represent all sections, it remained essentially a conservative grouping that reflected well the power structures in rural and urban India, with the leadership comprising lawyers, prosperous agriculturists, and others with a stake in the class and caste status quo, with funding from nationalist businessmen.

Nehru's talk may have been of socialism, but the party was solidly mainstream conservative; in any case Nehru meant state socialism, not revolutionary socialism. After Independence in 1947, rentiers like the zamindari class (landowners and revenue collectors during the British Raj) were abolished, and the Congress Party swept election after election. Nehru therefore had the elbow room to focus on building a "developmental state," with the middle class being the main beneficiary of an expanding higher education system and new jobs in a plethora of government-owned companies that were set up. The poor got short shrift: though the overwhelming majority was not literate at Independence, primary school education never got the same attention as higher education and the elite new technology institutes. The class and caste bias in such choices was evident.

The truth is that India's politicians have been snake-oil salesmen. They have appealed to the poor for their votes, taken protection money from the rich, and represented middle-class interests more than any other—though that is not how these last saw it, especially after 1969. That's the watershed year in which, when faced with a serious political challenge, Indira Gandhi felt forced to lurch into a more radical brand of legislative socialism. With that began the only period when the still-tiny middle class felt politically abandoned.

Mrs. Gandhi put in place a populist political paradigm with restrictive labor laws, an expropriatory tax regime, and state takeovers that would be dismantled only slowly, in phases, over four decades. She nationalized the leading banks, insurance companies, coal mining firms, textile mills, and engineering units in a headlong rush between 1969 and 1973, and imposed severe constraints on private enterprise. She took the peak income tax rate up to more than 97 percent.[9] Hardly anyone paid the top tax rate, of course, because tax evasion and avoidance flourished. The poor therefore got little out of Mrs. Gandhi's socialism, and not just because economic growth was at its slowest in the 1969–74 phase; but they remained her solid support base even as the policy pendulum swung back ever so slowly from left to middle-of-the-road and then somewhat right-of-center.

Elsewhere, populism was the politician's response to the failure to deliver real change in people's lives. The DMK in Tamil Nadu (called Madras state at the time) swept the 1967 assembly elections with the promise of a rupee for a *padi* (about 1.5 kilos) of rice. N. T. Rama Rao repeated that feat in Andhra Pradesh in 1983, leading his newly formed Telugu Desam Party to a sweeping victory by promising rice at Rs 2 per kilo. M. G. Ramachandran, his counterpart in Tamil Nadu, offered free midday meals to schoolchildren. Though not all such promises were eventually delivered in full (starting with the DMK's 1967 promise, because it would have bankrupted the treasury), politics remained a mix of election-eve populism and a left-of-center stance on key economic issues, including solid support for a substantial degree of state capitalism. As mild economic reforms (dubbed by many at the time as anti-poor) were introduced, election-eve freebies became steadily more ambitious, moving from subsidized rice and saris for women to free electricity for farmers, and later from free bicycles for girl students to free TV sets and then free laptops for students.

In essence, these were paternalistic overtures, palliatives tossed out by parties representing the interests of the better-off (who, as one would expect, cornered most of the state subsidies announced in the name of the poor).

But the lower orders were beginning to assert themselves too. The Dalits and "other backward classes" (OBCs) began to form their own parties, even as those completely on the margins—the victims of "development" who had been evicted from their land and homes to make way for new industrial and mining projects—defected from mainstream politics to join a growing Maoist movement in the country's heartland. Over a half century the Lok Sabha saw a steady increase in representation for farmers and people from the backward classes, with the upper castes yielding ground.

Meanwhile, the lethal combination of fiscal populism and state socialism caused persistent underperformance on the economic front. At the same time, governments that were saddled with too many tasks, following the bid to expand the role of the state, failed to deliver on the basics. Consequently, politicians delivered neither freedom from poverty nor effective governance of the kind that the better-off desired. This didn't seem to matter because, as Pranab Bardhan has argued, oppressed people often found the acquiring of dignity more important than good governance, while corruption by their newly risen leaders was seen in some ways as leveling the playing field vis-à-vis the traditionally exploitative wealthy (usually from the upper and middle castes). Mayawati retained her support base among Uttar Pradesh's Dalits despite facing charges of having amassed unexplained wealth. Lalu Prasad, a colorful backward-caste politician who became chief minister of Bihar, achieved notoriety in the 1990s by asking voters at election rallies what they would do with good roads as smooth as the actor Hema Malini's cheeks, since they did not own cars. Politics had become more truly representative, even as BJP's L. K. Advani expanded the BJP constituency (till then upper caste and mainly urban) to undreamed-of spheres, building on the tempo of a movement to demolish a Mughal-era structure that had once served as a mosque, and build in its place a temple to the Hindu god Ram, whose birthplace it was believed to be. Different strands of the political narrative were coming together.

Axial Decade

The rallying cries of the time had to do with identity (caste and religious community), not governance. Advani and Lalu were the stars of the 1990s, which established two of the master narratives spelled out later by Ahmed and Varshney. In that sense, the 1990s were a decade that redefined Indian politics. The period before that was marked by a studied stability in voter behavior. The first three parliamentary elections, which the Congress Party fought under Nehru in 1952, 1957, and 1962, saw the party get an average 45.6 percent of the total vote. Subsequent elections, all the way to 1989, never saw the party get less than 40 percent of the vote, except fractionally when it lost power in 1989. The substantive exception was in the unique circumstances of the 1977, post-Emergency elections, when the party got 34.5 percent of the vote.

What reshaped Indian politics for good were the four Lok Sabha elections of the 1990s: those held in 1991, 1996, 1998, and 1999. The decline of the Congress Party was matched by the rise of the BJP, and by the birth and growth of a number of smaller parties. At the start of what might be called the axial decade of Indian politics, the BJP dramatically increased its vote share from a modest 11.5 percent of the total in 1989 to 20.1 percent in 1991 and further to 25.5 percent in 1998. There followed a drop when the Congress Party bounced back, until the BJP notched up its best performance, 31 percent in 2014. The BJP's rise found a mirror image in a drop in the Congress Party vote share, which dropped over successive elections from 39.5 percent to 25.3 percent before recovering, only to plunge in 2014 to 19.3 percent. Interestingly, though, the combined vote share of the two largest parties did not veer far from the 50 percent level. The end of the one-dominant party phase of Indian politics (1951–89) meant the birth of the coalition era.

Many offshoots from the Congress Party and the Janata Dal were born during the axial period—the Samajwadi Party in Uttar Pradesh, 1992; the Rashtriya Janata Dal in Bihar, 1997; the Biju Janata Dal in Odisha, 1997; the Trinamool Congress in West Bengal, 1998; and the Nationalist Congress Party, predominantly in Maharashtra, in 1999. The Bahujan Samaj Party, representing Dalits and with its base in Uttar Pradesh, was born in 1984 but came into prominence only in the 1990s. The vote share of these and other regional and caste-based parties climbed rapidly during the decade. These parties represented the primary political challenge to the Congress Party and the BJP in the northern heartland, just as the DMK and regional parties did in the south. Caste politics had become democratized.

Muslims the Losers

The constituency that lost out in a big way in the axial decade and later was Muslims. While caste-based parties flourished after 1989 and gave new political voice to both Dalits and large numbers in the "other backward classes" category, Muslim representation in lawmaking fell victim to the rise of Hindu nationalist forces. Though the Muslim vote continued to be coveted by the Congress Party, which likes to present itself as the trustee of minority interests, it was also sought by a number of smaller parties—in Uttar Pradesh the Samajwadi Party, and in Bihar Lalu's Rashtriya Janata Dal and Nitish Kumar's Janata Dal (United). But Muslim candidates began to be rejected by voters more than before.

Once again, the watershed year was 1989. The number of Muslims in the Lok Sabha came down from forty-nine in 1980 and forty-six in 1984 to half that number (an all-time low of twenty-three seats) in the sixteenth Lok Sabha (2014). There was no Muslim among the winning BJP's 282 members in the Lok Sabha. The Muslim strength in the house, at just over 4 percent, was less than a third of the 14.2 percent Muslim share of the national population. Twenty of the twenty-three Muslim Members of Parliament (MPs) came from just five states. Nearly a dozen major states, including Uttar Pradesh where Muslims account for perhaps a fifth of the population and up to a third in several districts, did not elect a single Muslim MP, though there was no shortage of Muslim candidates. Muslims were becoming unelectable in much of the country. Of sixty-four people in Modi's council of ministers, only two were Muslim.[10]

Meanwhile, the factor that gave the BJP its big boost—the Ram temple agitation—was pushed to the sidelines, at least for the time being. What established the BJP in the center of Indian politics was what Stuart Corbridge, John Harriss, and Craig Jeffrey[11] called "banal Hindutva," a concept that they use as a variation of Michael Billig's "banal nationalism."[12]

Billig wanted to distinguish between xenophobic nationalism and everyday, endemic nationalism—such as flags that flew unnoticed above public buildings, the singing of patriotic songs on particular occasions, and expressions of support for national sports teams. In the same way, suggested Corbridge et al., a Hindu nationalist ethos had penetrated the public discourse in a way that often went unnoticed. A quick look around provides plenty of supporting evidence. New towns or localities in the 1950s and 1960s would be given names that reflected the development ethos of the time and denoted progress or optimism, like Model Town and Vasant Vihar, or honored contemporary leaders (Gandhinagar and Tagore Garden). From the 1980s names were more likely to be from the Hindu epics, like Dwarka and Kaushambi—juxtaposed with gated communities called Belvedere and Hamilton Court, to please the tastes of a more Westernized elite—also those aspiring to be Westernized and be accepted into the ranks of this elite. The complex of meeting rooms attached to the prime minister's residence (built when the

BJP's Atal Behari Vajpayee was prime minister) was named "Panchvati," from the Ramayana. Equally, the singing of "Vande Mataram" (recognized as the national song but excluding some of its verses that have a religious context) and the adoption of traditional Hindu practices like breaking coconuts and lighting lamps on auspicious occasions, contributed to the banal Hindutva that had taken root. Vedic hymns were sung when warships were launched into the water. Newspaper headlines reflected the trend: the *Times of India* took a quote from an outgoing Reserve Bank governor to headline a story on the new governor Raghuram Rajan as follows: "Can Rajan, the Arjuna, get India out of Chakravyuha?"—assuming, perhaps correctly, that all its readers knew their Mahabharata.

Noting this trend is not to take exception; indeed, it is what one would expect in any country or society. In India itself, there was no shortage of Muslim place-names reflecting centuries of Muslim rule—names like Ahmedabad (which some would like to rename Karnavati) and Allahabad (an occasionally suggested alternative is Prayag, to mark the confluence there of the rivers Ganga, Yamuna, and the mythical Saraswati). Nor was there a shortage of "convents" called St. someone or other, which often had no connection to any Christian order; it was merely that Christian missionary schools established mostly during the British Raj were traditionally known to teach good English and impart a passable education. Also, place-names had been taken from Buddhism (like Buddh Vihar—a name chosen by a leader of Dalits, many of whom had followed Ambedkar and converted to Buddhism). A government medical college in the capital was named after Vardhaman Mahavira (the founder of Jainism). So there was plenty of eclecticism on display. Still, the swing toward what the BJP's former president, L. K. Advani, called "cultural nationalism" was unmistakable, accompanied by a more overt religiosity that manifested itself in the popularity of TV serials on the great Hindu epics and the growing attention to what had once been relatively minor religious observances like *karva chauth* (when wives fast for their husbands' well-being). It was to be expected that the aspiring classes, gaining enough confidence to assert their cultural roots, were in the front ranks of those rooting for precisely such cultural nationalism.

Viewed benignly, this was nothing more than a post-colonial, deracinated people rediscovering traditional moorings in a contemporary context. A key development perhaps was the holding in the late 1990s of the Supreme Court (with the respected J. S. Verma as the chief justice) that Hindutva did not automatically violate the constitutional bar on appealing for votes on the basis of religion, and that Hindutva was also a way of life. The political significance of this was that banal Hindutva could become a fertile hunting ground for parties that based their appeal on a majoritarian ethic spiced with anti-minority feeling. Within the ranks of such parties, there was always a determined core looking to push the majoritarian agenda one more step. So the Ram temple issue might have calmed down by 2004, but Hindutva was now on the map with new champions who sometimes made yesterday's hardliner L. K. Advani look like a toothless old uncle.

In the first year of Modi's rule, emboldened elements of the Hindutva brigade adopted aggressive postures on religious conversions (justified as a response to Christian evangelist activity), while a junior minister referred to non-Hindus as *haraamzadas* (bastards). These embarrassed a prime minister keener on his development agenda, but it was also a fact that the BJP's 2014 manifesto had said "India shall remain a natural home for persecuted Hindus and they shall be welcome to seek refuge here." Why not Sikhs, who used to be a visible trading community in a Taliban-ruled Kabul? Or the possibility of politically persecuted Maldiveans (who are Muslim) seeking refuge? Highlighting one community gave a communal color to what should have been a humanitarian issue.

In 2015, a special prosecutor handling a case where some Hindus stood accused of terrorist activity made headlines when she announced that she had been told to go easy on the case. State after state banned the sale, possession, and consumption of beef—innocent Muslims suspected of violating this were killed in mob activity. Allegations about the "saffronization" of education were aired frequently—and gained credibility when elements from the Hindutva forces were appointed to several key positions in educational and research establishments. Muslim victims of riots in the Uttar Pradesh town of Muzaffarnagar stopped cooperating with police prosecutors, complaining they had been threatened and that the police offered no protection. Liberal voices were flooded with abusive comments on the Internet from what a commentator called "Internet Hindus"; now the prime minister was prompted to ask for restraint. Meanwhile, civil society organizations (not always the most carefully administered when it came to governance norms) saw a squeeze on their sources of funding, and there were cases of pressure on the media to not step out of line. Though the hotheads were still only on the fringes of political action, the so-far banal could well lead to what Fareed Zakaria has called an "illiberal democracy"—a polity that has elected governments but with restraints on individual rights and constitutional liberalism.[13]

Absorbing and Accepting "Mandal"

Meanwhile, the issue that gave the smaller caste-based parties their calling cards—namely, caste reservations—had ceased to arouse the great passions it once did, though here too the issue remained a rallying point. The acceptance of the Mandal reservation formula for OBCs in 1990 (27 percent of all educational seats in colleges, and of government jobs, over and above the reservations originally provided for in the Constitution: 15 percent for Scheduled Castes or Dalits and 7.5 percent for Scheduled Tribes) had provoked violent and widespread protests in the north by upper-caste students. But a subsequent succession of constitutional amendments, all extending reservations in one way or other (some to reverse court judgments), was barely noticed. Thus, the Constitution was amended in 1995 for the seventy-seventh time, to enable reservation in promotions, not just at the job entry level. A few years later, the eighty-first amendment added Clause 4B to Article 16, to overcome the 50 percent limit stipulated by the Supreme Court as the maximum percentage of seats or jobs that could be put into reserved categories.

Then, in 2000, the eighty-second amendment added at the end of Article 335 that relaxation in qualifying marks and lowering of standards of evaluation could be done for giving effect to reservation in promotion to higher posts. And in 2002, the eighty-fifth amendment changed Article 16(4A) to add "consequential seniority" so that reservation in promotion would also give the beneficiary consequential seniority—a subject that caused much heartburn in bureaucracies because it upset the seniority tables (all bureaucrats live and die by seniority). Finally, in 2005, reservations were extended to all educational institutions, including private ones that had taken no aid from the government, with the solitary exception of minority institutions (which have a separate constitutional protection from government interference). Thus, over the ten years between 1995 and 2005, the Constitution had been amended no fewer than five times, extending the scope and definition of reservations in each case, with not even a whiff of political protest at any stage. Though there would have been quiet resentment in upper-caste circles, like Hindutva, "Mandal" too had become an inalienable part of the political terrain.

It would be simplistic in the extreme to assume that plain economics would take over where these other issues left off. No human being is just *homo economicus*, and politics goes beyond the wallet or pocketbook. India in any case is known for its multiple identities—defined by caste, language, ethnicity, and religion, as also by gender and age profile. All of these had influenced voting behavior in the past and would continue to do so. But as the country urbanized, as economic interests became progressively separated from caste identities in towns and cities, an underprovided mass of supplicants looking for free goods or services or preferential treatment from a paternalistic state morphed into citizens with rights and consumers with a voice. It was a transformation that came with higher incomes, greater literacy, rising aspirations, deeper mass media penetration, and greater awareness of the wider world; naturally, it came first with the young, especially in the cities.

That has not meant an end to the old political currency of populism. Indeed, the Aam Aadmi Party's two principal promises were populist: to cut electricity tariffs by half at the lowest consumption level, and to give 700 liters of free water daily to every household. However, the larger promise by both the Aam Aadmi Party (AAP) and Modi was to clean up government and politics, and to shift the focus of government to issues that bothered the middle class, such as the effective delivery of public services, and the rooting out of petty corruption at the citizen's interface with officialdom (getting an electricity connection or a driving license, registering a property transaction or simply births and deaths). India has a long record of the rich cornering subsidies in the name of the poor; a growing neo-middle class that thinks it has not gotten its fair due could make the situation worse by using its newly acquired numerical clout to wrest more concessions. And since resources are finite, this would be at the expense of the genuinely poor. Even more important, so long as the economy was growing at 8–9 percent annually, the system threw up enough opportunities to keep everyone busy and happy. If, on the other hand, growth were to stay in the 7 percent range that has prevailed from 2008—and the job market therefore failed to absorb the net annual increase of 8–10 million people entering the working age and willing to work—tensions could boil over.

The Shape of Public Opinion

As noted in the previous chapter, the growth of the middle class and an aspirational class in an urban setting helps create a public sphere, a la Habermas. Such a sphere is usually missing or too small in predominantly rural societies where the overwhelming majority is too poor and downtrodden to have an independent voice. A narrow elite is in charge, with or without popular sanction. But as incomes rise and the middle class comes into its own, especially in growing towns and cities, the public sphere expands to a point where political change results. India is unique in that it has been a full-fledged democracy (that is, with universal adult franchise) even when the country was overwhelmingly rural and its primary characteristic was large-scale poverty. Elsewhere, the expansion of the public sphere has meant that democracies replaced autocracies. This has been the story in parts of East Asia—specifically South Korea and Taiwan. More recently, over the past decade, there has been a broad trend toward (admittedly imperfect) democratic rule in about half of Africa, even as economic performance has seen a significant uptick.

The trend is easily explained because individualism is more at play in towns and cities than in villages, facilitated by a certain degree of anonymity. It is easier to canvass opinion and mobilize crowds in an urban setting—one reason the French Revolution began in Paris. As part of the broader process, the media acquire a larger catchment, ordinary people understand more about how affairs of state are managed, and they develop more-informed opinions, to which they give expression in a variety of ways. Also, civil society organizations mushroom and create organized channels for developing and articulating opinions that challenge or question the state. Established power structures are tested, and the old elite are pushed to the margin. Among other things, patriarchal power structures start breaking down as women assert themselves and seek greater personal freedoms.

All this and more has been happening in India. Traditional village councils of elders, like *khap panchayat*s (male dominated, inevitably), have tried to crack down on romantic liaisons between young men and women on various grounds, especially when they crossed caste and community barriers. Companies have begun to face a nascent shareholder activism, while the social media are capable of near-ferocity when they turn on someone who has expressed a politically incorrect thought. Indian politics has to come to terms with the ownership of hundreds of millions of smartphones.

The expansion and democratization of the public sphere in a multicultural, post-colonial society can thus take various forms. In India, as already observed, the middle and lower castes have gained political voice and occupy center stage. The process could as easily combine with revivalist pride and nativist assertion, take the form of a subaltern revolt against the old or privileged elite, or be an assertion of hitherto suppressed or quiescent majoritarian sentiment. Tolerance of artistic freedom and dissident writers could shrink—stray episodes are already present. Past examples of majoritarian assertion vary all the way from Sri Lanka's decision in 1956 to derecognize the minority community's Tamil as an official language to Malaysia's racially oriented "*bhumiputra*" policy, introduced in the 1970s to favor indigenous Malays. Even without comparable action, reduced tolerance of minority concerns in India could develop into a progressive challenge to the existing constitutional arrangements. Fortunately, such a prospect is still remote.

The reassuring fact is that the pursuit of power requires parties to give up extreme positions: the communists accepted parliamentary democracy, the separatist DMK in Tamil Nadu settled for state autonomy, and the BJP has stopped harping on some of its core issues of old, like a common civil code for followers of all religions—desirable in principle but resisted by the Muslim community, whose men retain the right to have four wives (one of the complaints of the Hindutva brigade, who think this helps the Muslim population grow faster).

The acquisition of power further plays a moderating role—the DMK has stopped looking for even autonomy, while the BJP has done the previously unthinkable by forming a coalition government with a Muslim-majority party in Jammu and Kashmir. As prime minister, Modi sounds very different from what he did as a divisive chief minister of Gujarat; he has spoken out repeatedly against anyone creating divisions in the name of religion. So the BJP may already have moved to a stage where hardliners exist but are confined by the party to its fringes—not necessarily out of conviction, but because it is politically expedient.

However, such broad political trends are seldom wholly unidirectional. The two master narratives that emerged dominant in the axial decade (caste-based social justice and Hindu nationalism) continue to have relevance and traction. These forces will ebb and flow as they find room in the new master narrative created by the rise of the neo-middle class. It is a fair bet that India might eventually settle for secularism with Hindutva characteristics, even as politics settles into a more clearly middle-class mold over the coming decade.

14

Growth or Environment

A FALSE CHOICE

IT WAS A winter morning in January 2011, and Prime Minister Manmohan Singh was upset. He had been asking his environment minister to meet a number of businessmen whose projects had been held up on environmental grounds—Ajit Gulabchand, whose Lavasa real estate project had been stopped mid-track on belated environmental objections; Naveen Jindal, who wanted a coal mine project cleared in what had been declared a "no-go" area for mining; and others like them. Jairam Ramesh, the minister concerned, had duly met all of them but found he could not bring himself to clear things like mining in the middle of a tiger reserve. Why does the prime minister send only businessmen to me, and never anyone who speaks for the environment? Ramesh had wondered to himself.

Singh called Ramesh aside after a cabinet meeting to reprimand him. An economy could move forward only on the basis of the animal spirits of its businessmen, he said. Productive forces had to be allowed freedom, or economic growth would suffer. Ramesh defended his record: he was clearing more than 95 percent of the industrial projects that came to his ministry, and clearing them within the stipulated time. He was stopping only those that involved serious environmental questions or violations. But the prime minister had his own problems: the press and political parties in the opposition had been criticizing his government for what they called policy paralysis. One way to deal with the criticism was to approve projects that were stuck for want of clearances, and he wanted to get things moving.

Some months later, when the environment ministry continued to stand in the way of projects involving influential businessmen, Singh called Ramesh and gave him a full-scale dressing-down. He couldn't get "men from Mars" to run things the way Ramesh wanted them, he said. The country was "in a stage of primitive capital accumulation," and compromises had to be made. He went on to say that he was at the end of his life and did not want to see economic growth suffer or the India story come to an end. "We can't have European standards," he declared as he asked Ramesh to be realistic. Finally, he warned that if there were very tight environmental rules, the environment ministry would end up creating a "new kind of licence–permit raj."[1]

The perception of conflict between protecting the environment and pursuing development and economic growth is an old one. Indira Gandhi, prime minister for sixteen years in two stretches between 1966 and 1984, had spelled out the dilemmas at the first United Nations conference on the environment at Stockholm in 1972. "We do not wish to impoverish the environment any further and yet we cannot for a moment forget the grim poverty of a large number of people," she said. "Are not poverty and need the greatest polluters? The environment cannot be improved in conditions of poverty." She then went on to add, "The inherent conflict is not between conservation and development but between environment and the reckless exploitation of man and earth in the name of efficiency."[2]

This nuanced and in some ways confusing (perhaps even confused) speech has been much quoted since then. At one level, it reflected the tension between multiple objectives. But Mrs Gandhi was also playing on the word "polluter," in that poverty is "pollution" of a kind, though it is the rich who pollute the environment far more than the poor. But then, how was one to square that with an annual country ranking done by wings of Yale and Columbia universities, in partnership with the World Economic Forum, which showed quite clearly that the countries that did best on an Environmental Performance Index (EPI) were the rich ones, while the poor countries did poorly?[3]

The index looks at two broad concepts. "Environmental health" measures the protection of human health from environment-caused harm; and "ecosystem vitality" measures ecosystem protection and resource management. Since rich countries have better air quality, better and cleaner water supply, and superior resource management, they automatically score better on the EPI. India in 2014 ranked 155th out of 177 countries. China was 118th, while Australia, Switzerland, Germany, and Sweden were in the top ten. So could it be as Mrs Gandhi had put it, that "the environment cannot be improved in conditions of poverty"?

If so, Manmohan Singh had a point. He, for one, was willing to "exploit man and earth" in the interest of capital accumulation through the use of non-"European" environmental standards. Ramesh was assigned to another ministry after a cabinet reshuffle, and the extent of the forest areas that had been declared "no go" for mining was sharply reduced. The Modi government that took office in 2014 reduced the area even further, to a few dozen coal blocks out of 793, with what was now called the "inviolate" area less than 8 percent of the original area assessed in 2010.[4] Standing in opposition to this approach, environmentalists have stressed that it is industrial development that pollutes air and water; motor transport that emits carbon gases, causing global warming; and excessive application of pesticides and chemical fertilizers that ruin the soil and also cause health problems. Far from the poor being "polluters," they are the ones doing the least environmental damage; it is those who "exploit man and earth" who have laid much greater claims on the earth's resources.

Unlike some of his predecessors, Ramesh took his work seriously, but critics said he had been targeting projects by businessmen who had links to the opposition: the pro-BJP Ajit Gulabchand, Gautam Adani, who is widely seen as someone close to Narendra Modi, and Vedanta promoted by Anil Agarwal, who had invested in Odisha that was run by Naveen Patnaik's Biju Janata Dal. The problem with this line of argument was that it didn't explain why the projects of Congress MP Naveen Jindal were being rejected too. Later, in the run-up to the 2014 Lok Sabha elections, Modi referred to a "Jayanthi tax" for getting environmental clearances. This was taken to be a reference to Jayanthi Natarajan, who had replaced Ramesh as the minister for environment and forests.[5] After Natarajan resigned, the *Indian Express* reported that no fewer than seventy files, relating to projects already cleared by her ministry, had been retained by Natarajan at her home, and returned to the ministry only after she resigned from office.[6] Natarajan eventually quit the Congress in 2015 because she said the party did not give her a fair hearing. But it seemed clear that the "licence–permit raj" that Manmohan Singh had warned of could take more than one form.

When the Modi government swept to power in the summer of 2014, its priorities were clear: get stalled projects moving so that investment could be revived and the economy nudged to pick up speed. The new environment minister, Prakash Javadekar, showed very quickly that he was no Jairam Ramesh clone. The rules were modified to reduce the scope for public hearings (required before projects were cleared); more powers were given to states to clear projects; and a committee of former bureaucrats, armed with loose terms of reference, recommended rewriting the country's environment protection laws. The signs were that environmental clearance requirements for projects would be diluted, decentralized, and rendered less effective—thereby also removing some roadblocks and reducing the scope for demanding payoffs. Javadekar quoted Indira Gandhi and declared that poverty was the "biggest polluter." A coal mining project in Maharashtra's Chandrapur area, which Ramesh had rejected because it was located in a tiger reserve, now got the green signal after it went through some modification. At the same time, though, cleaning the Ganga (the recipient of vast quantities of industrial pollution as well as urban sewage) was one of the new government's signature objectives. Defending himself against criticism, Javadekar asserted that he was enforcing many environmental laws and rules far more effectively than in the past.

Green Accounting

The growth-versus-environment debate is presented as a choice of one or the other largely because GDP calculations do not take environmental degradation into account, though nature is a primary asset for any country. Companies account for depreciation of capital assets as a financial cost. So, for that matter, do national accounts, since net domestic product (or NDP) is calculated as GDP minus depreciation of capital. But the definition of capital excludes natural resources like forests and rivers, not to mention clean air—all of which can and do suffer because of economic activity, and therefore degradation. Such damage in turn affects economic performance. Calculations of national income have traditionally treated such environmental damage as an "externality" and therefore does not take it into account. Given the extent to which this affects economic performance, however, such an escape route is no longer defensible. Hence the growing clamor for what has come to be called "green accounting"—which can produce numbers quite different from the economic growth that is conventionally reported.

In the summer of 2013, the World Bank came out with a three-part report on India.[7] This concluded that the environmental degradation that had taken place in 2009 was equal to Rs 3.75 trillion, or 5.7 percent of GDP in that year.[8] The authors said they had taken conservative estimates because of the inherent difficulties in doing such accounting and therefore followed a "defensible borders" approach. (These calculations do not mean that were there no environmental damage, GDP growth would have been higher by 5.7 percent, because there would be costs incurred to reduce the damage, and one would have to arrive at a net figure. However, in current accounting methods the cost incurred in reducing or undoing the damage would also add to GDP.)

A more radical assessment of how nations should do their economic accounting was recommended by a group of experts that the government set up in 2011, under the chairmanship of a Cambridge University professor, Partha Dasgupta. Its mandate was to recommend a framework for green national accounts. The group's report, in 2013, offered some radical conclusions. It argued that the country needed to go beyond "green accounts"—because GDP calculated income whereas the committee sought to shift the focus from income to wealth. It stated in its "central conclusion" that "the coin on the basis of which economic evaluation should be conducted is a comprehensive notion of wealth . . . not gross domestic product (GDP), nor . . . indicators of human well-being . . . such as the United Nations Human Development Index (HDI)."

Such a comprehensive notion of wealth would take into account three kinds of capital: physical capital (machinery, roads, etc.), human capital, and natural capital. The report argued that "changes in the circumstances of an economy should be judged on the basis of their effect on the economy's wealth per capita." Going further, it said "the coin on the basis of which we should judge policy changes—such as changes in taxes, trade, and the undertaking of investment projects—is also wealth." Therefore, "economic growth" should mean growth in wealth per capita, not growth in GDP (which is income) per capita. In elaboration, the report said "it can easily be that a society enjoys growth in GDP per capita and/or an improvement in its HDI even while experiencing a decline in its per capita wealth" (it adds that the reverse can happen too).[9]

From this, it is in principle a simple matter to see what kind of development is sustainable" in terms of inter-generational well-being (are we going to leave our children a country devoid of forests and rivers, and of wildlife?). Growth that eats into wealth, including natural wealth ("the social value of an economy's stock of capital assets"), is not sustainable. The argument has obvious force, but it is also worth keeping in mind that growth, conventionally defined, and high income improve a country's capacity to deal with both environment-related health issues and ecosystem vitality—the two components of the EPI referred to earlier.

Dasgupta separately assessed how the Indian economy had been growing its "comprehensive wealth." In a paper written jointly with the Nobel laureate Kenneth Arrow and others, Dasgupta argued in 2012 that comprehensive wealth included "reproducible wealth and human capital but also natural capital, health improvements and technological change." Based on a complex set of calculations for 1995–2000, the authors concluded that India's growth rate for comprehensive wealth, per capita, had been 2.70 percent[10]—well below the per capita income growth for that period of about 4.7 percent.[11] Jairam Ramesh cites another paper in which Arrow and Dasgupta and others came to the depressing conclusion that during 1970–2001, India's growth after taking environmental costs into account was only 0.31 percent per capita.[12] This compared with the official GDP growth per capita of about 3 percent for that period.

This new way of looking at economic performance was to be incorporated into national accounts, and the initial spadework has started. But the results of such an exercise would be a hard political sell. It would be difficult for any government to tell the Indian public that the handsome growth recorded in GDP in recent years has been accompanied by noticeably slower growth in net wealth. As for the Modi government in its initial months in office, there was an eagerness to get moving on stalled industrial and infrastructure projects and to show results in terms of reviving income growth, conventionally defined. If nature's capital was suffering damage in the process, the government would deal with that later.

Dilemmas and Conflict

This approach ignores the harsh truth, which is that India is caught in an ecological crisis that is rolling out in many directions. It has globally about the worst index for air quality, and is said to account for thirteen of the world's twenty most polluted cities. The situation of its water—once abundant—is moving steadily from "stress" to "scarcity" (more on these terms later in the chapter). Its tree cover, vital as a carbon sink and for preserving the natural habitat, is not growing, and some of it is now being sacrificed to access mineral and other resources. Soil quality is affected by the unbalanced use of chemical fertilizer and poor-quality pesticides. The country's carbon emissions per head could more than double in the next fifteen to twenty years. Even as global warming begins to look inevitable, the majority of the country's Himalayan glaciers are melting faster than before, while a rise in the sea level could affect 150 million people living along the 7,000-kilometer coast. There is an equity issue as well. It is the poor who pay the biggest price for environmental degradation; they are the ones most affected by water scarcity, their resilience is the weakest when faced with the health effects of air pollution, and they are almost always the ones touched most dramatically by projects that disturb local ecologies and cause the involuntary displacement of people.

A growing economy has the ability to cope with many of these issues—by improving general nutrition levels; increasing the supply of safe water and sanitation facilities; better monitoring of industrial pollution; upgrading the reach, scope, and quality of healthcare facilities; switching to cleaner forms of energy; reducing carbon intensity per unit of GDP; and progressing overall to better standards and improved management. Much of this is taking place in India, however patchily—as reflected in the progress on (though not complete achievement of) the Millennium Development Goals set for 2015.[13] In that sense, Indira Gandhi is being proved right: dealing with poverty is also helping to improve the quality of life, and thereby either reducing "pollution" or improving the ability to cope with it.

The problem with an approach that says every country can get rich and then clean up is the one that Mahatma Gandhi had outlined: "the world has enough for everyone's need, but not for everyone's greed." By putting greater strain on its ecology, India is increasing environmental stress in multiple ways. A basic cause is population density, which at nearly 400 per square kilometer is about eight times the world average of less than 50 per square kilometer. Such an adverse land–human ratio has to affect various indicators, especially when combined with poor policies. The story with regard to air pollution, for instance, tells of a disaster in the making—with private motorized transport growing faster than public and mass transport systems; truck movement growing faster than railway freight; the bulk of electricity being generated by using coal as fuel; and industries like steel and cement producing high rates of emissions. Delhi has been rated as one of the most polluted cities in the world because it has a score of 110–120 pm2.5 (concentration per cubic meter of tiny air particles smaller than 2.5 micrometers in diameter). That compares with 16 for London. Other Indian cities fare worse: Gwalior, Patna, and Raipur have pm2.5 scores over 130. The EPI score has put India at the bottom of a list of 132 countries when it comes to air pollution.

As for industry, in 2009 India's Central Pollution Control Board (CPCB) carried out an environmental assessment of eighty-eight important industrial clusters. Of these, forty-three were identified as "critically polluted" since their score was seventy or more (on a scale of 0 to 100). A moratorium on further industry was ordered in these forty-three clusters. At about the same time, the environment ministry (with Ramesh at the helm) responded to the fact that much of the country's mineral wealth lay under forested land and declared that half the area in coal blocks, which covered 6,000 square kilometers of land, would be off-limits so far as mining was concerned. This led to an immediate riposte from the prime minister's office. Eventually, overriding

Ramesh's protests, the prohibited areas were reduced to a small number of coal blocks. The Modi government brought that down further.

Would that cause conflict? The fact is that 90 percent of the country's coal and 80 percent of other mineral reserves are in (mostly forested) areas inhabited by tribals, who account for every thirteenth Indian and who constitute the country's most vulnerable sections. Large numbers have been evicted over the years to make way for both mining projects and hydroelectric dams, with the displacement numbers hotly contested. Estimates of those displaced vary from 21 million over four decades (1950–90) to 50 million, while a government statement in 1994 said that 10 million displaced people were awaiting resettlement.[14] Jawaharlal Nehru, India's first prime minister (1947–64), had often called hydroelectric dams the "temples of modern India." Arundhati Roy, a campaigner against dams, has quoted Nehru as telling villagers being displaced by the Hirakud dam, "If you are to suffer, you should suffer in the interest of the country."[15]

What if those asked to suffer choose to resist? It is neither accident nor a coincidence that the areas subject to a sustained Maoist challenge to the system are in the tribal, forested districts in the country's hilly heartland, spread over half a dozen states. New laws to protect tribal land rights (2006) and to make forcibly acquiring land for industrial and mining projects far more costly as well as procedurally more difficult (2013) were pushed through Parliament by the Manmohan Singh government, though the moving spirit was Congress president Sonia Gandhi. The Opposition (especially the BJP) went along. But once the BJP came to power in 2014, it responded to criticism that the new law would hinder industrial and infrastructure projects and moved to change the law, only to get embroiled in a political firefight and withdraw.

The Coming Water Crisis

The challenges and conflicts are no smaller on the water front. The issue is water security, defined differently for different levels of aggregation. At the household level, it is the extent of supply (whether for farming or domestic use) and sanitation facilities. In cities and towns, it is the state of urban water supply, wastewater treatment, and drainage systems. At the national level, the issue is overall availability as well as levels of toxicity in rivers and other water sources. In specific geographical zones, there is people's exposure to water-linked disasters. On virtually all of these, India comes up with dreadful scores that are at or near the bottom in rankings of nearly fifty countries done by the Asian Development Bank.[16] It does no better on the quality of water management—like the level of water tariffs, the management of large irrigation systems that have been created, the organizational structures for managing water and sanitation in cities, and much else. The country's overall score on national water security, at 1.6 on a scale from 1 to 5, is better than that of just three countries—Afghanistan, Bangladesh, and Kiribati.

Statistics put out by the UN's Food and Agriculture Organization (using data from its AQUASTAT information system) show that India has less renewable water per head than almost all parts of the world, with the exception of water-starved West Asia and North Africa. The official figure for India was 1,545 cubic meters per head in 2011. According to the internationally accepted water stress benchmark, a country with less than 1,700 cubic meters per head of water is "water stressed" while one with less than 1,000 cubic meters per head is said to be "water scarce" (a borderline example of water scarcity is Morocco). India, which had abundant water at Independence in 1947 (more than 5,000 cubic meters per head), is now water stressed and could be close to water scarce by the time its population stabilizes at more than four times the 361 million that it was in 1951. The dramatic shift from abundance to stress, and then to potential scarcity, has made little difference to the country's water practices or led to any credible action that would improve the situation.

The broad numbers on usable water are that its supply is estimated at 1,123 billion cubic meters (BCM), while demand by 2050 is expected to be 1,450 BCM. The rivers of the southern peninsula are already being tapped more or less fully for water use. Nationally, the bulk of the water is used for agriculture. Even as there is excess drawing of water, in a manner that is not sustainable, there has been little effort to use water as though it were a scarce resource—that is, to use it efficiently. Cropping patterns have developed such that water-intensive crops are grown in water-scarce areas—like paddy in Haryana state and sugarcane in Maharashtra. The financial incentive to save on water use is absent because groundwater is virtually free once a bore well and pump are in place, and irrigation water is no different (water usage charges are so low that they do not pay for even the maintenance of irrigation systems, much less the capital investment required). The efforts to augment supply and to reduce the runoff from rivers by building storage dams, linking river basins (not always a good idea), and taking measures to recharge groundwater have all been well short of what is required.

Meanwhile, the norm for household supply varies between 100 and 200 liters per capita per day (lpcd), depending on the circumstances. The Bureau of Indian Standards suggests a range from 135 to 200 lpcd (for cities with full flushing systems). Leading cities around the world, from Munich and Amsterdam in Europe to Singapore and Hong Kong in Asia, manage within these limits.

Strangely, many Indian cities claim to supply more than what is prescribed, but little seems to reach the consumer. Official agencies assume waste levels of 15–20 percent, while some reports talk of 40–50 percent waste (this is different from unbilled water supply, which is water that at least is used). In the case of Nagpur, waste is reported to be 70 percent. Estimating the gap between claimed supply and demand actually met is therefore difficult; the only reliable indicator would be the hours of daily supply—but hardly any Indian city gets more than six hours of supply in a day. The Delhi Jal (Water) Board, for instance, claims on its website to supply more than 50 (British) gallons (that is, 225 liters) per head per day, and Mumbai claims about the same (4 million kiloliters per day for 18 million residents, about 220 lpcd). Yet both cities restrict civic water supply to a couple of hours in the day, and residents live with a sense of irregular supply. In Delhi the water board says demand is 30 percent more than supply (or nearly 300 liters per head per day).

Part of the problem is the grotesquely unequal use of water. Delhi's official supply norm is 225 lpcd in "planned colonies," 155 lpcd for other areas (like low-income, high-density "resettlement" colonies), and just 50 lpcd for slums. Actual supply ranges from several thousand liters a day for ministerial bungalows in Lutyens's Delhi (the protected colonial heart of the city) to 50 liters or less per day in the city's slums. At some stage, the well-heeled will have to start using water with a greater sense of civic consciousness. The problem, it would seem, is not physical scarcity so much as what is called "economic scarcity" caused by mismanagement. Indeed, the irony is that the Delhi Jal Board, which is also responsible for sewage disposal, is a profitable enterprise. It used to incur massive losses (Rs 15.67 billion in 2007–08) but has been comfortably profitable since 2010–11, after water tariffs were doubled in 2009 (the increase was less at lower consumption levels, more at higher levels) and an unusually high sewage charge at 60 percent of the new water tariff was slapped on. While making profits, the board has remained unable to improve the city's water supply or sewage treatment. A quarter of the city's households don't have piped water, and barely half the city's sewage is treated, while only 40 percent of the water connections are billed, according to a damning report by the government auditor in 2013.

An experiment in the Nangloi area of southwest Delhi might provide some answers. The French company Veolia, in partnership with an Indian firm, has contracted with the Jal Board to supply twenty-four-hour-a-day potable piped water year round, and it estimates that doing so is possible with the existing level of total water supply, through better engineering and management practices. Veolia has also contracted to overhaul Nagpur city's water supply, after successfully running pilot projects in some of the smaller towns of Karnataka state. A site visit showed the company's officials busy replacing every existing water connection in Delhi's Nangloi (an area with a million-strong population) plus doubling the number of connections, so as to cover every household. If indeed Nangloi and Nagpur get what they have been promised, it would show that city water supply can be managed—including how to maintain constant pressure in water pipes so that extraneous matter does not enter the system and contaminate the water before it reaches the tap. It is because of the failure to maintain constant pressure that *E. coli* (pointing to the presence of fecal matter) is today traceable in virtually every urban water supply system in the country.

Even so, the alarming development is that India's cities, many of which were once able to more or less manage with nearby sources of water, are reaching out farther and farther to draw water for their populations, sometimes going out hundreds of kilometers. The Centre for Science and Environment, an NGO, points out that Delhi, through which the Yamuna River flows, now gets some of its water from the Tehri dam on the Ganga, more than 300 kilometers away. Delhi also proposes to augment supply by having a dam built near the Renuka Lake in Himachal Pradesh, some 325 kilometers distant. If the price of water were such that consumption levels dropped, especially for the better off, and if the supply system were better managed, the city would not have to reach out 300 kilometers for its water.

It is not just Delhi. The desert town of Jodhpur in Rajasthan used to reach out 85 kilometers into the interior to get its water. It later stretched out 140 kilometers to the Jawai dam. When extensive tapping of the surrounding groundwater also proved inadequate, the city had to reach out 205 kilometers —all the way to the Rajiv Gandhi Lift Canal. Chennai now gets part of its water from Veeranam Lake, 235 kilometers away, and from the Krishna River some 400 kilometers distant. Even relatively small towns like Tumkur in Karnataka, Dewas in Madhya Pradesh, and Aurangabad in Maharashtra now pipe their water from as far off as 150–200 kilometers. At some stage, as urbanization grows apace, such options will no longer be viable. What happens then? According to the Centre for Science and Environment, which has recorded these facts and numbers for different parts of the country, villages in Nalgonda district once objected to the diversion of water for Hyderabad city.[17] There could be more such cases in the future.

Growing shortages, meanwhile, are a very real fact of life. The level of water demand in Punjab is 30 percent more than supply; it manages the situation through 50 percent excess drawing of groundwater—which cannot go on indefinitely. Similarly, in Delhi's satellite development of Gurgaon, which has grown in a quarter century from a rural backyard to a boom town of 2.5 million people, groundwater extraction is nearly three times the level it should be. The groundwater table has been falling by seven to ten feet every year from the mid-1990s, and the bore wells have to be drilled deeper and deeper. Residents who moved into the area's new suburban developments during the 1990s talk of bore wells that used to go down thirty or fifty feet; now drillers have to dig 200 feet deep into the bowels of the earth before they find water. Predictions abound in the newspapers of the town's water running out in less than a decade.

The levels of bacterial contamination of rivers are getting worse, while the treatment of industrial effluents remains unsatisfactory, with the result that large water systems are polluted. Finally, concerning water security and disasters, the hill state of Uttarakhand suffered from a water disaster in 2013; in 2014 it was the turn of Jammu and Kashmir. In both cases, the scale of the disaster could have been reduced by an order of magnitude if water systems had been better managed over the years and if flood warnings had been heeded. In both cases, the state government was incapacitated and/or paralyzed into inaction, prolonging the crisis. Both states will take years to fully recover.

What Is to Be Done?

Solutions exist. Punjab and Haryana need to change their choice of crops and reduce the acreage for growing water-hungry rice. Paddy cultivation itself can be made less water-intensive. Growing sugarcane, an even more water-hungry crop than paddy, in water-scarce Maharashtra is equally contraindicated—especially since the country happens to have a surplus in sugar most of the time. Exporting sugar amounts to exporting water. While economizing on water use is vital, water will also have to be re-priced—substantially. Canal water is priced too low to cover even maintenance costs. Electricity for pumping out groundwater is provided free to farmers in many states, or at a fixed tariff irrespective of extent of use. Both encourage wasteful use.

While it may be too early to judge the results of a privatized water supply in Nagpur and parts of Delhi, the earlier experiments in some Karnataka towns have shown that supply has improved. Given the extraordinarily high levels of water wastage, improvement should not be difficult if a systems approach is followed, along with the application of contemporary technology. Rainwater harvesting is gaining momentum and is mandatory in new buildings—for which green ratings and standards are now available. More can be achieved if taps, flush tanks, and other household fittings shift to water-saving designs and if the excess use of water were to attract penal tariffs. Meanwhile, projects aimed at connecting river basins, for the better use of their water, have made little headway, and inter-state disputes over water sharing have proved ever more intractable (a sure sign of water stress).

On other fronts, cities need to plan for greater density of population (high-rise apartments, with public spaces), facilitate energy-efficient mass transport, and prevent the urban sprawl that comes with private motorized transport. Energy-efficient lighting and household gadgets can save significantly on the demand for electricity—perhaps 7–10 percent of total demand. Retrofitting the presidential residence, Rashtrapati Bhavan, has reduced its energy consumption by 23 percent.[18] Vehicle emission norms should be further tightened and hybrid vehicles encouraged. Energy-efficiency ratings should be mandatorily displayed for all electrical gadgets, as has been done for refrigerators and air conditioners.

Mining regulations should make it obligatory on mining companies to return the land to its original condition within a specified time frame—as has become standard practice in many countries. Industry should learn to locate projects on smaller parcels of land—the GMR group set up a power plant in Singapore on a fraction of the land it procured for a similar project in Andhra Pradesh. Even software service companies like Infosys have become accustomed to setting up sprawling campus-style offices that are far too land-hungry. Environmental regulations on effluent treatment, and more broadly on environment impact, have to be taken more seriously.

None of this is rocket science, but action to change a manifestly unsustainable situation is limited and inadequate. India's environmental challenges range across many other fronts. Whether these concern air, water, waste management, forest cover, or resource misuse, the challenge is the same: economic activity has to grow, but the management of its consequences has to improve. This underlines once more that the focus of government activity should be proper regulation and monitoring, and the strengthening of the public institutions (like the undermanned state water pollution control boards) that are charged with delivering clean water and air.

The Modi government signaled new ambition when it raised dramatically the target for solar energy capacity. The plan had been to take solar capacity from 3,000 megawatts in 2012 to 20,000 megawatts by 2022—which, given the planned sixfold increase, was ambitious enough. Seeking a change of scale, a feature of his approach to his work, Modi has upped the target to 100,000 megawatts, while simultaneously raising the target for wind-generating capacity to 60,000 megawatts (the country's total generating capacity from all sources is currently 276,000 megawatts).[19] Actual power generation using the sun and wind will be less than these numbers suggest because of lower capacity utilization than in the case of coal-fired thermal stations. It is not certain that the numbers will be achieved. What is encouraging, though, is that the cost of solar power has been coming down steadily as the efficiency of solar panels has improved. The price of solar power is now competitive, especially when compared to the power tariffs paid by industrial and commercial users in most parts of the country. Even if the eventual capacity increase falls short of an outsize target, it would be a significant step forward in adopting low-carbon growth strategies.

If India is to tackle its development and growth objectives without creating an environmental disaster (poisonous air, water scarcity, and a breakdown of natural habitats), it has to tailor its development strategy so that nature's assets are protected and harvested sensibly. From the viewpoint of global climate change negotiations too, a low-carbon growth strategy is essential. An ambitious clean energy program would make a difference. But that is only a small part of what needs to be done. Anyone who pretends that environmental concerns can be pushed into the background while economic growth is made the primary focus is asking for trouble, especially for the poor.

India and the World

15

Default Choice or a Defaulting Power?

MYANMAR IS ONE of those countries that once fell off the world map, like Afghanistan did. It sits at one end of the Indian subcontinent, at the junction of South and Southeast Asia, just as Afghanistan sits at the other end, on the boundary between South, Central, and West Asia. (Please consult the map of India at the front of the book.) Roughly equal to Afghanistan (or France) in size, Myanmar shares its borders primarily with India, China, and Thailand. Subjected for many years to economic and financial sanctions, the country has a paltry GDP of $65 billion (equal to that of the Dominican Republic) and a per capita income level that comes near the bottom of world rankings. But like Afghanistan it is resource rich and has much that its neighbors are hungry for: oil and gas, timber and rubber, the promise of massive hydroelectric power, and the potential to mine tin, copper, and coal. Above all, like Afghanistan, it can serve as a strategic gateway for its bigger, more powerful neighbors. Just as Afghanistan to India's northwest was the focus of the Great Game between imperial Russia and colonial Britain for two centuries, Myanmar could become similarly important in a smaller way to India's northeast.

That explains why different deep-sea ports are being built simultaneously on the Myanmar coast with investment from its principal neighbors—with an eye to shipping coming up through the Bay of Bengal, carrying goods headed through Myanmar to and from their respective territories. China has been working toward a land route directly into the Bay, and Kyaukpyu (meaning "white rock") Port will be at one end of 1,000-kilometer oil and gas pipelines that go all the way to Kunming in its southwestern province of Yunnan. That would sidestep the long, circuitous route farther south via the potential choke point of the Malacca Straits, which serve as the gateway from the Indian Ocean to the South China Sea.

India in its turn has been developing Sittwe Port—less than 100 kilometers to the northwest of Kyaukpyu, as an entry point for the transport of goods up the Kaladan River and then by road into Mizoram in the landlocked northeastern part of the country. Thailand has its own infrastructure dream near Myanmar's southern leg: the Dawei Port on the Andaman Sea, connected by highway to Kanchanaburi, west of Bangkok. Dawei in its grander vision is meant to serve the Greater Mekong Subregion, an economic area. Meanwhile, the India–Myanmar–Thailand highway that is being built will for the first time connect India by overland route to Southeast Asia.

The regional competition for using Myanmar as a transport gateway is matched by the keenness of its neighbors to exploit the country's natural resources, though dealing with Myanmar has not been easy. India thought it had negotiated a major deal for the gas to be produced at Shwe, but it dawdled over the transport link; China quickly secured the gas. Beijing, too, has faced setbacks, like being asked to stop work midway on a massive hydroelectric project on the Irrawaddy River in 2011. But there is little doubt that China enjoys pole position. India's trade with Myanmar is only a quarter of that country's trade with China, which also showers Myanmar with financial resources, while Indian companies operating in the country suffer from a lack of coordination as well as resources. If Chinese ships begin to move up and down through the Bay of Bengal, it would give Beijing a role and stake in India's neighborhood waters that it has never had till now. The strategic calculus would change. For anyone looking at the evolving roles of India and China in Asia and also Africa, Myanmar shows in microcosm what it could mean in practice as China gains the upper hand.

The rise of China, on a scale and at a speed that has no precedent in history, is the most significant global power shift in half a millennium. Just as India's Look East policy was launched in the early 1990s following the collapse of the Soviet Union, a great deal of what has changed in India's international relations over the 2005–15 decade is the backwash effect of China's spectacular rise. One merely has to look at where Indian and US interests converge and diverge to understand the centrality of China in the new level of Indo–US engagement. To the east of India, there is an alignment of interests. Both India and the United States want the existing power balance to be disturbed as little as possible, with countervailing forces minimizing the power shift that must necessarily accompany the rise of China. Both want open sea-lanes to be maintained, the South China Sea not to be converted into a Chinese lake, and China to play by the accepted rules. Both wish for strategic cooperation with and between the other regional powers.

To the west of India, however, there is considerable divergence in Indian and American approaches and interests. Whether it is Iran, Afghanistan, or Pakistan, the "Arab Spring" or Palestine/Israel and Syria, the two countries' perspectives are more divergent than convergent. And on multilateral issues, like trade and climate change, the differences in interests and negotiating positions are plainly manifest. These differences are softened by the, well, soft issues—the large and influential Indian diaspora in the United States, the fact that both countries are democracies, and the substantial and growing business links. But the breakthroughs on hard, strategic issues, like the civil nuclear agreement of 2008 and Indian access to American advanced technology and defense supplies, have been direct by-products of the China factor. Robert Blackwill, a former US ambassador in New Delhi, puts it with typical bluntness: "Without the rise of Chinese power, there would have been no dramatic change in the US–India relationship."[1]

That goes for India's relationships with Japan and Australia as well. The two countries were among India's worst critics when it conducted nuclear tests in 1998 but have since warmed significantly to India. In a rare irony, Australia has even agreed to supply uranium for civilian use, while Japan has been India's most munificent financier of infrastructure projects and also joined in trilateral naval exercises with India and the United States. It is an interesting aside in this context that when the Soviet Union had suggested joint naval exercises with India during the days of the Cold War, India had not been receptive to the idea.

Sphere of Influence or Encirclement?

China's rise has impacted India's neighborhood ties as well, but not to India's advantage. The tiny island nation of the Maldives, lying barely 600 kilometers off India's southern tip in the Indian Ocean, had long been considered a nation dependent on Indian support and goodwill; after a coup attempt there in 1988, India flew out paratroopers to rescue the president. But the Maldives slipped unnoticed out of the Indian fold after Chinese tourists started flocking in large numbers to the country's white beaches and turquoise waters. Tourism accounts for 28 percent of the Maldives' GDP and 60 percent of its foreign exchange earnings. The 330,000 Chinese who took the eight-hour flight from Beijing and Shanghai in 2013 accounted for 29.5 percent of the total tourists choosing the Maldives for a holiday.[2] There were few tourists from India.

The new equations were driven home when the Maldives arbitrarily canceled an airport development contract with India's GMR group in 2012. This was shortly after an elected government seen as pro-India had been forced to step down. New Delhi was paralyzed in inaction when the government changed hands and merely asked the new government in the capital of Male to honor its airport contract—to no effect. Two years later, China's president Xi Jinping visited the Maldives, the first visit to the islands by a Chinese leader, while Modi felt obliged to skip the Maldives on his Indian Ocean tour because India (like many Western nations) disapproved of the treatment being meted out to the ousted president. Soon the Maldives gave its airport project to a Chinese firm.

Xi Jinping crisscrossed his way through India's neighborhood in 2014, visiting not just the Maldives but also Sri Lanka and Pakistan, even as Afghanistan's new president, Ashraf Ghani, made Beijing his first overseas port of call within a month of winning the election in 2014. Modi was busy too, visiting Nepal, Bhutan, and Bangladesh, and also the Indian Ocean island nations of Sri Lanka, Seychelles, and Mauritius. He signed agreements with the last two on maritime surveillance, naval listening posts (some were already in existence), and landing strips, and negotiated naval docking rights. Packaged along with other elements as Project Mausam, the initiative was clearly a response to China's ambitious Maritime Silk Road project, which India has refrained from joining. A new Great Game has begun in the Indian Ocean region.

Over the centuries, India and China have functioned in different spheres. The Himalayas were a virtually impenetrable land barrier, and the existence of smaller buffer states (including, most importantly, Tibet till 1951) meant there was virtually no common land border. The Chinese navy never came into the Indian Ocean until 2008, except briefly in the early fifteenth century. India came to see all of South Asia as its sphere of influence, defined so by size and geography. It has also seen its natural area of naval interest as defined by the Indian Ocean littoral, stretching from East Africa at one end to Singapore and Indonesia at the other, with West Asia a near-abroad. Indian traders have navigated this substantial space for centuries, while the powerful Chola empire's navy from southern India made repeated incursions into Southeast Asia in the eleventh and twelfth centuries. Indonesia's currency is the rupiah (also the Hindi word for the rupee), while Oman replaced the Gulf rupee with the rial only in 1970; the rial comprises 1,000 baisa (in India 100 paise make a rupee). It is not without reason that the Indian Ocean is so named.

But as the world's economies have become more connected, and transport systems and weapons of war have increased in range and scope, regional geography and distance have lost some of their defining importance. Simultaneously, China's transition from self-sufficiency in energy to dependence on large imports of oil and gas (mostly from West Asia) has given it a stake in the Indian Ocean through which 90 percent of its oil imports must pass. Chinese naval ships first entered the Indian Ocean in late 2008, on their way to Somalia to join the international anti-piracy campaign.

Also, China as a rising power sees no reason to acknowledge Indian supremacy in South Asia. As John Garver wrote in 2001, "To China India is a regional hegemonist that presumes to block the natural and rightful expansion of China's relations with its neighbours."[3] In the same vein, a Chinese admiral told an Indian diplomat, "The Indian Ocean is not India's Ocean." In turn, India's South Asian neighbors see in China a useful counterpoint to India's (sometimes unwelcome) weight, and have played it as such.

China has therefore built and now taken charge of operating Gwadar Port on Pakistan's coast, near the mouth of the Persian Gulf. It has developed and part-financed Sri Lanka's Hambantota as the island nation's second-largest port (India declined to do so when invited), and more recently committed to building a deep-water container facility at Colombo Port. Chinese submarines started calling at Colombo and then Karachi for fuel and supplies. A controversial $1.4 billion port city project at Colombo was part of the broader Chinese plan in Sri Lanka but was put in abeyance after a change of government in Colombo. Later, however, it was cleared with special laws for a "financial and business district".

Beijing nearly pulled off another coup in 2014: a contract to finance and build for Bangladesh its first deep-sea port, near its southeastern tip bordering Myanmar, at a place called Sonadia. What was potentially a second Gwadar, which would have caused headaches for India's navy (whose new submarine base is being built not too far away, on the Andhra coast), was called off at the last minute. While Sonadia's future remained to be decided, China had already become the largest military supplier to Bangladesh, providing tanks, artillery, fighter aircraft, frigates, and two submarines. India's worry is not Bangladesh's military power but China's influence over an important neighbor.

India has scrambled to get its act together. Diplomatic pressure was brought on Bangladesh at the eleventh hour to prevent it from contracting with a Chinese company to develop Sonadia Port (Bangladesh decided eventually to engage with Japan for another port project nearby, in effect putting Sonadia on ice). China meanwhile has increased the pressure by pushing its ambitious proposal for a Maritime Silk Road through the Indian Ocean (and also a Silk Road "Belt" by land through Central Asia to Europe), touching various points on its littoral. As part of the Belt project, it has agreed with Pakistan on developing the Karakoram Highway that links the two countries across the Karakoram mountains (through territory that India claims) into a multimodal transport network and economic corridor from Sinkiang (or Xinjiang) all the way down to Karachi and Gwadar ports near the mouth of the Persian Gulf. Nepal, nestling in the Himalayas between India and Chinese Tibet, has also seen a growing Chinese presence, with the prospect now of a railway line connecting Lhasa in Tibet to the Nepalese capital of Kathmandu farther south. New Delhi's tensions with Nepal over its new Constitution have not helped bilateral relations.

Virtually all countries of the region trade much more with China than with India, buy its armaments (India has been a reluctant arms exporter), and respond to its varied overtures. India would have noted in 2014 that Nepal and Sri Lanka joined Pakistan in supporting China's bid for membership in the South Asian Association for Regional Cooperation (SAARC). Pakistan has of course been a long-term beneficiary of nuclear and missile technology from China. During his 2015 visit to Pakistan, Xi Jinping announced investment in various civil infrastructure and defense projects worth an astonishing $46 billion—equal to more than 18 percent of Pakistan's GDP. Already, Chinese companies are involved far more in Pakistan than in India, and almost as much in Sri Lanka. Overall, Chinese investment and projects in India's neighboring countries (whose economies taken together are equal to less than a third of India's) stands at more than $38 billion, more than three times the Chinese figure for India ($11.9 billion).[4] Whether it is trade, arms supplies, investment, or contracts to build infrastructure, India's involvement with its immediate neighbors is now overshadowed by China's influence.

There are limits to what China can do, given the dictates of geography. In the past, New Delhi has reacted decisively when it has seen its core interests threatened. In 1974, when the ruler of the Indian protectorate of Sikkim reached out to China in a signal for greater independence, New Delhi stage-managed a smooth annexation of Sikkim as an Indian state. In the 1980s, after Nepal ordered anti-aircraft guns from China, New Delhi closed the usually open border between the two countries, leaving open just two transit points provided for by treaty, for onward access to Indian ports. Nepal plunged into an economic crisis and quickly fell in line. Again, when Sri Lanka bucked Indian pressure to negotiate with its restive Tamil minority, Indira Gandhi began training and arming rebel Tamil guerrillas. Later, Rajiv Gandhi used air force planes to drop relief supplies over the Tamil-populated Jaffna peninsula without informing Colombo or seeking its consent. But India's dispatch of a peacekeeping force to Sri Lanka was to prove a misadventure; after its withdrawal, Rajiv was assassinated by a Tamil guerrilla.

As for the Maldives, for all the tourist traffic from China, the island nation's citizens need visas to visit India for the extended stays required for medical care and higher education. Indeed, when the Maldives ran into a water crisis in 2014 (Male's only desalination plant broke down), it was India that quickly shipped water to the city in naval ships and air force planes; China followed in due course. However much China might make inroads into the region, geography still places limits on what it can do.

Equally, though, the new extent of China's presence in the region must prompt India to be more circumspect and more sensitive to the concerns of its smaller neighbors. Some of the strong-arm methods of the past may no longer be feasible, or advisable even if they are feasible. A country that, in the early part of the new century, still saw itself as an equal to China (in the narrative of two Asian giants rising together) now feels hemmed in by a more powerful and assertive China in its home neighborhood. In this new phase, New Delhi can more often than not be in a reactive mode, if not a defensive one—and not just on the disputed land border, along which China has superior forces and much easier mobility because of the terrain and superior border infrastructure. If China's game of encirclement gains momentum, the choice for India could become quite stark. As Garver noted at the turn of the century, "Unless India is able to alter its lacklustre development record, and to work out a skilled and confident programme employing India's national capabilities in the South Asian region, India could well conclude that the prudent way to enhance its security is to assume a role as junior partner to an emerging Chinese superpower."[5]

Indians may have bristled at the thought in 2001, but the country has become China's junior partner in the BRICS Development Bank (now called the New Development Bank) and in the Asian Infrastructure Investment Bank, both based in China. It has not joined the "Belt and Road" initiative but may eventually feel obliged to do so; if the objective is to link the European and African economies with Asia and specifically with China, how would India benefit by being out of the loop? Signaling Chinese perceptions of changing power equations, a prominent Chinese scholar said at the World Peace Forum in Beijing that his country's relations with Moscow improved after Russia reconciled itself to China's greater wealth and power. And the foreign minister, Wang Yi, told a Japanese questioner that Sino-Japanese relations would improve once Japan reconciled itself to the fact that China was a greater economic power. What then of India?[6]

Comprehensive National Power

Hainan Island lies off the southwestern coast of China, jutting into waters stirred by controversy. At its southern tip, China has built a massive naval base with subterranean hiding places for nuclear submarines and long piers for parking the aircraft carriers it will build. The South China Sea stretches from there into territory claimed controversially by China and contested by smaller Southeast Asian countries. Hainan is also touted as China's answer to Hawaii, another sunny spot where a key naval base exists side by side with sandy beaches and palm-fringed holiday resorts. Flights land at Hainan's Haikou airport from all corners of the region. Bullet trains speed you from the airport in the north to the holiday resorts in the south.

Midway lies Boao, which boasts broad, well-paved roads; lush tropical greenery; a large conference center; and several hotels in which uniformed hostesses move around in single file and clap in unison whenever a VIP enters or leaves. In 2002, Boao began hosting an annual conference called the Boao Forum for Asia. At the second such conclave, in late 2003, Zheng Bijian spelled out for the first time his thesis on "China's peaceful rise." Zheng had been a longtime adviser to the Chinese leadership and vice principal of the Central Party School. He said the previous rise of new powers had resulted in changes in global political structures and war because they "have followed an aggressive path of war and expansion. Such a path is doomed to failure." He said China should rise peaceably, never seek hegemony, and help maintain a peaceful international environment.[7] A year later, at the 2004 Boao conference, Hu Jintao as president amended the phrase to the more innocuous "peaceful development."

The talk of a peaceful rise or development came not far from the site where the new naval base was under construction, and from where naval ships set sail for Somalia in 2008. Before long, China's rise threatened to be anything but peaceful as it claimed virtually all of the South China Sea which Hainan abuts. Underlying the claim is the potential for oil and gas offshore, but economics is only one reason. Chinese foreign policy is manifestly dictated by an irredentist nationalism, fed by memories of unfair treatment and territorial loss in the nineteenth and twentieth centuries.

The Western hope has been that China would mature into what Robert Zoellick, the US trade representative and later World Bank president, described as a "responsible stakeholder" (which begs the question of how responsible Western stakeholders have been during their period of ascendancy). Still, the Western powers have been leery of China's mercantilist trade and currency policies, its brazen violation of intellectual property rights, the repeated hacking of government and defense websites, and the treaty-violating support given to rogue friends like North Korea. Martin Jacques asserts in a forcefully argued book that China will never be a normal power, in the way the West understands the term.[8] In turn, Lee Kuan Yew of Singapore told Graham Allison and Robert Blackwill: "It is not possible to pretend that China is just another major player."[9] Lucian Pye famously talked of China as a "civilizational" state pretending to be a nation-state. The Chinese civilizational view includes the Confucian idea of harmony as a hierarchical order, with everyone accepting his or her place in that hierarchy—which means that China does not deal with other countries as its equals but as its tributaries, or as entities that should be tributaries. Nothing about the country's civilizational consciousness has changed just because it suffered a two-century eclipse or has a different political system.

China measures power and national security through a matrix that it calls Comprehensive National Power. Among the factors taken into account are the economy, technological development, natural resources, military power, population, and diplomacy. A 2014 ranking of comprehensive national power put the United States at the top, with Russia and China next. After that, in a lower league, came four countries bunched together: India, Britain, Japan, and France. Germany, Brazil, and South Korea followed lower down. Another ranking that used a combination of population, urbanization, steel production, energy consumption, military expenditure, and military strength put the top three as China, the United States, and India, in that order. Earlier rankings, in 2006, had put China in only sixth place and India in tenth.[10] The changes in rank since then show the rise of both China and India, naturally with China as the superior power.

Arvind Subramanian compiled his own Index of Economic Power, with the index of all countries in the world totaling up to 100. India in 2010 scored 3 percent, while China and Japan were level at 11 percent, and the United States at the top of the list with 14 percent.[11] Subramanian and Martin Kessler also argued in 2013 that China's yuan was already challenging the primacy of the dollar in East Asia. They contended that a yuan bloc was already in place, since the currencies of seven out of ten East Asian countries "track(ed) the yuan more closely than the dollar."[12] Perhaps and perhaps not, because the yuan was accepted by the International Monetary Fund as the world's fifth reserve currency only in late 2015. Some commentators have observed that even this was premature. Nor does the Chiang Mai Initiative—conceived after the Asian crisis of 1997 and which has evolved into a multilateral arrangement for managing short-term liquidity problems for ten member countries in East Asia—represent a serious challenge to Western financial arrangements. Still, when the United States imposed trade sanctions on Russia and the ruble took a tumble in 2014, China invited Russia into its zone of influence by offering a generous market for Russian gas, and then a currency swap arrangement. The wooing of Russia also took the form of a rail project, to connect Beijing and Moscow (around 8,400 km) with travel time of just forty-eight hours.[13]

So is India on its way to becoming a Great Power, as these rankings on national power suggest? Or has it begun an inexorable slide into China's shadow because of the growing imbalance of power between the two? The subject came into focus in March 2005 when Condoleezza Rice, on a visit to New Delhi as the new US secretary of state, told Prime Minister Manmohan Singh that the United States would help India "become a Great Power in the twenty-first century." A somewhat different thought came from Martin Wolf, who characterized China and India as "premature superpowers," potentially front-ranking nations because of their size even as they struggled with the stubborn challenges of widespread poverty and inadequate economic, technological, and institutional development.[14]

China has substantially emerged out of that duality, having become the world's largest manufacturer and merchandise exporter, with its eyes set now on mastering advanced technologies. India, in contrast, is still caught in old dualities. In PPP terms, India's per capita income in 2015 ($6,162)[15] put it noticeably out of line with the other BRICS economies. China was at $14,107, Brazil at $15,615, and Russia at $25,411. South Africa, an afterthought addition to BRICS, was at $13,165, while the global average was $15,638. India might hope to become a Great Power, but it has the chains of poverty around its ankles. India has the world's largest number of absolute poor, the largest number of malnourished, and an overall score on the United Nations Development Programme's Human Development Index that makes it feature well below most other large economies.

Yet India is undeniably the world's third-largest economy in PPP terms, and the seventh largest in nominal dollars. It is a nuclear weapons power with the ninth-largest defense budget.[16] It has a growing share of world trade: annual export growth in the first decade of the twenty-first century (at 19.3 percent) was topped only by China (20.1 percent). In seven years since the Western financial crisis of 2008, its economy has averaged 7.1 percent annual growth—which places it second only to China among the large economies. China has now slowed down and is likely to slow further, even as it faces daunting challenges including the risk of instability. Meanwhile India has stepped up its pace and could entrench itself in its new slot as the fastest-growing among the large economies. This adds to the weight of the country's landmass and population (including a growing middle class), while its geographical position gives it a strategic value that is hard to ignore.

It is inevitable, then, that countries looking at the emerging Asian picture should view India as a possible counterweight to China, the "default option"[17] if you look for balance of power. The problem with such a view is that India has been falling short of what is required for such a role, in terms of overall economic, technological, and military performance—becoming a defaulting power, so to speak, rather than the default option. Still, it is remarkable how the country's relations with the other leading powers of Australasia have been transformed over the past decade—in part because of its growing importance as a market, in part because of the rise of China, and in part because of the Indo–US nuclear agreement of 2008. As Manmohan Singh once told me, many doors open once you are seen as America's friend. India was no longer seen as the "leader of the awkward squad," as a British High Commissioner in New Delhi once termed it, referring to its refusal to be drawn into either camp during the Cold War and unwillingness later to become an "honorary white" nation, so to speak.

The Default Option

Rewind to 1990–91. India's finance minister, Yashwant Sinha, was in Tokyo in search of desperately needed foreign currency, as the country teetered on the edge of international payment default. His Japanese counterpart, Ryutaro Hashimoto (later to become prime minister), was cool to India and had only reluctantly given the finance minister an appointment. When Sinha reached Hashimoto's office, the Japanese minister shook hands, said he had to rush off to another meeting, and asked Sinha to deal with the officials in his ministry who were present. Sinha chose to leave too, thereby avoiding a further protocol indignity, and left his own accompanying officials to parley with their counterparts. As things worked out, Japan did help India with badly needed foreign currency loans. The Indian ambassador, Arjun Asrani, recalls a Japanese official explaining to him later: "We had no choice, we were your biggest creditors and we could not afford to have you default."

Gratuitous insults to a visiting Indian finance minister would be unthinkable today. The clearest signal of a change in approach came when Prime Minister Shinzō Abe addressed India's Parliament in August 2007. In a landmark speech that he titled "Confluence of the Two Seas" (harking back to the title of a book authored by the Mughal prince Dara Shikoh in the seventeenth century), Abe articulated his concept of a "broader Asia" and proposed an informal security alliance between four countries: Japan, Australia, India, and the United States. He visualized "an arc of freedom and prosperity" and said, "We have rediscovered India as a partner that shares the same values and interests."[18] Beijing immediately saw the "Quadrilateral Initiative" as an

"Asian NATO" that was meant to encircle China, and protested; Australia under a Sinophile prime minister (Kevin Rudd) was sensitive to China's concerns, and America's ardor cooled too. Indeed, President Obama had thought briefly in terms of a G-2 (the United States and China as a club of two) until he received a Chinese rebuff. What survive are joint naval exercises and a trilateral dialogue among India, Japan, and the United States, with Japan making its strategic intent clear by opening its purse for India. Over the last decade it has lent an astonishing $40 billion on repayment terms soft enough for the loans to be considered virtual grants. More is in the works, including the financing of India's proposed bullet train service to cover the 500-kilometer distance between Mumbai and Ahmedabad in a couple of hours.

Abe kept up his interest and came visiting between his stints as prime minister, getting a warm reception from his hosts. In 2013, when he was back in office, New Delhi immediately invited him to be the chief guest at the annual Republic Day parade, which is used as a show of military muscle. Earlier, in 2010, when China used its market dominance in rare earths (critical for the electronics industry) for some diplomatic arm-twisting of Japan, New Delhi and Tokyo began cooperation in the production of rare earths, for which India has the raw material.

In 2013, the Japanese emperor also came visiting—a symbolically important event. And Narendra Modi visited Japan more than once as the chief minister of Gujarat. Japan was one of the first countries that Modi visited after becoming prime minister, offering a special clearance facility for Japanese investment. Notwithstanding the growing warmth, though, there is as yet no real strategic relationship. But the "arc of freedom and prosperity" might yet find new expression, especially if Japan continues its belated defense buildup in response to a more assertive China. Steadily more ambitious bilateral naval exercises involving the Indian and US navies also saw the Japanese coming back as exercise partners in 2014 and 2015, after a gap following participation in 2007 and 2009.

Australia, on its part, has seen a new convergence with India on both soft and hard issues. Like Japan, it had taken a particularly hard line when India conducted nuclear tests in 1998, but Prime Minister Julia Gillard buried that issue when she visited New Delhi in October 2012 to announce that her country was willing to sell India uranium. Later, Gillard's successor Tony Abbott struck up a good relationship and sealed the uranium supply agreement. A white paper, "Australia in the Asian Century," looked ahead to a time when Australian schools would start teaching Hindi![19] Meanwhile, new bilateral naval exercises were held in 2015, focusing on anti-submarine warfare.

Across a Southeast Asia that has been unnerved by the Chinese claim to 90 percent of the South China Sea, countries have been boosting their defense budgets and armaments, and looking for new ballast. India has started playing a small role. Vietnam is to get four patrol boats and training for naval (including submarine) staff, plus a line of credit for defense supplies. There have been speculative reports of Vietnam wanting BrahMos cruise missiles, capable of Mach 3 speeds, but supplying them will need Russian agreement since it is an Indo-Russian project. In turn, Hanoi has offered the use of its naval facilities at Nha Trang, and improved the terms on which it invited investment in oil exploration, in order to keep India interested in drilling in the waters off its coast. India has decided to continue drilling despite Chinese protests, but refrained from using the naval facilities that Vietnam has offered.

So while India may have been temporarily eclipsed by China's stellar performance over more than three decades, now, due in part to India's own ascendancy, New Delhi has found its diplomatic and strategic options expanding. The growing tensions between the established superpower that is the United States and the challenger that is China have brought India into new strategic calculations for a number of countries in Asia, not to mention the United States itself.

Wary Alignments

For all the alignment of interests in Asia, the Indo-US relationship has not been a smooth one. A domestic liability law in India prevented the nuclear agreement from bearing fruit for quite a few years; a way was found to get around it only in early 2016. Meanwhile trade disputes have mushroomed. US companies have been exasperated by the vicissitudes of the Indian business scene—new kinds of protectionism, retrospective tax demands, and the like. A new rapprochement was signaled when Obama became the chief guest on Republic Day in January 2015. A joint statement was notable for referring to the South China Sea, but the reference was dropped in subsequent joint statements.

The problem with constructing a relationship cultivated partly to balance a third force is that interests might diverge at some point. India would rather not play second fiddle to anyone in what it sees as its sphere of influence, but it recognizes the need for defense cooperation and for access to the latest technology and armaments. Yet it is unwilling to be drawn into a strategy that China might view as hostile, especially since it has vulnerabilities on the disputed land border with China—where China has periodically tested India's response in small skirmishes.

India also remains wary that the United States will go back to the G-2 formulation attempted without success in the early Obama years, wherein the two leading powers (the United States and China) might decide to cooperate in a power-sharing arrangement rather than compete for influence. The Indo-US relationship has broadened and deepened, but the United States has far stronger, deeper relationships with China on almost every front than it does with India. The two countries may be strategic rivals, but a new manifestation of G-2 occurred when the United States and China, who between them account for nearly half the total emission of greenhouse gases, came to a bilateral agreement on modest reductions in emissions—putting India (which earlier had joined in common cause with China against the rich countries) under pressure to announce cuts of its own, though its total emissions were less than a fourth of China's. If more such G-2 agreements materialize, India would find that it has become collateral damage as the United States pursues its own interests.

Indian diplomats recall that when President Obama first visited India in 2010, he had urged India to join the Western campaign to isolate Myanmar, then run by generals. Soon afterward, the United States changed its position on Myanmar. If India had followed Obama's advice, it would have been left stranded diplomatically vis-à-vis an important neighbor. The United States has also blown hot and cold on Afghanistan. It has repeatedly advised India to lower its profile in that country in order to allay Pakistan's concerns; at other times it was glad that India had continued to engage with Kabul. It was the same with the Quadrilateral Initiative; the United States was in favor of it at first but later advised India to cool off on the idea at a time when the United States was more engaged with China. Indian diplomats acknowledge that the United States as a global power has the freedom to change its positions in pursuit of its interests. India therefore would have to use its own judgment on where its interests lie, and act accordingly.

The risk is that either country might not deliver what the other had bargained for. The calculations on India as the default choice for being the balancing factor, or swing power, in Asia assume that India will, to some degree, match China as a rising force. And further, that India's underperformance in the past will change because of new demographic patterns (China's working population has started to shrink, while India's will continue to expand for another couple of decades). But the stronger India becomes, the less it will think it needs the United States in an anti-China play; and the weaker

New Delhi becomes, the less useful it will be for Washington in its pivot to Asia.

Pakistan and Other "Stans"

India's strategic handicap to its northwest is the lie of the land, as Robert Kaplan has argued. He points out that India, like China, is possessed of geographical logic, but its northwest is "the least defined and protected" of its frontier regions. He quotes Halford Mackinder, one of the founding fathers of geopolitics, as saying in the early twentieth century that "In the British Empire there is but one land frontier on which warlike preparation must ever be ready. It is the Northwest Frontier of India."[20] That corner of the map is now identified as the old Afghanistan and a new Pakistan. Both are seriously troubled countries, topping the Asia list of the Fragile States Index,[21] and ranking seventh and tenth in the global listing of such states in 2014. Additionally, the existence and creation of other smaller states in the subcontinent deprives India of complete geographical coherence and has provided China with the opportunity to make inroads into contestable pockets of influence.[22]

And what of Pakistan, which according to Kaplan creates for India an "existential" fear? The sixty-seven-year-old dispute over Jammu and Kashmir has simmered down after the short border conflict of 1999 on the heights above Kargil. The cease-fire along the Line of Control, which separates the Pakistan-occupied portion of Kashmir from India, has mostly held since 2003, though the most recent years have seen more cross-border action than earlier. Separatist activity and militant violence in the India-held Kashmir valley have stayed on low boil, but there have been a couple of high-profile terrorist strikes against defense installations, with the one on the Pathankot air force base in Punjab in early 2016 causing the postponement of bilateral talks that it had been hoped would break a long-standing diplomatic stalemate. The risk of all-out war is low—even if there is another scaled-up terrorist strike against India. India has conventional military superiority, whereas Pakistan has been building a bigger nuclear arsenal and has sought to neutralize India's conventional arms superiority by developing short-range, tactical (as opposed to strategic) nuclear weapons. India's response in the form of a missile defense has made little headway so far. Whether tactical nuclear weapons can be used without rapid escalation into all-out nuclear war is very much in doubt—as war game scenarios have shown. So peace between the nuclear-armed neighbors is an imperative, especially since it must be clear to everyone in Pakistan that the Line of Control that divides Jammu and Kashmir is not about to disappear from the map. Meanwhile, growing concern about the spread of jihadist forces in that country and possible radicalization at lower levels in the Pakistan army suggest that the issue is not Kashmir but Pakistan itself.

Despite its unflattering ranking in the Fragile States Index, Pakistan is a functioning state, although faced with serious internal challenges to its stability and cohesiveness. Its post-financial crisis growth of per capita income has been barely 1 percent annually (5.7 percent annually for India over the same period). With an investment rate of 11 percent of GDP (a third of India's), rapid growth is impossible, and the country has lurched from one International Monetary Fund (IMF) loan to another. With a defense budget that is one-seventh of India's, the military imbalance between the two countries can only grow—increasing Pakistan's sense of vulnerability and therefore lowering its nuclear threshold.

The underlying problem, as Husain Haqqani, a former Pakistan ambassador to the United States, has argued, is Pakistan's "elusive quest" for parity with India, ignoring the obvious lack of symmetry—and not just in defense budgets or size of economy. In his article, Haqqani points out that 94 percent of Indian children finish primary school compared to 54 percent in Pakistan. Indians get more doctorates in a year in the sciences than have been awarded by Pakistan's universities since Independence in 1947. Pakistan publishes 2,581 books in a year (including religious texts and children's books), while India publishes 90,000. As for Jammu and Kashmir, according to Haqqani, the last effective UN Security Council resolution on the subject was in 1957, and Pakistan is the only one from among 193 UN members who mentions the issue in the General Assembly.[23] The world has moved on.

The irony in India–Pakistan ties is that the bigger power seeks status quo, while the smaller power seeks to wrest territory. But since Pakistan is not India's equal—India has moved from being six times Pakistan's economy to eight times—it has resorted to asymmetric warfare, a soft term for exporting terrorism. But the policy of subjecting India to "death by a thousand cuts," in the form of repeated cross-border terrorist strikes, has resulted in Pakistan itself becoming the victim of a homegrown terrorism that its army now fights to contain. Growing insecurity with regard to a resurgent India also drives Pakistan into China's arms. In recent years, the embrace across the Karakoram Range has become noticeably warmer and tighter.

Meanwhile, frustrated by Pakistan's refusal to allow movement of its goods in transit to Afghanistan—and by the instability that seems to mark Afghanistan's foreseeable future—India has pushed for access to Central Asian energy resources and markets farther north through road and rail networks that start in Iran, to the west of Afghanistan. The proposed north–south multimodal transport corridor will begin at Iran's Chabahar Port, which India will help to develop, and go north to the Caspian Sea and from there to Central Asia, southern Russia, and Europe. A separate 900-kilometer spur is planned by India, from Chabahar into Afghanistan. The Chabahar option has been in the cards for years, and was formally approved only when Modi visited Tehran in the summer of 2016.

As it happens, China has already moved into the Central Asian "stans" like Kazakhstan and Uzbekistan, securing mining and energy contracts, pumping in tens of billions of dollars, and building impressive railway lines even as it seeks to create a New Silk Road Belt. As India looks for answers to the problems of geography, both natural and artificially created, to the point of taking some decidedly risky bets in unpredictable terrain, China is already there, sewing up deals.

A New "Race for Africa"

Competition for natural resources is also being played out in an economically resurgent Africa, where the Chinese grabbed the first-mover advantage at the turn of the century. Rich in untapped natural resources, characterized by underdeveloped negotiating capabilities and all too many corrupt leaders, and yet blessed with enormous growth potential, Africa has for quite a few years been another theater in the unequal contest for influence. China's cumulative outbound investment and projects from 2005 to 2014 amounted to $870 billion, with sub-Saharan Africa getting the largest share. By the summer of 2014, Chinese investment (including contracts) in sub-Saharan Africa had grown to $150.4 billion—the focus clearly being on energy and minerals.[24] Almost inevitably, China has become Africa's biggest trading partner, with the overwhelming bulk of African exports being commodities and raw materials to feed China's manufacturing sector. China gets a third of its oil from Africa, though the continent accounts for only a tenth of world output. India has played the game on a smaller scale; but both countries came unstuck in their gambit for oil out of Sudan, as detailed by Luke Patey.[25]

The Chinese state has moved in behind its companies and announced funding on a scale that India cannot match: $20 billion over three years (India has offered $1.87 billion annually over five years), plus training 30,000 Africans and giving scholarships to 18,000.[26] The under-reported corollary, not always state-supported, has been that a million Chinese have migrated to Africa in recent years, the number to increase tenfold over twenty years.

Chinese companies have also been in the lead when it comes to taking over agricultural land for commercial farming—a subject that has developed into a contentious issue in countries like Ethiopia. In 2006, Michael Sata, the opposition leader who was to become the president of Zambia five years later, went so far as to say that he didn't want Africa to become the dumping ground for China's unwanted people and goods.[27]

Greg Mills, head of the Brenthurst Foundation in South Africa, described the nature of investment deals that China typically combines with construction contracts thus: "In September 2007, for example, the Congolese government and a group of Chinese state-owned enterprises signed a bilateral investment and trade agreement, under which the Chinese committed to constructing a number of roads, railways, and hospitals. The work was to be carried out by Chinese companies and financed by loans from the Chinese Exim bank estimated at $6.5 billion. In return, to guarantee repayment of the loans, a Congolese–Chinese joint venture with Chinese majority participation was to be created to extract and sell Congolese copper, cobalt and gold." As Mills went on to explain, the deal was of no help to Africa in its desire to diversify its economy away from raw material production, and loans to "kleptocratic" governments only hindered development.[28]

Nor is China reticent about using the leverage that it acquires. After a face-off with Japan in 2010, mentioned earlier, Beijing began rationing the supply of rare earths that are vital raw material for many industries and for which China is a dominant supplier. It clinched the gas deal with Myanmar in 2006, taking it away from India, after China used its veto in the UN Security Council to stop a resolution condemning Myanmar's human rights record. At the time of the face-off with the Philippines over Scarborough Shoal in 2012, China stopped buying Philippine bananas, citing health reasons; further, it stopped the flow of Chinese tourists to that country. And, as the Brenthurst report has it, when the Argentine president Christina Kirchner slapped a duty on cheap shoes being imported from China, it promptly suspended a contract for 2 million tons of soybean oil.

India has been a quiet player as China has flexed its muscles and gained ascendancy in the broader region. Its "development partnership" program has grown in size, with the overall spending target raised to about $3.5 billion annually. The money is small in relation to China's spending, but the ratio (0.175 percent of GDP) compares with the bilateral aid budgets of wealthy members of the OECD, these having averaged 0.3 percent of GDP. Indian officials say they seek to gain goodwill rather than leverage, by focusing on schools and hospitals, capacity building through technical training programs, and constructing roads and railways. Among other things, New Delhi has consciously avoided linkages to resource supplies; most of the Indian investment in extraction industries overseas (largely coal and iron ore but also copper) has been by private-sector players like Tata, GMR, GVK, Adani, Lanco, and Aditya Birla, in places like Australia, Indonesia, and Mozambique—manifestly commercial transactions designed to source supplies for plants back home and, unlike China, without any visible supporting hand from the state. The exceptions have been oil and gas, where the players are mainly (but not solely) in the public sector. But India's resource-driven investments have simply not been on a scale to rival China's appetite for such deals.

Thus, while some of the $129 billion invested overseas by corporate India during the last decade has gone into the resources sector, money has also been invested in acquiring brands and gaining access to markets and technology in the United States and Europe. Tata, for instance, became the largest private-sector employer in the United Kingdom after its acquisition of Jaguar and Land Rover, and Corus. As in so many other spheres, the fundamental differences in the nature of the two states and societies have found reflection in India's and China's strategies for development funding.

India's Choices

Where do the outcomes and prospects in different theaters leave India's search for strategic autonomy in the face of China's challenge, and the country's attempts to establish a footprint beyond South Asia? In a rapidly evolving situation, especially as China wobbles, it is hard to predict long-term outcomes. Based on the long-range evidence since 1950, a reasonable conclusion would be that the Chinese ascendancy has and will continue to overshadow India's rise, placing the two countries in different power orbits—China a global power, India only a regional one. Will this constrict Indian plans? Almost certainly yes, even if by 2025 India has become the fourth-largest economy and third-largest military—precisely because all power is relative and China will have retained its relative superiority.

Even in testing situations, though, the natural instinct for a country of India's size is to rely on its own economic and military strengths; that is the logic of the country's desire for strategic autonomy. In 2015, with the prospect of improved economic performance and a more active diplomacy under Narendra Modi, strategic autonomy still is a viable policy framework. But should the power imbalance with China grow and create a sense of increased vulnerability in India, it would make the attractions of greater alignment with the United States, Japan, and perhaps Australia shine brighter. And yet India will always be held back by nervousness about provoking Beijing and the desire to avoid a fresh border conflict with China in a mountainous terrain where defense is not to its advantage. Conversely, the prospect of an Indian–American embrace could encourage China to play its cards more circumspectly with India.

Whenever China has taken a misstep (as with its aggressive posture in the South China Sea), India's diplomatic options have expanded in the region. New Delhi could profit from American support for its objectives, like breaking into the missile and nuclear technology clubs, but the larger challenge to Indian diplomats will be complex. How can they exploit the growing alignment with the United States and Japan without antagonizing China? And how do they sidestep the potential pitfalls of a policy that might be defined as "nobody's ally, everyone's friend"? In a crisis, no "friends" might come to help—as happened during the 1962 clash with China and the 1965 and 1971 wars with Pakistan.

And yet there may well be no conflict. Henry Kissinger writes about the difference between chess (which originated in India; each player seeks the other's capitulation) and the Chinese game of *wei qi*, where a player seeks relative advantage, with the goal being strategic encirclement.[29] If China can manage the encirclement of India, it will have contained India without the risk of hostilities—just as Sun Tzu advised in the ancient treatise *The Art of War*.

Troubling as these thoughts are from the Indian perspective, there is a more sanguine view, that Chinese ascendancy needs to be understood in the context of the key constraints it faces: the simultaneous rise of other powers around the world; the existence all around China of semi-hostile powers that might increasingly coordinate their actions on the basis of shared threat perceptions about a new hegemon (as a senior Australian diplomat put it, "China invites containment"); the vulnerabilities of a system that is a one-party autocracy with elements of a kleptocracy; and finally the fact that growth must slow as its productive population shrinks. All of this suggests that China's ascendancy will face some headwinds.

Can China be contained? Almost certainly not. As the largest trading partner of most of the countries in the region, with regional integration of production chains creating complex dependencies, with a currency that is gaining traction, and with assertive naval power, it could eventually "Finlandize" some of the countries in the region—precisely the result that the United States hopes to prevent with its "pivot" to Asia. India, in contrast, can count on more soft power, more friends, a natural zone of influence in South Asia, and in much of East Asia general goodwill with regard to its non-threatening ascendancy. All of that helps to explain why India would be the default choice as the main balancing power in the region—if it measures up, that is.

Rapid economic growth remains the best foreign policy. If India can improve its economic position, it will strengthen its overall position vis-à-vis China and also provide the "balance" for which other countries look to it. If India falters economically, China will encroach on its space more than it has already—just as a *wei qi* player would. It would be a strategic failure if India eventually has to reconcile itself to functioning in China's shadow. That would mean limiting its power ambitions, or being forced to seek additional ballast through yet closer ties with China's rivals. Either way, it would probably be compromised in its goal of strategic autonomy. The prospect of that unpalatable choice should help focus India more sharply on achieving rapid economic growth.

16

The Race to Re-Arm

IN 1938 MAO Zedong wrote what became one of his better-known aphorisms, that power flows out of the barrel of a gun. Twenty-four years later, he drove home that lesson to India. During a month-long engagement over a disputed land border, the Chinese army routed unprepared and poorly led Indian forces on the eastern front, moved into large swaths of vacated territory, then abruptly announced a cease-fire and pulled back. More than half a century has passed, but India has not forgotten the humiliation. Several minor border skirmishes have punctuated the years that have followed, and India has mostly stood its ground diplomatically and militarily, most notably in the standoff at Sumdorong Chu in 1986. But every such episode, the latest being one in 2014 (oddly, when Xi Jinping was in India), has raised old anxieties in the public mind about having to confront a superior fighting force. The intermittent talks on settling the border dispute have delivered little progress.

The two countries' soldiers face each other across a 3,448-kilometer "Line of Actual Control" that runs across virtually the entire length of the Himalayas. Both countries maintain programs to upgrade their military capabilities on their respective sides of the line. On the Indian side, there is a painful awareness of China's better state of defense preparedness, including its greater mobilization capabilities on terrain that is to China's advantage—capabilities bolstered by the building of an impressive, high-altitude railway line that reaches Lhasa and extends farther south, to points not far from the border.

New Delhi has tried to speed up construction of its neglected border roads, positioned heavy fighter aircraft (Su-30 MKIs) at new air bases closer to the border, and focused on building the army's counter-strike capability as a deterrent. In the last few years it has added two mountain divisions (35,000 troops) to the existing ten, and announced the formation of a new mountain strike corps, adding to the three in the plains focused on Pakistan. But opinion is divided on the wisdom of the expensive new corps, which for want of funds will be created only in phases. China's overall mobilization capability (both numbers and speed) remains far superior.

To overcome the limitations of surface connectivity, India has looked at quick mobilization by air. Heavy transport planes and heavy-lift helicopters have been acquired from the United States for airlifting troops and material, and forward air bases have been developed or reopened. Extended negotiations have been under way for light howitzers that can be lifted to the front at short notice. To reach decisions on these and other long-delayed acquisitions, such as a new assault rifle and night-fighting capabilities, takes many years. The result is that the country's defense preparedness is never what it should be. If this does not ring alarm bells, it is only because no one expects serious conflict. But it does leave the country vulnerable and its soldiers at a disadvantage when there is the occasional face-off.

Meanwhile, the Indian Ocean has become a new area of contested influence. Chinese naval ships have slowly ratcheted up their presence in India's neighborhood waters, starting with anti-piracy operations in 2008 and most recently docking submarines at ports in Sri Lanka and Pakistan. The carefully calibrated nature of the naval thrust is evident in a sixteen-character exposition of Chinese policy: "Select locations meticulously, make deployments discreetly, give priority to cooperative activities and penetrate gradually."[1] In line with that prescription, China's naval outreach has involved Pakistan, Myanmar, Bangladesh, and Sri Lanka.

Indian naval ships have made their own separate forays east of the Malacca Straits, showing the flag at ports in Vietnam, the Philippines, South Korea, and Japan. India has expanded the scale and scope of its trilateral naval exercises with the United States and Japan, and has begun regular exercises with Australia. Both China and India are in the middle of a naval buildup and a maritime thrust. This chapter looks at India's military response to the Chinese threat, its scale and quality, its successes and failures—all of which show up the strengths and weaknesses of the Indian system.

Key Handicaps

Three factors have bedeviled India's attempt to build a defense force that is equal to the country's external security needs. One is lack of funds, the second is an accident-prone weapons import system, and the third is the very mixed record in the domestic manufacture of defense hardware—so far almost exclusively in the public sector. A fourth factor, less focused on, is perhaps the most important: a mindset in the military that is largely tied to old ways of thinking about battle.[2] China has in 2016 followed the example of the United States and other countries by integrating commands across the defense services in each theater, but India's generals and air marshals continue to play at turf protection and operate in silos.

On the equipment side, the country has always been at least a decade behind on its weapons program. The air force is down to thirty-four or fewer operational fighter squadrons (typically with eighteen aircraft each) instead of the sanctioned forty-two squadrons.[3] Of the thirty-four, thirteen MiG-21 and MiG-27 squadrons are waiting to be replaced, having run their full life. Against this, the proposed acquisition of 126 medium-combat aircraft (the French Rafale) was scrapped in 2015, eight years after bids had been invited. Instead, thirty-six aircraft would now be bought on direct negotiation with the French supplier. These negotiations have already taken another year, for the same reason: the Rafale is forbiddingly expensive.

The cost of the domestically built light-combat aircraft, Tejas, is about a tenth of the Rafale and these planes are supposed to be the replacements as more than 200 MiGs get phased out. But development of the Tejas, while creditable, has been inordinately delayed; it has yet to get its final operations clearance for combat flying. Volume production of the Tejas waits for a new model with important modifications that will satisfy the air force. The different schedules for retiring and acquiring aircraft suggest that the number of fighter squadrons will drop further before it picks up. Meanwhile, the air force's mainstay, the Su-30MKI fighter-bomber, has a low serviceability rate of barely 50 percent for what is intended by 2018 to be a fleet of 272 aircraft. The defense minister, Manohar Parrikar, promised in March 2015 to raise the serviceability rate to 75 percent.[4] Seeing will be believing.

Meanwhile, the navy has not grown in size over a quarter century in terms of the number of major combatant ships; most of the ships to be built over the next decade will be replacements for ones that are due to be decommissioned, though the new ones will be superior in size and capability. As for the army, it is still without essential night-fighting capabilities, and does not have a comprehensive air defense network. In the event of hostilities, ammunition and stores will last for twenty days or fewer—half of what is needed. Planning has been undertaken for creating a more modern infantry, but there is little real change, while no major acquisition of artillery has occurred for thirty years. The country has also been late in acknowledging the dangers and opportunities presented by cyberwarfare.

Of the three services, the navy has been the most proactive in working with domestic production units (shipyards) to get the ships and submarines they need built indigenously. The navy has also received the most attention from the Modi government. While the government's shipyards have been building steadily more ambitious vessels, from nuclear submarines to an aircraft carrier, the shipbuilding program has been subject to the same delays as everything else. Many ships in the fleet date back more than three decades and are overdue for replacement. The submarine fleet has been particularly depleted, with no more than seven or eight out of a conventional fleet of thirteen said to be operational at any time; the requirement is twice that number. The minesweeping fleet is down to six vessels, more than a quarter century old; again, double that number is needed.

So when the destroyer INS *Kolkata* was commissioned in 2014, it was the first such addition to the navy in thirteen years—a period in which the Chinese navy was adding a destroyer to its fleet almost every year. The submarine INS *Kalvari*, due to be commissioned in late 2016, will be the first since 2000, other than the INS *Chakra* loaned from the Russians in 2012. Even among corvettes, INS *Kamorta* (commissioned in 2014) was the first to join the navy after one in 2004. Meanwhile, INS *Viraat*, the aging aircraft carrier, has been sent to the scrapyard. The new (rather, extensively refurbished) Russian-built carrier INS *Vikramaditya* arrived six years behind schedule, in 2014, while the *Viraat*'s replacement (INS *Vikrant*), being built at Cochin Shipyard, will not be commissioned before 2018. It is only when a third carrier is built, in the 2020s, that the navy will become the two-carrier fleet that has been talked of since the 1980s (one of the three carriers will usually be in harbor for maintenance and repairs).

Meanwhile, INS *Arihant*, the nuclear-powered ballistic-missile submarine built at Visakhapatnam, was launched in 2009 but has yet to be commissioned into the navy as sea trials continue. A second nuclear submarine, INS *Aridhaman*, is behind schedule on its launch, even as work has started on a third. These nuclear submarines (whenever they eventually join the navy) will represent second-strike capability and give credibility to India's no-first-use nuclear doctrine. However, the intermediate-range (3,000 km) missile that can provide effective deterrence has been delayed and will not be integrated with *Arihant* before 2017. What will be deployed in the interim is the K-15, with a 700-kilometer range that makes it an unsatisfactory substitute.

Defense manufacture involves the development and integration of complex technologies and is subject to notorious delays and cost overruns everywhere, especially when a country is on a steep learning curve. There is a price to be paid for this, and in India the delays have stymied defense plans and handicapped the defense forces. The government has struggled to speed up the time-consuming acquisition process, without success. For instance, it decided in 1999 to build half a dozen conventional diesel–electric submarines by 2012, and another half dozen soon after; but the first of the original six will be commissioned only in 2016, and the order for the second lot of six has yet to be placed.

The delays and squeezed budgets have meant that in the five calendar years 2005–09, the navy added a solitary frigate to its fleet of major combatant vessels. The last five years (2010–14) have been better, with the addition of ten such ships (mostly frigates). The new pace of two major combatant vessels every year is likely to be maintained through to 2020 (mostly submarines), and then scaled up to perhaps three new ships annually—budgets permitting. The problem is that many of the new ships are without essential accompanying equipment because of delays in ordering ship-defense missiles, active towed array sonar, torpedoes and submarine-hunting helicopters. The ships have an impressive presence but are less than combat-ready—prompting the wisecrack that India has a peaceful navy!

Still, the acquisition of long-range Poseidon surveillance aircraft from the United States, Barak surface-to-air missiles from Israel, and the Indo-Russian BrahMos supersonic cruise missile, the fastest and heaviest in its class, has meant that the navy's capabilities have grown substantially in recent years. The steadily more ambitious shipbuilding program that is under way could see the navy grow from a total fleet size of about 320,000 tons (counting submarines and combatant ships of at least 1,000-ton displacement) to more than 450,000 tons—which would make it comparable in tonnage (though perhaps not capability) to the Japanese navy, the world's fourth largest.

That expansion will mean a lot of work for the five government-owned shipyards, though indigenization has so far not extended meaningfully to ship propulsion systems and weaponry, other than some missiles. A visit in late 2013 to Mazagon Dock, the government's premier builder of naval vessels, showed that shipbuilders had never been busier. Located deep in Mumbai's docklands, the yard was also busy expanding its facilities. Two giant destroyers were being kitted out in a "wet basin" while the first two of six Scorpene submarines were being built in covered sheds that opened out onto a vast new "wet basin" twice the size of the first one. In the slipways close by, two other destroyers were in their early stages of hull construction. Next to them, a giant shed to help build ships on a new, modular pattern (to save time) was nearing completion. A 300-ton crane for lifting ship modules out of the shed (equipped with a sliding roof) and onto the slipways dominated the skyline.

But it has been taking Mazagon eight to ten years to turn out a ship, and that is a few years too long—in part because repeat orders are rare. With its expanded facilities, it can simultaneously work on half a dozen ships and deliver at least one ship or submarine every year. Apart from saving time, repeat orders also save up to 30 percent on costs, but the defense acquisition program moves jerkily. Budgeting is an ever-present constraint, and ordered components never come on time, disrupting smooth production schedules.

Meanwhile, other shipyards were busy too, and upgrading. Garden Reach Shipbuilders in West Bengal was building bigger corvettes and frigates, while Goa Shipyard was building large patrol boats and readying to start work on minesweepers. Cochin Shipyard was busy constructing its first aircraft carrier, while the nuclear submarine facility at Visakhapatnam was working on two submarines after launching one. Private shipyards were doing smaller jobs. Larsen & Toubro as well as Reliance Defence had shipyards that could build and repair large ships; the former was already doing submarine hulls and had set up a submarine design center. With the new emphasis on encouraging private-sector defense production, both yards can hope to bid for new contracts to build entire ships and submarines.

Budget Squeeze

The country's National Security Advisory Board had looked at the appropriate level of spending on defense, given India's security challenges, and determined some years ago that the defense budget should be 3 percent of GDP. Except briefly in the 1980s, this level has never been reached. Indeed, a rush of armaments imports in the 1980s is believed to have been one of the reasons for the foreign exchange crisis of 1991—after which finance ministers have become parsimonious. Defense expenditure was between 2 percent and 2.5 percent of GDP through much of the 1990s, then dipped to below 2 percent, and in the most recent years to 1.75 percent.[5]

The more relevant figure, when looking at money for buying arms, is perhaps the budget for acquiring weapons. In the 1990s, this was routinely about 0.65 percent of GDP. As new weapons acquisition orders flowed during the Manmohan Singh government's two terms in office, the capital budget for defense jumped sharply to 1 percent of GDP before sliding back to 0.75 percent. For the most recent years, the figure was down to 0.70 percent of GDP or lower. This points to a brief flush of spending and now a return of the fiscal squeeze, and therefore a slowdown in the pace of fresh arms acquisitions—for which there is a long-pending list. Still, the record shows that expenditure on arms purchases grew rapidly, with a compounded annual growth rate of nearly 17 percent for the decade.

The other factor causing delays is the recurring problem of illegal payoffs when it comes to arms purchases. The first military scandal, as early as 1948, involved the purchase of jeeps—an issue that the Nehru government rode out. A 1981 submarine contract with Germany's HDW was restricted to four boats following allegations of bribery. After another bribery scandal hit a Bofors artillery contract in 1987 and effectively destroyed Rajiv Gandhi's prime ministership, subsequent governments have been sensitive to allegations of payoffs on defense purchases. A. K. Antony, defense minister for nine years till 2014, was particularly concerned to preserve his reputation for probity. The result was blacklisting of a variety of arms suppliers from Singapore, Israel, Italy, South Africa, South Korea, and elsewhere, sometimes on the basis of little hard evidence; the result was derailing of contracts for artillery, helicopters, rifles, missiles, and minesweepers. The more recent arms purchase scandals have not had political color, but the global arms bazaar is inextricably linked to payoffs.[6] India's risk-avoidance strategy in recent years has been to source contracts bilaterally, as with Russia, or in the case of the United States at prices already negotiated with suppliers by the US Department of Defense. Competitive bidding has become a rarity for big-ticket purchases; the Rafale too is now being negotiated directly with the supplier.

Apart from delayed contracts for helicopters, light howitzers, and combat aircraft, orders are pending for light tanks and new minesweepers, and the development of a battlefield management system, with a digital wireless network that integrates frontline battlefield formations with real-time voice and data communication systems. In its initial months, the Modi government moved forward on important items of military hardware, preparing the ground for final purchase orders—helicopters, new conventional submarines and frigates, field guns, trainer aircraft, and missile systems. But financial reality has reasserted itself, and the modest defense acquisitions budget for 2015–16 showed once again how vital rapid economic growth is for generating the revenues that will pay for a credible defense force.

One change in recent times has been the stepped-up shipbuilding program; another has been the choice of overseas suppliers. For many decades, the Soviet Union and then Russia was the principal source of India's defense hardware, from aircraft to tanks and ships, not to mention advanced rocket technology. However, India's growing dissatisfaction with delays in Russian delivery schedules, poor spare parts support, and also mid-contract renegotiation of price came at a time when the United States made a determined bid to get into the Indian defense equipment market, in 2005. Soon India was buying a variety of American aircraft for heavy transport, maritime surveillance, and airborne early-warning radar, as well as engines and other components for the indigenously developed Tejas light-combat aircraft. American companies also acquired the contracts for attack and heavy-lift helicopters. Israel became an important supplier of ship-defense missiles and unmanned aerial vehicles, plus airborne early-warning radars. And the French have their corner of the market, including the contracts for Rafales and submarines.

For all the diversification of supplies, however, the largest fleet of fighter aircraft in the Indian air force is and will remain for many years the Russian Sukhoi 30 MKI, even as the bulk of the armored corps comprises Russian T-90 and T-72 tanks. India and Russia have also collaborated to develop the BrahMos supersonic cruise missile and have agreed to jointly develop a fifth-generation stealth fighter. India remains Russia's largest market for defense equipment; it is now Israel's largest market too.

Modi's Three-Pronged Thrust

Shortly after assuming office, the Modi government initiated a threefold policy thrust. It announced a "Make in India" policy in which the localization of manufacture was a key component. India had acquired the dubious distinction of being the world's largest arms importer, with some 60 percent of the annual $15-billion budget for hardware acquisitions going to finance imports. Modi declared he wanted to reduce that to 30 percent in five years' time. To facilitate this, he took the second step of raising the limit on foreign direct investment in defense manufacture from 26 percent to 49 percent. Before long, Bharat Forge announced a joint venture with Israel's Rafael to make missile systems. After the government canceled a large contract for nearly 200 light utility helicopters, and announced that they would have to be made in India, Airbus announced that it had started negotiations with three Indian business houses for a joint venture to make helicopters in India. Sikorsky's parent, United Technologies, also expressed its willingness to locate helicopter manufacture in India if it got orders for supplying Sikorsky Seahawk choppers for anti-submarine warfare and other naval uses. Among the smaller companies, Samtel (once a maker of cathode ray tubes for TV sets) tied up with France's Thales for avionics and helmet-mounted display systems for fighter pilots.

The third element in the new government's policy thrust was a complementary push for domestic private-sector involvement, with some hardware acquisitions all but reserved for manufacture in the private sector. As a visit to the Aero India show in Bengaluru in early 2015 made clear, all the weapon systems made in India were by public-sector entities like Hindustan Aeronautics Ltd. (trainer and fighter aircraft), Bharat Dynamics (missiles), Bharat Electronics (radar and other systems), and Mishra Dhatu Nigam (special metals). As milling crowds at Aero India gawked at the Tejas, at HAL's prototype light-combat aircraft, at the BrahMos supersonic cruise missile, and at the aircraft that overseas suppliers had brought for aerobatic razzle-dazzle, marquee private-sector names like Tata and Mahindra, Godrej, and Larsen & Toubro featured only as suppliers of components or subsystems, along with a couple of hundred small and medium enterprises that displayed everything from wire harnesses to machined steel components.

Yet all four large business groups have long been eager to get into the defense hardware business. Tata already makes parts for at least three Western aircraft manufacturers, including cabins for Sikorsky helicopters, while Godrej supplies parts for the BrahMos and other missile systems. Private shipyards built by Larsen & Toubro and Pipavav (acquired recently by the Anil Ambani group and renamed Reliance Defence) could handle more defense orders. If the private sector were allowed to play a larger role, a more diversified production base for defense equipment would be a growth area for the economy and add to strategic capability.

A major incentive to localize production is that domestic supplies tend to be cheaper, despite massive cost overruns, often to the extent of 100 percent and more over the original cost estimate. The problem has almost always been delays and questions about the combat-worthiness of weapon platforms—as with both the Tejas and the tank developed by the Defence Research and Development Organization. In both cases, though, the doubts in the minds of high military officers about combat-worthiness seem to be getting laid to rest following product modifications. The additional benefit of localizing defense manufacture is the acquisition of technologies and mastery of special materials that offer civilian spin-off benefits, especially when complex projects like the development of fighter aircraft are undertaken.

An India–China Dance

The Western media like to portray Pakistan as India's "archenemy," but that country is too weak to be a conventional military threat—it is outgunned in the air, on land, and in the sea. Pakistan's logical response has been to focus on deterrence through the acquisition of a nuclear missile armory and the threat of a tactical nuclear response even at a low threshold of conflict—to which the Indian response has been that any use of tactical battlefield nuclear devices would quickly escalate to an all-out nuclear exchange. Meanwhile, Pakistan's focus on asymmetric action by supporting terrorist activity in India (not just in the Kashmir valley but in the rest of the country as well) has been delivering diminishing returns, even as its failed gambit to grab territory in Kargil in 1999 lost it international goodwill. A new theater of terrorist activity directed at Indians is in Afghanistan, given Pakistan's determination to keep India out of that country once the United States has withdrawn its forces. It is possible that as world attention shifts away from Afghanistan, a Pakistan that feels more secure on its western border may give renewed attention to sponsoring militant activity in Kashmir—where there is already a latent threat of more radical militancy.

Still, India's primary concern is the military imbalance with China, which it sees as the country's main strategic threat, and against which its strategic objective is to maintain credible conventional deterrence. China uses Pakistan to try to keep India off balance, including supplying Pakistan with nuclear and missile technology (in violation of international control regimes), pointing to a Sino-Pak axis that defense planners in New Delhi have to factor into their calculations.

As might be expected, China has been well ahead in the armaments game, with an official defense budget three and a half times India's (unofficial estimates say it is even bigger), and a much larger navy that has begun looking beyond its earlier focus on coastal defense. While Indian companies have been gearing up to make standard defense hardware, China in 2007 had already demonstrated anti-satellite warfare capabilities, and in 2012 showcased a fifth-generation strike aircraft. It has developed guided missiles that can sink aircraft carriers—the intention being to keep the carrier-based US navy at bay. The assessment at senior levels in the Indian armed forces is that the imbalance in military power between the two Asian giants might reduce for a while but could increase again. The strategy to deal with the imbalance, to quote a former service chief, "is to never allow asymmetries with China to go beyond the point where it would encourage war."

This stance assumes that China will opt for conventional methods. Observers have noted that India's army brass is still wedded to traditional, troop-intensive ways of thinking, even as inter-service rivalry prevents the creation of fully integrated command structures for specific theaters. In contrast,

China's white paper on defense, issued in the summer of 2015, talked of modular units for multidimensional, trans-theater operations and an "air-space defence force structure," and put this structure into practice in 2016. Earlier white papers had mentioned high-technology wars and "winning local wars under conditions of informationization."[7] India, in comparison, has remained stuck in twentieth-century thinking about positional warfare. One result is that far too much of the defense budget is spent on paying and maintaining more than a million low-tech troops (then paying pensions in their long years of retirement), and precious little is spent on preparing for new methods of warfare. India's army brass does not have a great record of strategic thinking or of being ready for the kind of military challenges the country might face. When asked by the political leadership for military options after the attack on Parliament in 2001 and on Mumbai in 2008, the service chiefs could offer none.

Meanwhile, the navy is getting ready for greater Chinese naval penetration of regional waters. One of the western fleet's naval bases, on the Karwar coast, is to double its capacity to base thirty major combatant ships. A subterranean submarine base is under construction at Rambilli on the Andhra coast, not far from the eastern fleet's base at Visakhapatnam. Air and naval bases have been created farther afield, in the Andaman and Nicobar Islands, including INS Baaz (Eagle) which is 300 kilometers south of Port Blair and therefore nearer the entry to the Malacca Straits—for better monitoring of the traffic coming through the Straits.

Beyond Indian terrain, a monitoring station has been set up at Ras al Hadd in Oman, barely 400 kilometers across the mouth of the Gulf from Pakistan's Gwadar Port (the station will listen to low-frequency signals to submarines and monitor port traffic). Other monitoring and listening stations have been established on an island off Madagascar, not far from the African coastline, and in Mauritius, to monitor traffic in the southern Indian Ocean, where submarines like to hide from detection. Seychelles has now been pulled into the effort; Mauritius and Seychelles have agreed to let India build landing strips and secure docking facilities on their territory.[8]

Moves and countermoves, thrust and parry: the Indian Ocean region has become the new theater for an India–China dance that has just begun and which will continue for some time. The Chinese maintain that India is excessively sensitive to the presence of Beijing's ships in India's neighborhood waters, while New Delhi calculates that it needs to retain naval superiority in waters through which Chinese oil supplies must pass, for neutralizing the country's vulnerabilities in a land war. That objective would be better served if the three Indian forces could get their armaments programs in order.

17

Dealing with the World

TIME TO GROW UP

ANY SIGNIFICANT POWER shift changes attitudes. The old masters of the universe, the wealthy Western countries, are now challenged by low rates of economic growth, high unemployment, and unsustainable welfare systems. As they look at rising economies like China's and India's, with their rapid growth rates, new capabilities, and also new assertiveness, the old attitudes to yesterday's poor countries have changed. Protectionist instincts now coexist with selective free trade rhetoric. The focus on development assistance, never munificent despite the ideological tussles for "mindspace" in poor countries during the Cold War, has given way to demands that the new centers of production match Western labor and environment standards, lest they undercut employment in high-wage "home" markets.

This is hard diplomacy, and it affects real lives. Yusuf Hamied, chairman of the Indian drug company Cipla, created a global stir when he declared in 2001 that he could sell anti-AIDS drugs for a dollar a day—compared to $30 a day that the global pharmaceutical giants were charging. A mighty battle ensued. Hamied won and many African countries found a new ally in their battle against AIDS. Hamied has gone on to wage price wars in drugs for treating stomach cancer (charging Rs 6,500 for thirty tablets, compared to a competitor's price of Rs 280,000) and bird flu. The big pharmaceutical companies saw it differently and sued Cipla and others for patent infringements.

Even without Cipla's challenge, these have been testing times for some global pharmaceutical companies as they have found their patent cupboards getting slowly emptied. The inability to discover new blockbuster drugs has threatened profit margins even as Indian firms like Sun have specialized in replacing drugs going off patent with much cheaper generics. Some firms have responded by trying to "evergreen" patents, using marginal changes in product and effectiveness. In the big recent battle on drug patents, fought in 2013 in India's Supreme Court, Novartis was denied a patent on an anti-cancer drug because the new drug was found to be a case of evergreening.[1] The fallout was intense US pressure because of what Washington saw as inadequate Indian legal protection for intellectual property rights.

The new terms of multilateral engagement, therefore, have influenced diplomacy on everything from patent law and trade to climate change. The free pass once given to poor countries on trade obligations and carbon emissions has been withdrawn; what is asked for now is matching action by everyone: rich, middle-income, and poor. Some of the change of approach is warranted; countries that benefited from special rules when they were poor or needed help should expect the rules to change when their circumstances and capabilities improve. But some shifts involve Western countries backsliding out of commitments, such as contributing to a fund to help poor countries cope with climate change. There is also a broader shift in the pattern of fund flow to poor or emerging market economies. What used to be the World Bank's smallest money window, its private-sector lending arm (the International Finance Corporation), was by 2014 giving out more money than the Bank's soft-loan window, the International Development Association (IDA), which at one stage was India's biggest non-trade source of foreign exchange.

Similarly, the early rounds of trade talks delivered preferential market access to poor countries in the 1960s and '70s, through such devices as the Generalized System of Preferences. But what began in 2001 as the World Trade Organization's Doha Development Round, to introduce fairer trading rules for developing countries, including those in agricultural trade, stalled because—among other things—it became clear to the emerging market economies that the wealthy nations were not about to reduce high agricultural subsidies in their domestic markets (e.g., on cotton in the United States and sugar in Europe). The developed economies, on their part, saw little coming back to them in return for the concessions they were being asked to make; their attempts to enlarge the Doha agenda to include issues of interest to them were blocked.

It has been no different with climate change negotiations. The Kyoto Protocol of 1997 that followed the 1992 Earth Summit at Rio de Janeiro had said that poor countries were not required to make any commitments on reducing carbon emissions. The successor agreement to Kyoto will make no such concession—once again, because the world order has changed. Emissions by the emerging market economies like India and China now account for a much larger share of emissions than they did two decades ago.

It is perhaps inevitable that India, along with China, should be cited most often as among the countries that should assume greater responsibility for the global commons because of its increased role in both trade and emissions, and because many countries continue to see India's markets as among the more protected ones. India's problem is familiar—of being a premature power. It has taken large strides in the past quarter century and has become a leading economy, but it continues to have more poor people than any other country in the world and a level of per capita income that puts it in the lowest quartile in a global country listing. When it comes to agricultural subsidies, on which the country has faced pressure to change, the subsistence-level farming that is the everyday reality on over 100 million farm holdings prevents the government from being flexible. As New Delhi sees it, it is the United States that is being stubborn in not addressing issues like its cotton-growing subsidy.

If India had made more progress on agricultural productivity and been more trade-enabled by having efficient ports, roads, and power supply, it would have had room to be more flexible in its trade negotiations. The rigidity in its approach to trade negotiations is a by-product of its failures in economic management at home. Most of the country's free trade agreements are quite restricted in their scope and depth, but even these have caused domestic producers to protest the limited market access that counterparty countries are permitted. The Modi government has ordered a review of all free trade agreements. There is little domestic realization that this is putting India on the wrong side of the fence.

The hard fact, which New Delhi cannot sidestep any longer, is that India is one of the significant markets with potential, and will be treated as such. While India has distanced itself from old "Third World" groupings like the G-77 (all the world's poor and developing economies), it has felt the need to make common cause with Brazil, South Africa, and China in trade talks. Mistakenly, it also made joined with China in climate change discussions at Copenhagen in 2009, though the two countries' emission levels are not comparable on any metric. The Chinese were under concentrated fire at Copenhagen and asked India for support; Manmohan Singh obliged in the hope of a larger bilateral payoff.

Negotiating Climate Change

Nowhere is the contradiction inherent in the notion of a "premature superpower" more apparent than in climate change negotiations. When the Kyoto Protocol was hammered out in 1997, future cuts in the emission of six greenhouse gases were to be compared against baseline data for 1990. The cuts were to be achieved by forty-three rich countries (listed in Annex 1 to the Protocol and therefore known as the Annex 1 countries), which had been responsible for the bulk of the emissions through history, and therefore for the buildup of greenhouses gases in the atmosphere—the cause of the climate change problem. Also, these countries continued to be the primary emitters of these gases. In the base year, India's CO_2 emissions totaled 578 million tons[2]—less than the figures for many of the major economies, including the United Kingdom, West Germany, Japan, Russia, and of course the United States and China. Fifteen years later, when negotiations for a successor agreement to Kyoto were under way, India's emissions had more than trebled; it was now the third-largest emitter, behind only China and the United States (though the European Union, if taken as a unit, had a much higher figure). China's emissions had grown even faster than India's, nearly quadrupling from 2.27 billion tons to 8.55 billion tons.

While these increases were being logged by the emerging giants, many Annex 1 countries had managed to reduce their emissions—though by much less than had been discussed. The United Kingdom, Germany, and Italy had all reduced total emissions. Some developed economies went the other way and increased their emissions, including the United States, Japan, Canada, Australia, and the Netherlands, while France had static numbers. For its part, the European Union (EU) had cut its emissions by 2012 to 18 percent lower than 1990 levels and was comfortably on course to reach the target of 20 percent reduction for 2020. In late 2014, the EU stretched that to a 40 percent cut by 2030 (with 1990 as the base), which most observers considered a comfortably achievable target; indeed, there was criticism of the EU for aiming too low.

Meanwhile, the late developers were increasing emissions—not just China and India but also Indonesia, Mexico, and Brazil. Any progress that the rich countries made in containing or reducing the emission of greenhouse gases was therefore being more than neutralized by the increased emissions from the late developers. By 2012, global emissions were up 51 percent from the Kyoto reference year of 1990. But whereas in 1990 the rich countries had accounted for 62 percent of emissions, and the poor countries for 34 percent (the remaining 4 percent was accounted for by shipping and aviation), now the roles were reversed. The rich countries in 2013 accounted for only 36 percent of emissions and the poor and emerging countries for 58 percent (of which China accounted for half). It was obvious that further cuts in emissions by the rich countries were not, on their own, going to be an adequate solution, given their declining share in total emissions. The emerging economies would henceforth have to lift some of the weight. For instance, the 40 percent reduction in emissions promised by the EU for 2030 could be swallowed up by the expected increase in India's emissions. The world as a whole would be no better off.

On a second metric, of emissions per person, it was the rich countries that remained virtually off the charts. The global average in 2013 was reckoned at about 5 tons of emissions per person in a year, but the figure crossed 10 tons in Holland and more than 15 tons for the United States and Australia. India, with its lower levels of production and consumption, had emissions per person of less than 1.7 tons, while China was at 7.4 tons, not very different from the European Union's average.

If the first metric was total emissions, and the second emissions per head, a third metric was emissions per unit of GDP (using the PPP measure). In 2013, India's share of emissions (7.1 percent) was slightly higher than its share of global GDP (6.7 percent). As for China, while its GDP was marginally lower than that of the EU and the United States, its share of emissions was 29 percent, compared to 10 percent for the EU and 15 percent for the United States. It has been argued, though, that a good bit of China's emissions (as of other emerging economies) is because of goods produced for rich country markets, and that emissions should be measured on the basis of consumption, not production. But even on the consumption metric, China's share of emissions was 23 percent in 2013, compared to 13 percent for the EU and 16 percent for the United States, with India following at 6 percent. On all three metrics, China was in a position where it had to show improvement in its emissions record—total emissions, emissions per head, and emissions per unit of consumption-GDP.

The effort to prevent climate change is within the framework of pursuing the global good of humankind and of protecting the global commons. But national agendas have surfaced in the familiar rich–poor divide and a win–lose context in which "your loss is my gain." Each group therefore has used the numbers that suit its convenience. The rich countries have pointed to the growing emissions by the emerging markets, while the latter have pointed to inequalities in emissions per head. The only neutral measure fair to all would probably be the third metric, that is, emissions per unit of consumption-GDP. Adopting this as the relevant yardstick would be fair to both rich and poor, early developers and late arrivals, provided the late arrivals are helped with the relevant technologies and funding to facilitate adopting of low-carbon growth strategies. It would not require correction by only one group (which is of course problematic in that it ignores the historical question of past emissions). Nor would it ask late developers to accept a cap on their economic growth, any more than it would ask people in rich countries to accept a drop in their standard of living. Such an approach would therefore sidestep some of the primary sticking points in the climate change negotiations. This approach can be translated into a mutually reinforcing strategy; as each country drops its emissions intensity in relation to the global average, others would be required to drop theirs. Those with emissions intensity above the world average would have to buy carbon credits from those with a better average. Failing to pull your weight in saving the global commons would therefore carry a price, which would inevitably mean higher taxes. Countries and their citizens would then have to choose which they prefer.

Adopting emissions intensity as the norm from which to work out an agreement for tackling climate change will address the question of equity, especially if the late developers are allowed a transition period before their total emissions peak and helped with technology and financing. But that will not be enough. There has to be a plan to reduce this intensity to sustainable levels as quickly as possible. This may mean that European countries may have to accept a much greater cut than a 40 percent reduction in emissions by 2030—which then would put pressure on others to lower their emissions intensity too. Outliers like the United States and China (who agreed to a bilateral deal that promised too little) will face the challenge of having to do more. Many supporting measures will have to be worked out—like carbon capture and storage, the imposition of carbon taxes, and a workable international trading system for carbon credits.

China raised the stakes in the run-up to negotiations in Paris in late 2015. Repeating its intention to reach peak emissions by 2030, it promised to reduce its emissions intensity per unit of GDP by 60–65 percent, with 2005 as the base year (when the country's emissions totaled 5.2 billion tons). China's GDP has trebled since 2005 in PPP terms and could double again by 2030. With GDP in 2030 at six times what it was in 2005, and with a 60–65 percent cut in emissions intensity, Chinese emissions in 2030 would be 20 percent more than in 2012. Commendable as that would be, it would still account for about a third of the safe global limit for emissions. So China would continue to account for the greatest amount of emissions, which in relation to the world total would also remain higher than China's likely share of world GDP. Hence, its emissions intensity would also remain out of line. Finally, Chinese emissions per capita would stay well above the current world average of about 5 tons, a level considered unsustainable. On all three metrics, therefore, even an ambitious emissions control program would not help China make the cut by 2030.

India, for its part, is comfortable on the per capita emissions front, which is the reason that Manmohan Singh as prime minister committed in 2007 to the goal that India's emissions per head would never exceed those of the rich countries. An expert group chaired by Kirit Parikh, appointed by the Planning Commission to outline a low-carbon growth strategy for the country, looked ahead to 2030 and said in its April 2014 report that India's emissions per head would climb from 1.4 tons per head in 2010 to 3.6 tons in a baseline growth strategy, or stop short at 2.6 tons if a low-carbon strategy were followed. Either way, the number would be lower than the global average of about 5 tons per head, and less than half the Chinese figure of 7.4 tons per head in 2013.

Still, following the mistaken clubbing of India and China, most countries expect India to do more—hence the importance of the government's commitment to reduce emissions intensity by 30–33 percent by 2030, with 2005 as the base year. This commitment falls midway between the two scenarios in the Parikh report. Parikh's assumption was that overall GDP growth would be at 7 percent per annum in the baseline case, and at 6.9 percent if a low-carbon growth strategy were adopted, even as the population grew by 24 percent. On the baseline track, Parikh said, emission intensity per unit of GDP would drop by 22 percent, and on the low-carbon track by 42 percent (with 2007 as base year). This means that, for India, the commitment given at Paris is not a stretch target but one that can be met. It also compares very well with the likely result of the Chinese goal of a 60–65 percent reduction, because India's starting point on emissions per unit of GDP is much lower than China's and will remain lower in 2030.[3]

Still, it is worth pointing out that the difference between Parikh's two scenarios works out to between 1.5 and 2 billion tons per head—close to the country's current emissions total. Given that humankind's carbon footprint is already larger than what is considered sustainable, it is vitally important to follow the low-carbon strategy, not as a favor to the world or as a gift to bigger emitters of carbon gases, but primarily because India would be more affected than most by climate change—with melting Himalayan glaciers that would affect river flows across the Gangetic plain, rising sea levels that would hit large coastal populations, and less predictable monsoon weather patterns. There is also the heavy price to be paid by the effect of air and water pollution on people's health and productive capacities.

However desirable it may be as an outcome, low-carbon growth will not come cheap. Parikh has estimated an additional investment of $834 billion in 2011 dollars (about half of India's GDP in that year) to keep emissions down while the economy grows in the two decades till 2030. Should it expect financial help from the rich countries? In earlier climate change negotiations, they had promised financial assistance to help poorer economies transition to low-carbon strategies, but only small sums have been put on the table. India may continue to wrestle with large-scale poverty, but its premature projection as an economic power means that for India to expect significant help, if indeed any help at all, is probably delusional.

A key question is when the late developers should be expected to reach peak emissions. China has settled unilaterally on 2030. India can hope for perhaps ten or at most fifteen years beyond 2030 before its total emissions are expected to start falling. In all such negotiations, the iron constraint on any Indian government is that nothing will be domestically acceptable that translates into a de facto cap on growing the country's per capita income, especially since this income even in 2030 is likely to be below the global average, in PPP dollars.

If India is to successfully negotiate a late year for peaking on total emissions, it is vital that the country deliver on the promise of cutting emissions intensity and demonstrate that it is following the low-carbon strategy that has been laid out. It earned points on the road to the Paris climate summit in December 2015 by taxing carbon fuels while also reducing subsidies on them and by upping its targets for producing clean energy—both solar and wind. Solar energy capacity had grown from a low base to 2.6 gigawatts in just three years, and the target for 2022 had been to multiply that eightfold to 20 gigawatts. The Modi government has taken up that target in a quantum leap, to 100 gigawatts, and for wind energy from next to nothing to 75 gigawatts. If achieved in substantial measure, these would be transformational. Preparatory action has been slow, but the tempo has been picking up, while solar power costs have been coming down to the point that they seem fully competitive with coal-based electricity, despite the sharp drop in international coal prices. Companies have bid to supply solar power at as little as Rs 4.30 per unit (about 6.3 cents). However, coal will remain the country's primary source of fuel for the foreseeable future.

Trade Talks

Through the different phases of its development, India's approach to international negotiations on trading rules has changed. The initial phase saw the country join with all poor and developing economies in the G-77, as it was called. The late 1980s saw the formation of the G-15, comprising the largest members of the G-77, who now saw their interests as being somewhat removed from the larger, more motley grouping. That did not go very far because little bound the G-15 together (think Algeria and Peru, Malaysia and Senegal, Sri Lanka and Chile). Attendance at summits was sub-optimal, the talk of south–south trade achieved little, and the group had little or no influence on issues such as reforming the International Monetary Fund. However, the idea that the larger developing economies could become a more potent group took root.

Following the Asian crisis of 1997, the G-8 club of rich countries recognized that issues flowing from the greater multi-polarity of the world economy would have to be discussed and new financial rules agreed on. Thus was born the G-20 grouping of major economies, which at one stage was heralded as having become more important than the G-8. However, while the new grouping was useful, especially in the immediate aftermath of the 2008 financial crisis, it has delivered only modest dividends in terms of setting global rules.

In recent years, alignments in international negotiating forums have become more tactical and therefore fluid. India might team up with China in climate change talks and be distanced from the interests of the least-developed countries. The rich countries would then pit the least developed against the emerging markets—as they have sought to do in talks on both trade and climate change. During the Doha Round, four of the BRICS countries (India, China, Brazil, and South Africa) came together to call for an end to protectionist policies and trade-distorting practices by the developed economies. This mushroomed into a G-20 negotiating bloc of emerging market economies (different from the G-20 group of major economies), to respond to US and EU positions on agricultural trade—the EU's common agricultural policy and the US's agri-subsidies having become contentious issues that were important causes of the Round's stalemate, if not outright failure.

The message from the new groupings of the larger emerging market economies was that the developed economies could no longer agree on new rules and then get the rest of the world to sign up. The emerging blocs now had sufficient weight to be able to say no—but not enough power to force the rich countries to concede real ground. Since the negotiating rules were that nothing was agreed until everything was agreed, a "no" was the same thing as a veto. Every negotiating forum began to see negotiations getting stalled; something had to give.

The move to break free from the logjam has come in the form of "coalitions of the willing" on the trade front—a proliferation of bilateral and regional free trade agreements. The most significant for India is the Trans-Pacific Partnership (TPP), negotiated successfully (but not yet entered-into-force) by a dozen economies that account for 40 percent of world GDP. The TPP proposes to extend the rules on trade to include what are called "WTO-plus," beyond-the-border issues like labor standards, pollution control norms, and public-sector reform where Western economies feel the emerging markets gain a cost advantage because of lax standards. Meanwhile, the Transatlantic Trade and Investment Partnership (TTIP) will take longer to negotiate. If that too is concluded in the next couple of years, countries that are unable to join either might feel the pressure of market exclusion.

Not being part of the TPP would put India at a disadvantage in having access to the North American market, as well as to that of Japan, although existing free trade arrangements provide limited access routes. The target country in the TPP exercise is mainly China, which is seen by the United States as having escaped lightly with the terms on which it joined the WTO. The TPP will set stiffer conditions. It is worth recalling that even Japan had hesitated before entering the TPP tent, but Beijing in recent months has indicated that it is up to the challenge of meeting any stipulated conditions for joining what will be an important new trading club.

In preparation for eventually signing up for TPP membership, China has started negotiating a bilateral investment treaty with the United States and started work on a Shanghai free-trade zone, the first on mainland China. This is to experiment with economic and social reform—including unrestricted Internet access, full capital account convertibility, and international labor and environmental standards. In addition, China has joined the negotiations for the Trade in Services Agreement (TISA), a US initiative that now includes fifty-one countries, including members of the European Union; they account for 70 percent of international services trade. The focus once again is on areas that India has been reluctant to open up—like banking. China sees participation in such forums as stepping-stones to TPP membership, even as the ruling faction in the Chinese Communist Party uses the trade policy agenda to push more domestic reform.[4]

India, less prepared to deal with such issues and therefore less able to adjust, might get caught out—though it might be argued that if Vietnam is comfortable being one of the countries negotiating the TPP, there is no reason the task of adjusting should be beyond India's capacity to deliver. In turn, Pakistan is taking part in the TISA negotiations. India, for its part, has shied away from negotiating a bilateral investment treaty with the United States, its free trade negotiations with the European Union have run aground, and its focus in recent months has been on reviewing existing free trade agreements in response to complaints from local producers about imported competition. India's many concerns about joining the TPP include what it might imply for competition law, policy preferences that favor the public sector, blocking of cross-border data flows for e-commerce, and harmonization of standards—among others. Yet commentators have noted that the TPP has gained critical mass, with the longer-term prospect of the TPP forming the basis for rewriting WTO trade rules.[5]

A less demanding forum, though falling short as an alternative to the TPP in Asia, would be the Regional Comprehensive Economic Partnership (RCEP) idea, proposed originally by the ten-member ASEAN, with six leading countries of the region joining in, including Japan, China, and India. RCEP is less ambitious than the TPP in what it seeks to do, but even here the word is that India is keenest on reducing the initiative to the minimum possible. Irrespective of the forum, when it comes to trade reform, India is a foot-dragger. It adopts an attitude that is the opposite of China's, which has used the conditions for entry into trade forums to drive domestic policy change—as it did when joining the WTO in 2001. India does the opposite; it uses the lack of reform at home as the reason for trying to limit the scope of international trade agreements. This is an approach that may have run its course in terms of utility, because the country's major trade partners are signing deals among themselves. Whether India likes it or not, it will have to start negotiating differently if it wants to join the world's most important trading clubs—or be left out in the cold. The phase when it could demand concessions and commitments without offering any in return is over. So is the era of special rights and privileges on grounds of poverty.

New Negotiating Era

The first phase of global negotiations was one in which the developed economies wrote the rules and made some minor concessions to the poor economies to keep them in the tent. The second phase, now coming to an end, has been marked by more assertive emerging market economies developing the power to block one-sided deals. The result in recent years has been that no deals have come to fruition. Now the world has entered a third phase, where coalitions of the willing strike deals and then invite others to join on terms that have already been set. This gives the naysayers less of a voice and makes domestic reform action more productive than grandstanding in negotiating forums. There will be less and less percentage in being an outlier.

A case in point is the climate change framework. The US–China agreement on emissions reduction—however minimal and easy the numbers, dates, and targets—put India in the spotlight. At the Paris meeting toward the end of 2015, it was the country's domestic agenda, including the clean energy program and the broader low-emission growth strategy, that provided crucial talking points in tough negotiations. The lesson to be taken home was that simply saying "no" would not work anymore: you had to deal.

That India was becoming more flexible became clear in the summer of 2015 when it withdrew its long-standing opposition to discussing the phasing out of hydrofluorocarbons (HFCs, used for air-conditioning and refrigeration) under the Montreal Protocol. The country's preference till then was to negotiate HFC phase-out within the framework of climate change talks. The difference is that developing countries like India get no special rights under the Montreal Protocol. This, therefore, was an example of India's indicating willingness to carry its share of the burden.

The overall message is clear: whatever the multilateral (or, for that matter, bilateral) forum, a country's negotiating strength depends primarily on the extent of domestic reform it has carried out. Defensive responses of the kind that India has been famous for, with reliance on pure negotiating skill, serve little purpose in the new scheme of things. Failure to reform at home merely weakens the country's hand abroad. China has learned that lesson well; India has just started doing so.

Looking Ahead

18

The Next Ten Years

EVERY COUNTRY THAT is on the ascendant feels the need for a "coming out" party. In the last half century, that need has been met most often by hosting the Olympic Games. Japan did it in 1964. South Korea followed in 1988 and China in 2008. The Olympic itch seems to come in the wake of economic growth that takes per capita income to the vicinity of $6,000—as was the case with Japan and China when they played host, and not far off the mark for Korea. It was true for the Soviet Union (which hosted the 1980 Games) as well. Only Mexico among the emerging markets was ahead of the curve; its per capita income at the time of the 1968 Games was barely $4,000.[1] Sometimes, the Olympics were not a stand-alone showpiece project. Japan timed the launch of its Shinkansen bullet trains for the Tokyo Olympics and China started its high-speed trains a year ahead of the Beijing Olympics.

India's per capita income, calculated on the same basis (see note 1), was $3,372 in 2009–10 and can be expected to get to the $6,000 mark before too long. The itch for showpiece projects like high-speed trains is already evident in India; one has been proposed, to link Mumbai and Ahmedabad. It is a fair bet that if the economy fares well over the next few years, whichever government is in office in 2019 will feel compelled to bid for the Olympic Games of 2028; by then some high-speed trains should be up and running. That will be presented as a statement of India's "arrival"—and serve also to bury memories of the scandal-scarred Commonwealth Games of 2010 in Delhi.

But long before any Olympics, a country on the ascendant should see a hundred flowers bloom—entrepreneurs flourish; audiences and markets grow for film and music, sports, art, and books; and the country attempt a more ambitious external outreach. The Jaipur Literary Festival began in 2006 and now attracts audiences from across the country and authors from around the world. At least a dozen other cities now hold annual literary festivals. The print runs for books are small by global standards, but their growth has been explosive. The popular storyteller Chetan Bhagat has reportedly sold 2 million copies of his latest novel, *Half Girlfriend*. Self-help books and romance novels have sustained sales in the hundreds of thousands, while non-fiction "bestsellers" are expected to sell not 10,000 copies as of old, but multiples of that number. India is now the third-largest market for books in English; by one estimate, 90,000 titles are published annually.

The art market is thinner but also buoyant, with sales by art galleries and auction houses reflecting growing interest and fetching much better prices than in the past. The highest price at a Mumbai art auction in the late 1980s was a record Rs 1 million for an M. F. Husain (about $65,000 at the time); against that, Christie's two auctions in Mumbai in 2013 and 2014 fetched $2.8 million for a Tyeb Mehta and $3.7 million for a V.S. Gaitonde, with combined sales of all works sold topping $27 million. The growth of professional sports is another marker. Indian cricket's governing board has become the game's financial powerhouse; domestic professional leagues exist now in hockey and football (soccer) as well as the homegrown *kabaddi*, once a strictly rural sport with no urban following. Private ownership of newly formed clubs and teams and the support of satellite television have made the difference. The inaugural year of the *kabaddi* league delivered a viewership of over 400 million, not too far behind that for the mega-sports event, the Indian Premier League (involving privately owned teams that play 20-over cricket).

Then there is the flowering of entrepreneurial talent—not just the emergence of e-commerce poster boys like Flipkart (touted as India's answer to Amazon), its rival Snapdeal, the mobile ad player InMobi (funded by SoftBank and others), and online furniture businesses like Urban Ladder (supported by Ratan Tata) and Pepperfry, but also scores of others. The rush of investor money into these and other firms has produced instant wealth for the founders, but with suggestions of a pricing bubble; the homegrown cell phone marketer Micromax promised extra-long battery backup and quickly became the second-largest vendor in a booming market. The company, dependent on imports from China and Taiwan, has started local assembly and exports to Russia. Business newspapers devote special pages to start-ups, and one has announced a set of annual awards in the category. Bengaluru's residents used to take pride in being a tech city; they now talk of its start-up culture—the city is said to attract 30 percent of the total angel investment in the country.

A confident indigenous ethos shows in films and popular music groups too—though the money outside of mainstream commercial cinema is still very limited. Citizen engagement reflects in the growth of civil society activism as large numbers of youngsters commit to careers in non-profit, public-interest activities. The millennial generation's attitudes are noticeably different and more freewheeling, compared to the safety-first approach of the country's post-colonial generation, with its focus on conventional careers and traditional family values. Nielsen's consumer confidence surveys (which track the mood with regard to jobs, spending intentions, and changing habits) consistently show that Indians with access to the Internet are the most optimistic in the world; except for the first quarter of 2009, the country has never ceased to be optimistic since the tracking began in 2005. The optimism rides high even when half the respondents think the economy is in a recession![2]

Still a "Work in Progress"

The problem with defining the emerging India by using these parameters, however indicative they may be of the direction of change, is that the country does not offer a neat narrative about bullet trains and the Olympics—not when large numbers of people travel by train in Bihar by squatting on the roofs of overcrowded coaches; and not when the average speed of a goods train has remained static at 25 kilometers per hour for decades. The fact is that you can still approach the India story from fifteen different angles and get multiples of that many different narratives.

Markets for consumer goods are expanding in breadth and depth, but half the country is still outside the pavilion in which consumers have voice and choice. Rural land prices in some states have gone through the roof, but in many parts of the country farming remains essentially unviable—with newspaper reports of farmer suicides almost routine. Agricultural growth rates have risen, but the yield per hectare of some crops is barely half of what it is in other countries.

India takes pride in its premier institutes of technology and management, which have been expanding even as they mentor new ones. Seventeen IITs now turn out 10,000 engineers every year. But one Technion in tiny Israel has 10,000 undergraduates, and is partnering Cornell to set up an applied science and engineering campus on Roosevelt Island in New York—something that no IIT could hope to do (if it wanted to, that is).[3] In any case, the IITs account for less than 1 percent of the total number of fresh engineering graduates in the country, and leading companies say that the majority of people emerging with engineering degrees and diplomas are in effect unemployable. Three-quarters of the 1,000 officially certified business schools would not pass muster in any proper certification process; their alumni can hope at best to find work as frontline sales staff. And lest one forget, the ground-level fact is that the average number of years of schooling in India was just 5.4 (for China it was 7.5), so claims of the country being an intellectual powerhouse are strictly for the home crowd.

India has taken belatedly to building a navy, with almost all new fighting ships now being built in domestic shipyards. But China builds a guided-missile destroyer in two years, less than a third of the time it takes for Mazagon Dock in Mumbai. India's 2013 law on land acquisitions stipulates processes that could require up to four years to release land for an infrastructure project. That's more than the two and a half years that it took China took to finish building its 1,318-kilometer Beijing–Shanghai high-speed railway line.

The defense could be that India is a democracy and that the state cannot ride roughshod over people; indeed, the country has been an early exemplar among poor countries for sustaining governance by consent. While democratic processes can be slow, to many citizens the state seems predatory enough, being a systematic violator of basic human rights. Torture is routinely used during police interrogation, and at least half of those in jail should never have been put there.

New Internet entrepreneurs grab the headlines, but old-style conglomerates still subvert the rule-making system; their mishandled projects in steel, power, and road-building have left the country's banks in a mess. India's share of world trade has been rising, but the country remains defensive in world trade talks (a reflection of internal weaknesses) and unprepared for the next round of rule changes through supra-regional trading arrangements. It is seen as an emerging power, but the grittiness of everyday Indian reality and the extent of open defecation cast a bad odor over any comforting narrative.

Joan Robinson, the British economist, is frequently quoted for her pithy comment "Whatever you can rightly say about India, the opposite is also true." So you can spin a hopeful narrative about the delayed blooming of India while someone else spins a depressing story about all the things that are still wrong. In almost every way that you can think of, India is very much a "work in progress."

Getting from Here to There

How does one direct such a complex, even contrary, country along the long road to Olympic heights? The truth is that there is no real probability of anyone trying to effect much of the change agenda spelled out in these pages. A basic, underappreciated problem remains the country's unwillingness to let market forces determine prices in competitive fashion. This is born out of the foreignness of the notion to the bulk of the political class (also to academics and intellectuals) that open, competitive markets are as much a public good as clean water and unpolluted air, and that regulated markets too should have rational pricing. The electricity distribution business is bankrupt because tariffs are too low; the result is that cash-starved distribution companies (discoms) can't buy power from generating companies, thereby disrupting supply to consumers. This is a supreme irony because for the first time in more than half a century, the country has the capacity to generate all the electricity it needs. The sugar industry has been rendered unviable by artificially pegged cane prices, so the government has raised the import duty from 18 percent to 40 percent to try to boost sugar prices and has borne the interest cost on loans given to clear farmers' dues. The high cane prices make the crop attractive to farmers who otherwise might have grown less-water-intensive crops, especially in stretches where water is not abundant. But one price distortion leads to another, and then another.

Next, there is a continuing reluctance to break the egg in order to make an omelette—as the *reformistas* used to phrase it in the 1990s till making the point became pointless. The labor market has to be made more flexible and not segregated into artificial categories by legal definitions, but the government in New Delhi does not want to upset organized labor and the trade unions. Government schools must provide better education, but the teachers in those schools (often absent or not teaching when present) cannot be held to account. There are public-sector companies whose revenues are less than half their costs, still the government will not think of either closing or selling them. A Food Corporation loader can be paid almost as much as a senior civil servant, but a committee report that calls for change is quickly buried. Close to half a century after the Swedish economist Gunnar Myrdal called India a "soft state,"[4] reformers still have to tread gingerly on not just eggshells but whole eggs. This is not because of any innate quality of "softness"—the Indian state is perfectly capable of being tough with Naga rebels, anti-nuclear activists, Kashmiri separatists, and Maoist insurgents. Softness creeps in only when existing power structures have to be challenged or when change requires having to tack away from the prevailing political wind.

The operative phrases therefore are "reform by stealth" and "opportunistic reform"; if you spot an opportunity to change something, use it. Sometimes the opportunity comes because the larger play of social and economic forces has created the space for it—as happened to some extent in 1991. What India does not have is reform flowing from political conviction, as when a political leader campaigns and creates the climate for change. The easy choice in an environment of minimalist change is to accept only relatively painless solutions—like the application of technology to deliver government services faster, better, and cheaper.

Arvind Subramanian, chief economic adviser in the finance ministry, may have a point when he argues that radical reform happens only when there is a sense of crisis. The reality in India is that there is no sense of crisis or of an urgent need for change, especially after the Central Statistics Office (CSO) upped economic growth rates by about 2 percentage points from what was being reported earlier.[5] GDP growth of more than 7 percent (the average after 2007–08) sounds like good going, especially when every other large economy is now growing more slowly. To compound matters, governments continue to believe in an inevitable reversion to the mean—that the economic growth rate will return to what prevailed before the financial crisis of 2008, forgetting that the world was different then. Such comforting assumptions militate against any push for radical reform.

If, despite the very partial reform that India has seen so far, the economy continues to notch up passable progress every year, it will be because of two factors. First, the country still invests about 30 percent of its GDP. If it can invest that money profitably and find ways to improve the productivity of investment in infrastructure, that should underpin annual economic growth no slower than what has been achieved in the last quarter century, that is, about 6.5 percent. Indeed, future growth should improve on that record because the investment-to-GDP ratio is significantly higher now than it was in the 1990s.

The second reason for expecting a creditable growth rate is that the constituency for reform is no longer politically irrelevant, being influential beyond its very limited numerical strength. That will not deliver radical reform, but incremental change is always in the cards. If one looks at elements of the immediate agenda, tax policy is likely to be rewritten with the introduction of the goods and services tax; defense manufacture, through localization, is likely to become a growth area; the progressive replacement of subsidies with cash payouts will deliver better bang for government buck; and the widespread application of technology in many sectors will improve speed, accuracy, and efficiency. In addition, the steady (if slow) improvement in literacy and education attainments will improve human productivity, and the expansion of the middle class will make for scale efficiencies in manufacturing. All of these will contribute to productivity gains and therefore to economic growth, as will the slow takeover by the private sector of those areas of economic activity that are still dominated by relatively unproductive government-owned companies.

However, while optimists like the finance minister, Arun Jaitley, talk of getting to double-digit growth, it is worth bearing in mind that no country has achieved this on a sustained basis without rapid export growth—which, in an uncertain world economic situation, is not likely to materialize, especially with the continuing deficiencies of India's physical infrastructure. But, as we said at the beginning, rapid economic growth of the East Asian kind is not essential to the story. India has both economic weight and creditable speed, the two combining to generate a momentum that only two other countries can match. Steady, incremental change is enough to sustain economic growth that over time achieves transformative results.

Three Mega Trends and a Question

Looking to the future, one can profitably emulate John Naisbitt and identify key "mega trends" for the coming decade. The first and most obvious is that markets will change in scale—something that has already happened in sectors like telecom, where India has more than 900 million connections, but will happen much more across the board. India has so far been a 25–30 percent economy: roughly that percentage of households belongs to the middle class, and about that number own a private vehicle and have active bank accounts. Also, just under 30 percent of the relevant age cohort acquires secondary education certification (after ten years of schooling) every year. The big change coming over the next decade is that the 30 percent figure could nearly double. That would be a seismic change for society and the economy, compressed into a short decade; bear in mind that the number of college-going students has already multiplied from 8 million to 20 million in less than a decade.

If the economy grows at an annual average of 7 percent over the next decade, the median family income for what should be a 1.4 billion-strong population would have grown from Rs 22,500 in 2015 to about Rs 40,000 in constant rupees—comfortably above the $10 PPP benchmark for qualifying to become part of a "global" middle class. The numerical growth of this class—from 340 million in 2015 to perhaps 700 million in 2025—combined with greater purchasing power for each one of those 700 million, and buttressed from below by a strong neo-middle-class cohort, means that the markets for all manner of goods and services will explode.

The car market, for instance, could become the world's third largest—ahead of Japan, today's number three, with twice India's current annual sales of

2.6 million. Housing construction, retailing, financial services—these foundational sectors of any modern economy will all witness dramatic growth. Many markets will grow at sustained rates of 10–12 percent, trebling in size over a decade—as indeed has happened in the past with, for example, the sale of trucks. Outbound tourist traffic in 2013 was 16.6 million, three times what it was a decade earlier. It is easy to imagine what will happen to the aviation business if the number trebles again in the next decade, to 50 million. This is not fanciful; Chinese outbound traffic is already more than 90 million. There is a reason why India's aviation market too is forecast to become the world's third largest. The important point is that if the economy does well, these will not be exceptional stories.

The Retreat of the State

The second mega trend will be the unwilling retreat of the state. Already, 43 percent of schoolchildren go to private schools.[6] That number is growing by 1.5 percentage points annually; by 2025, therefore, 60 percent of school-age children could be going to private schools. Beyond class eight, the majority of students are already in private schools. The same is true for post-school education in degree and diploma courses. This is unprecedented: no country has seen public education reduced to a smaller component than private education. That it has happened in India serves as a measure of the failure of the country's public programs. Such a switchover has already happened in medical care, with 60 percent of hospital beds now privately owned. In education, the factor driving the change has been perceived differences in the quality of education provided in public and private schools. In medical care, the issue is a plain shortage of public hospitals, so patients often don't have a choice when they need hospitalization.

These switchovers are mirrored in other service sectors like telecom and aviation, where new private providers have displaced erstwhile state-owned monopolies. The next important sector for such a consumer flip to the private sector could be banking. It is likely that private banks will grow faster than government-owned banks which are caught in a crisis because of accumulated bad loans, and currently account for 70 percent of banking activity. Future lending will be constrained by stressed balance sheets (even though the government has pumped in Rs 586 billion as additional capital in 2011–14 and intends to infuse a further Rs 700 billion over 2015–19). As more private bank licenses are issued and new kinds of banks (such as payment banks) are born, it is plausible that in a decade's time, the 70:30 public–private ratio might swing closer to 60:40, or, in an extreme scenario, to 50:50.

What remains as areas of public-sector dominance are mining, energy production, and defense. In the last of these, the private sector is about to make its first serious forays. As for mining, Rio Tinto, allowed to do diamond prospecting, is confident that it will produce multiples of the 84,000 carats of diamonds that the government-owned National Mineral Development Corporation (NMDC) extracts from the country's only operating diamond mine. The Bunder mine in Madhya Pradesh, which Rio Tinto hopes to develop, has just one of seven rock pipes in the area, with a reported promise of 27.4 million carats of diamonds.[7] In comparison, NMDC's entire cumulative output so far has been a million carats. Gold mining, shut down as being unviable for many years, could see a revival in the private sector.

In the electricity component of the energy sector, the private sector emerged as a significant player in both generation and distribution over the last decade. Coal is still a government monopoly, but inroads have been made as captive mining of coal by private companies had been allowed. It is not a big step from here to allowing private companies to compete with Coal India. Imported competition is already permitted, so why not domestic competition? In the emerging energy scenario, gas is likely to be a mainly private-sector business, as is solar and wind energy. Even in areas like urban water supply, private (including foreign) companies have made an initial entry into what has been an unsatisfactory government-provided service. If a significant difference in the quality of private water supply becomes established, the resistance to privatizing water might well give way, as in other areas.

In macroeconomic terms, the public sector accounts for a fifth of GDP, half from the government and the rest from state-owned enterprises. Over the years, the broad trend would continue to be for state-owned enterprises to shrink in size relative to private-sector providers. Think Air India, which has lost Rs 360 billion in seven years up to 2013–14, or Doordarshan, the state-funded television broadcaster which has lost out to private cable and satellite providers despite having a monopoly in terrestrial broadcasting. Ranked on viewership, Doordarshan's channels are in the bottom quartile—whether news, entertainment, or education.[8] The organization has more than 30,000 employees and an annual revenue of about Rs 10 billion, leaving additional costs of Rs 18.5 billion to be picked up by the taxpayer—most going toward employee cost.

While public-sector enterprises may shrink or lose market share, growing economies usually see an increase in the tax–GDP ratio; that means government budgets will grow in size relative to the economy. This should translate into expansion of government and public or constitutional institutions, because there is a clear need for more policemen, judges, and schoolteachers. Cash payouts ("direct benefit transfers") could conceivably account for an increasing chunk of government expenditure, as a proper social security system is born. Still, if a broad policy switch takes place, from "make" to "buy" (that is, governments no longer provide services like education and water supply but pay for such services from private providers), the growing private-sector dominance of productive economic activity will continue.

It is important to recognize these trends as being out of line with the political mood. The private sector occupies the "commanding heights" not because it is supported by ideological conviction in the political world but because the public sector has failed over the decades to meet consumer demand and expectations—whether for watches or scooters (at one stage, half a dozen state governments were busy assembling the latter). The political desire for control, and the power to intervene in everything from airline fares to private school fees, remains strong.

This desire for interventionist power (often exercised arbitrarily, as in the banning of Nestle's Maggi noodles, which the court overturned after finding it a violation of natural justice) coexists with a virtual abdication of responsibility. There is relative inaction on improving the quality of, and capacity for, regulatory oversight and proper certification in both education and health care as well as in sectors like mining and energy. Ensuring safety standards of food and drugs, and even water, is not a priority. If the state gets rolled back, it will simply be because people choose the private sector as their service provider and supplier. However, the state will need to play the role of regulator and quality certifier—as in, say, teacher education. The way to turn the situation to an advantage in terms of superior outcomes, therefore, would be to recognize that state capacity is limited, and that government ought to focus on doing better what it alone can or should do. Pressure on the state to perform key roles better (as with ensuring good air quality) will have to come from civil society activism.

Shifting Centers of Gravity

The third mega trend is the shift of the center of gravity from New Delhi to state capitals—and therefore the creation of distributed centers of gravity. This manifests itself in many ways, starting with the end to one-party dominance in Parliament (no party has had complete control of both houses of

Parliament since 1989) and the rise of strong state-level leaders in national parties (Modi was one, the late Y. S. Rajasekhara Reddy of the Congress Party another) or as leaders of their own parties.

Then there is financial power. State governments used to be debt-laden and constrained by large deficits and therefore unable to spend much program money till the restructuring of state finances in 2003 and the much greater share of tax funds that now goes to the states. Most states are now fiscally comfortable and have greater freedom to spend money as they wish because of the reduced role for discretionary transfers from the central government—a change facilitated by Modi's decision to abolish the Planning Commission, which used to prescribe policies for states to adopt.

Economic reform has contributed to the decentralization of political power. The abolition of industrial licensing and many other controls leaves little if any role for the central government in many investment decisions. As private-sector players take the lead role in more sectors of the economy, and in the provision of more services, the central government's role will shrink further.

Finally, the plain fact is that in most areas of action it is the state government that has to execute policy—whether in education or health care, soil monitoring or identifying the poor, providing land for infrastructure projects or attracting industrial investment. This is logical because democracy at the national level is a bit like politics from the rarefied height of 33,000 feet. The average Lok Sabha constituency has 1.6 million voters; it is next to impossible for an MP to have any real political (as different from an electoral) relationship with his or her voters—the numbers, costs, and distances are simply too daunting. Assembly constituencies, in contrast, have about 200,000 voters, so state election issues tend to deal more with ground-level issues. Many states are in fact the size of fairly large countries. Tamil Nadu (the eleventh-largest state) is the size of England and has a 30 percent larger population.

The extent of federalism provided in the Constitution may not have been evident in an era of strong national leaders like Indira Gandhi who commanded overwhelming parliamentary majorities, leaders who did not hesitate to dismiss chief ministers in blatant misuse of power. Today, such arbitrary action would be unthinkable, not least because it has been blocked by the Supreme Court. Especially in the last few years, when getting legislation through both houses of Parliament has proved difficult, it has become apparent that change is easier to introduce at the state level simply because chief ministers are more in control.

The combination of constitutional federalism, greater financial autonomy, and centrifugal political trends means that state economic growth rates and human development indicators, not to mention industrial investment, can vary depending on the quality of governance at the state level. Chief ministers who are seen by voters to be delivering are reelected often, in some cases repeatedly—which becomes an incentive for them to continue in the same vein. It is not for nothing that at least two BJP chief ministers declined invitations from Narendra Modi to join his cabinet in New Delhi, preferring to stay where they were as state bosses. One, from the tiny state of Goa, was later persuaded to take over as the nation's defense minister.

A logical corollary to this shift to greater federalism should be the empowerment of local government bodies, especially in urban areas where no city has a directly elected mayor. The steady growth of urbanization, the programs for urban renewal, "smart cities," and the like will all focus attention on empowering the third tier of government. The number of "urban agglomerations" with million-plus populations had reached fifty-three in 2011. Some Indian cities now have larger populations than states like Jammu and Kashmir and Uttarakhand. They also have bigger budgets and far more wealth. The absence of proper urban governments will therefore become increasingly untenable.

A Liberal Democracy

Finally, there is the question of whether the country's constitutional liberalism will gradually give way to a less-than-liberal democracy. The country has a long tradition of being trigger-happy when it comes to banning uncomfortable books and films, and more recently websites. Free expression, it has been generally accepted, should not cause religious offense (the reason for banning Salman Rushdie's *The Satanic Verses*). But, as Rushdie has argued, this can be the start of a slippery slope. There is the case, therefore, of a book on the Maratha warrior Shivaji (who fought the Mughals and is therefore a nationalist hero) being banned because a vigilante group protested and attacked a library in Pune. Publishers refrain from publishing specific books or sometimes even withdraw them from the market in response to protests. The painter M. F. Husain could not exhibit in India toward the end of his life because objections were raised to his portrayal of Hindu goddesses, leaving the country to live and eventually die in Dubai.

The state has moved against inconvenient civil society activists and whistleblowers exposing corruption, sought to restrict the protection given to the latter while attempting to whittle down the scope of the Right to Information Act (RTI), and made moves to reduce autonomy in academic institutes while filling leadership positions with candidates who have poor credentials but are ideologically faithful. Parties in opposition that argued for giving autonomy to a variety of institutions, including the state-funded broadcaster and the government's criminal investigation agency, give up those positions when they gain political power. The media are often constrained in the role of watchdog by the interests of their owners or by financial pressures.

Some of the points of conflict are the result of social churn that is linked to modernization. Traditional hierarchies, boundaries, and authority get challenged in a more freewheeling world where more women work, where youngsters mingle without concern for caste or community, and where old identities are fused into new ones that might seem deracinated. Countertrends do exist, such as an increase in overt religiosity and the disappearance of women behind the veil in parts of the country where this was not the practice earlier. The backlash is often led by subalterns who have not been swept up by the new processes, and takes the form of physical attacks on individuals (women in pubs or those celebrating Valentine's Day) as well as moves to reassert old patriarchies (by *khap panchayats* [male-dominated community organizations that have objected to inter-caste marriages] and through the "Ghar Wapasi" [homecoming] drive for religious conversions to Hinduism).

Individual rights are not always given effective protection by statutory institutions; the commissions that have been set up for protecting human rights and different kinds of minorities (women, Dalits, and religious minorities) are not the most effective. The courts are a more effective bulwark, but their process is extremely slow. The reassuring fact is that the spirit of the age is one of greater freedom, supported by new and liberating technologies. At the same time, one should not rule out the danger of complicit majorities operating to impose constraints on different minorities. As James Madison warned in the eighteenth century, "In our governments the real power lies in the majority of the community, and the invasion of private rights is chiefly to be apprehended, not from acts of government contrary to the sense of its constituents, but from acts in which the government is the mere instrument of the major number of the constituents."[9]

These different trends are manifestations of a society, polity, and economy caught in a process of evolution, with change at multiple speeds. When there are many forces driving change on a grand canvas, tensions and conflict are inevitable by-products. The reassuring facts in a broadly hopeful scenario are that the directions of change are overwhelmingly positive and that the system as a whole has a bedrock of stability that is not affected by the surface turmoil. That is why each generation of Indians has been able to say with confidence that the life of the next generation will get better for larger numbers—not at optimum but at what appears to be acceptable speed, and not wholly but very substantially.

Notes

CHAPTER 1

1. Angus Maddison, *The World Economy* (Academic Foundation, by arrangement with the Organisation for Economic Co-operation and Development—OECD; Indian two-in-one edition, 2007), tables B-18 and B-21. Numbers are in 1990 PPP $ (1990 constant international dollars using purchasing power parity rates).
2. International Monetary Fund, *World Economic Outlook*, January 2016.
3. Martin Wolf, "India's Elephant Charges on through the Crisis," *Financial Times*, 2 March 2010.
4. World Development Report 2009, hrrp://openknowledge.worldbank.org.
5. CO_2 emissions (metric tons per capita) for 2011, World Bank, http://data.worldbank.org/indicator/EN.ATM.CO2E.PC/.
6. *Trends in CO_2 Emissions: 2014 Report*, PBL Netherlands Environmental Assessment Agency, http://edgar.jrc.ec.europa.eu/.
7. Andrea Matles Savada and William Shaw (eds.), *South Korea: A Country Study* (Washington, DC: US Government Printing Office for the Library of Congress, 1990).
8. According to the 2011 Census of India, literacy was 74 percent. Human Resources Development Minister M. M. Pallam Raju set a target of 80 percent for 2015 (*Times of India*, 18 July 2013).
9. Organisation Internationale des Constructeurs d'Automobiles, quoted in *LiveMint*, 23 June 2015.
10. The 2011 Census; the figure in the 2001 Census was 2.5 percent of households.
11. Foreign Agricultural Service, US Department of Agriculture.
12. For 1951–61, 41.3 years; 1986–91, 58.6. Source: Ministry of Health and Family Welfare (www.infochangeindia.org).
13. *Economic Survey, 2014–15*, Ministry of Finance, Government of India.
14. Maddison, *The World Economy*, tables 5c and 6c.

15. Three countries with lower per capita incomes in 1979 now have higher incomes than India: Laos, Bhutan, and Vietnam. A larger number of countries listed with higher incomes in 1979 have since dropped below India in the rankings.
16. Conforming broadly to Michal Kalecki's intermediate classes and regimes. *Collected Works of Michal Kaleki*, Volume V (Oxford: Clarendon Press).
17. *The Growth Report: Strategies for Sustained Growth and Inclusive Development* (Washington DC: World Bank, 2008), https://openknowledge.worldbank.org/handle/10986/6507.
18. Calculated using World Bank data for 1988 and 2013, http://data.worldbank.org.

CHAPTER 2

1. International Monetary Fund, World Economic Outlook database, http://www.imf.org/external/pubs/ft/weo/2015/01/.
2. In PPP terms, too, India's per capita income in 2014 was the lowest among the forty large economies, at less than half the world average; its country ranking in PPP terms was 125th, against 142nd when using nominal dollars.
3. Propounded in the 1950s by Alexander Gerschenkron.
4. Convergence (or catch-up) is also helped by the fact that diminishing returns on capital investment have not set in.
5. Thorstein Veblen, *Imperial Germany and the Industrial Revolution* (New York: Macmillan, 1915).
6. The Indian diaspora—6 million in West Asia, 3.2 million in the United States, 1.5 million in Britain, 1.2 million in Canada, and 25 million in all—has had a separate, independent influence on host countries.
7. International Air Transport Association, IATA air passenger forecast, 26 November 2015,, http://www.iata.org/pressroom.
8. John Sarkar, "India Will Be 3rd Biggest Market for Pernod Ricard," *Times of India*, 16 June 2015.
9. Bombay Stock Exchange (BSE) data, http://bseindia.com.
10. *Business Standard*, 15 March 2014.
11. India follows an April–March financial year.
12. Figures from *Economic Survey, 2014–15*, Ministry of Finance, Government of India.
13. *Doing Business 2015*, World Bank. As it happens, the numbers for the developed OECD countries are not very different, http://www.doingbusiness.org.
14. *Doing Business 2015*, World Bank: China $823, Mumbai $1,120, Delhi $1,520 (these numbers exclude shipping costs).
15. *Doing Business 2015*, World Bank.
16. Car manufacturing companies' annual reports, and author's conversations with car manufacturers.
17. World Bank figures, for Malaysia 5.9 percent (2011) and for Thailand 7.6 percent (2012).

18. Human Development Report, United Nations Development Programme. Numbers for 2013: India 4.4 years, Pakistan 4.7, Bangladesh 5.1. The average number of schooling years for "medium human development" countries like India is 5.5 years.
19. By Pratham, a non-government agency.
20. Figures for 2010 from World Development Report, 2013.
21. *Agricultural Statistics at a Glance 2014*, Ministry of Agriculture, Government of India.
22. Because of large year-to-year fluctuations in output, the choice of period makes a noticeable difference to growth rates. For some periods, the growth rate is close to 10 percent.
23. Its share in all-India foodgrain procurement rose from less than 1 percent to more than 13 percent in the decade to 2013–14.
24. Occupational Wages around the World Database 1983–2008 (using ILO October Inquiry data).
25. wageindicator.org.
26. Prasanta Sahu and Siddhartha P. Saikia, "DBTL Weeds Out 3 Crore Bogus LPG Connections," *Financial Express*, 27 April 2015.
27. Performance Evaluation of Targeted Public Distribution System, Planning Commission, Government of India, March 2005.

CHAPTER 3

1. These figures are from Angus Maddison, *The World Economy* (Academic Foundation, by arrangement with OECD; New Delhi, Indian two-in-one edition, 2007), using 1990 US$.
2. Dominic Wilson and Roopa Purushothaman, "Dreaming with BRICS: The Path to 2050," Goldman Sachs Global Economics Paper No. 99, 1 October 2003.
3. All figures from the World Bank.
4. *The Globalist*, 23 November 2012.
5. Growth of Electricity Sector in India from 1947 to 2015, Central Electricity Authority.
6. USITC Executive Briefing on Trade, August 2012.
7. World Aluminium Institute (world-aluminium.org).
8. Peter Foster, "China to Get New Skyscraper Every Five Days for Three Years," *Telegraph*, 8 June 2011.
9. All figures from *Trade Profiles 2014*, World Trade Organization.
10. Mentioned in *China and India 2025: A Comparative Assessment* (Santa Monica, CA: RAND Corporation, 2010).
11. World Trade Organization numbers for 2013: $313 billion for India, $305 billion for Taiwan.

CHAPTER 4

1. Peter Lindner and Sung Eun Jung, "Corporate Vulnerabilities in India and Banks' Loan Performance," IMF Working Paper WP/14/232, December 2014.
2. Manufacturing index for 2014–15, 186; for 2010–11, 175.7. These are data from the old-time series, not new data which is available only for 2014–15, a component of Index of Industrial Production, http://mospi.nic.in.
3. R. Sreeram, "Companies' Efficiency in Using Assets at Multi-Year Low," *Mint*, 6 March 2015.
4. Reliance's refining margin for the March 2015 quarter was $10.1 per barrel of crude, compared to the benchmark Singapore gross refining margin for complex refineries of $8.5: from Kalpana Pathak and Ujjval Jauhari, "Refining Business Helps RIL Post Highest Quarterly Profit in 7 Years," *Business Standard*, 18 April 2015.
5. NASSCOM (National Association of Software and Services Companies), a lobby group for India's software industry; http://www.nasscom.in.
6. From newspaper reports and http://Mahindra.com.
7. National Stock Exchange, http://www.nseindia.in.
8. Tataadvancedsystems.com.
9. The oldest and perhaps most widely recognized international quality award, established in Japan in honor of W. Edwards Deming, who had helped Japanese industry establish statistical quality control methods after the Second World War.
10. Joseph Schumpeter, *Capitalism, Socialism and Democracy* (London: Routledge, 1942).
11. A derisive term coined by the free-market politician C. Rajagopalachari to describe Nehru's system of industrial policy controls; the term was a play on "British raj," or rule, used as shorthand for British rule in India.
12. The total in the years 2006–12 was $96 billion: *Economic Survey, 2012–13*, Ministry of Finance, Government of India.
13. UK Trade and Industry, Inward Investment Report 2014–15; India was third in terms of number of projects and also impact on jobs.
14. "Bharti Completes Acquisition of Zain's Africa Biz for $10.7 bn," *Times of India*, 8 June 2010.
15. From newspaper reports, company websites, and author's conversations with group chairman Shashi Ruia.
16. Luke Patey, *The New Kings of Crude: China, India, and the Global Struggle for Oil in Sudan and South Sudan* (London: C. Hurst, 2014).
17. P. C. Parakh, *Crusader or Conspirator? Coalgate and Other Truths* (Delhi: Manas Publications, 2014).
18. Raghuram Rajan, "Why India Slowed," *LiveMint*, 30 April 2013.

CHAPTER 5

1. "The amount involved is Rs 40,000 crore (1 crore = 10 million). I can change the face of India's irrigation with that Rs 40,000 crore."—quoted in "Govt to Press Ahead with Rs 40,000 cr Tax Demand on FIIs: Jaitley," *Hindu Business Line*, 14 April 2015.
2. Editorial in *Business Standard*, 27 April 2015.
3. Companies are allowed to make political contributions, and some report check payments. But political parties prefer cash because they feel the need to circumvent Election Commission rules that cap expenditure on elections.
4. James Crabtree, "India's Billionaires Club," *Financial Times*, 16 November 2012.
5. "CIL to Reduce Selling Coal through e-Auctions by Almost Half," *Economic Times*, 3 September 2014.
6. "Apocalypse Now," research note for Macquarie Research by Suresh Ganapathy and Sameer Bhise, January 2016.
7. http://research.religarecm.com/INDIA/India%20Banks%20-%20Sector%20Report%204Jan16.pdf.
8. "Pipavav Debt Is Recast Days before Deadline," *Financial Express*, 27 March 2015.
9. "PM Narendra Modi Seeks End to Lazy Banking," *Economic Times*, 3 January 2015.
10. Manojit Saha, "Public Sector Banks in a Fix over Selective Capital Infusion," *Business Standard*, 13 February 2015.
11. Francis Fukuyama, *Trust: the Social Virtues and the Creation of Prosperity* (New York: Free Press, 1995).
12. "Government to Discuss National Optical Fibre Network with States," *Times of India*, 24 May 2015.
13. Daron Acemoglu and James A. Robinson, *Why Nations Fail: The Origins of Power, Prosperity, and Poverty* (New York: Crown, 2012).
14. William J. Baumol, Robert E. Litan, and Carl J. Schramm, *Good Capitalism, Bad Capitalism and the Economics of Growth and Prosperity* (New Haven, CT: Yale University Press, 2007).
15. Raghuram Rajan and Luigi Zingales, *Saving Capitalism from the Capitalists* (New York: Crown Business, 2003).

CHAPTER 6

1. These ratios are based on the new set of GDP numbers for 2014–15; see "Indian GDP Growth Expands by a High 7.5 Percent in Q4FY15 . . .," Information and Credit Rating Agency paper, May 2015, table 5, p. 9.
2. Countries with 16–18 percent of GDP from manufacturing include Bangladesh and Vietnam, Sri Lanka and Turkey, Egypt and Cambodia. Those at 15 percent or less include Russia, Brazil, Pakistan, and South Africa.
3. World Bank database, http://data.worldbank.org.

4. The ratio of non-agricultural to agricultural income per head in manufacturing-oriented China is not very different from India's, at more than 4:1.
5. Directorate General of Employment and Training, Ministry of Labour, Government of India.
6. For an amusing yet dispiriting account of these clearances, read Mihir Sharma's *Restart: The Last Chance for the Indian Economy* (Gurgaon: Random House India, 2015).
7. Jagdish Bhagwati and Arvind Panagariya, *Why Growth Matters: How Economic Growth in India Reduced Poverty and the Lessons for Other Developing Countries* (New York: Public Affairs, 2013).
8. Gurcharan Das, *India Grows at Night* (New Delhi: Penguin/Viking, 2012).

CHAPTER 7

1. Refined petroleum goods are now the largest export item, but the value addition to the cost of imported crude is quite small, as a result of which net export earnings are less than for textiles.
2. Apparel Export Promotion Council and Christopher Ruvo in Wearables-digital.com, June 2013—both cite WTO data.
3. Author's conversation with industry sources.
4. "Bangladesh's Ready-Made Garments Landscape: The Challenge of Growth," McKinsey report, November 2011; an updated version is at http://www.mckinsey.com/industries/consumer-packaged-goods/our-insights/bangladesh-the-next-hot-spot-in-apparel-sourcing.
5. Author's conversation with industry sources.
6. Union Budget of India, 2015–16, available at http://indiabudget.nic.in/budget.asp.
7. The Mahatma Gandhi National Rural Employment Guarantee Act (MGNREGA) created 2,108 million days of work in 2012–13; the figure is expected to have dropped in subsequent years. Assuming that a person would work for 260 days in a year (person-year), the 2012–13 figure translates into 8.1 million person-years of work; if 300 days of work make a person-year, it would mean 7 million person-years.
8. Data from Technopak.com. In six years up to 2013–14, total foreign direct investment was $184 billion.
9. Author's discussions with company officials, and company annual report on car output and employee strength.
10. Society of Indian Automobile Manufacturers, http://www.siamindia.com.
11. The hourly wage rate in India in a car factory is Rs 180; in the United States, it is a minimum of $30, or Rs 1,920. The saving on work per hour is Rs 1,740; the man-hours going into a car are 30. Thus, the saving per car is Rs 1,740 × 30 = Rs 52,200.
12. Auto Component Manufacturers Association of India, http://www.acma.in.
13. Author's discussions with company officials during plant visit.

14. "Taxman Claims Rs 21K cr from Nokia," *Times of India*, 10 December 2013.
15. "Planning Rs 3 lakh cr of Road Projects in 6 Months: Gadkari," *Business Standard*, 19 May 2015.
16. See Chapter 5.
17. Author's conversation with company officials.
18. "Aricent Buys Chip Design Co SmartPlay for Rs 1,100 cr," *Times of India*, 11 August 2015.

CHAPTER 8

1. Adrian Levy and Cathy Scott-Clark, *The Siege: The Attack on the Taj* (New Delhi: Penguin Books India, 2013).
2. Karl Marx, "The Eighteenth Brumaire of Louis Bonaparte," in Robert C. Tucker (ed.), *The Marx–Engels Reader*, 2nd ed. (New York: W.W. Norton, 1978), p. 594.
3. Press Note by Election Commission, March 2014, which organizes state and national elections in the country.
4. The Mars Orbiter Mission cost Rs 450 crore, or about $75 million; *Gravity* had a production budget of $100 million.
5. Kumbhmelaallahabad.gov.in.
6. The project was launched in 1973, after the first tiger census in 1972 reported a tiger population of no more than 1,800, less than 10 percent of what it had been at the turn of the century. A 2015 census by the ministry of environment and forests reported the existence of 2,226 tigers.
7. *Statistical Year Book 2014*, Central Statistical Office, Ministry of Statistics and Programme Implementation, Government of India.
8. "A Third-Rate Police Force Cannot Be a First-Rate Anti-Terror Force," *New Indian Express*, 17 March 2013.
9. Statement of 1 June 2015, Department of Justice, Ministry of Law and Justice, Government of India.
10. "Govt. SOS to HCs to Fill Vacancies in Lower Courts," *Times of India*, 12 November 2014.
11. President Pranab Mukherjee in an address to Advocates' Association of Western India, 9 February 2014.
12. *Manpower Planning in Judiciary: A Blueprint*, 120th Report, Law Commission of India, Ministry of Law and Justice, 31 July 1987.
13. Prison Statistics 2013, National Crime Records Bureau, Ministry of Home Affairs, Government of India.
14. Specified under the law on Right to Education.
15. Smriti Irani, Minister for Human Resource Development, in an answer to the question in Rajya Sabha (upper house of India's parliament), 4 August 2014.
16. "Nine in 10 Flunk CBSE's Test for Elementary Teachers," *Tribune*, 3 April 2015.

17. Lant Pritchett, "Is India a Flailing State? Detours on the Four Lane Highway to Modernization," HKS Faculty Research Working Paper Series RWP09-013, John F. Kennedy School of Government, Harvard University, available online at the Digital Access to Scholarship at Harvard website, dash.harvard.edu/handle/1/4449106.
18. "Battling India's Malaise of Corruption," address to the India CEO Forum, available online at the Central Vigilance Commission website, www.cvc.nic.in/CEO.pdf.
19. "Full Text of Modi's Speech at Aero India 2015," *The Hindu*, 18 February 2015.
20. These and the following numbers are from *Millennium Development Goals: India Country Report 2015*, Social Statistics Division, Ministry of Statistics and Programme Implementation, Government of India, released in February 2015.
21. Gross enrollment would be higher because it includes students who are older or younger than the typical age enrolled at that level.
22. For sobering comparisons with Bangladesh and other countries on key socioeconomic parameters, read *An Uncertain Glory: India and Its Contradictions* by Jean Drèze and Amartya Sen (London: Penguin/Allen Lane, 2013).
23. Abhijit V. Banerjee and Esther Duflo, *Poor Economics: A Radical Rethinking of the Way to Fight Global Poverty* (Noida: Random House India, 2011).
24. Ayushi Gudwani, Palash Mitra, et al., *Indian Healthcare: Inspiring Possibilities, Challenging Journey* (McKinsey & Company, December 2012), prepared for the Confederation of Indian Industry.
25. The United States and the United Kingdom have about three beds per 1,000 people.
26. *World Health Statistics, 2009*, World Health Organization.
27. The Central Bureau of Health Intelligence lists the country as having 0.92 million allopathic doctors and 1.56 million nurses and midwives, for a total of 2.48 million, or about two health professionals per 1,000 people. In addition, there are 0.69 million doctors practicing other systems of medicine, most of them in Ayurveda and homoeopathy.
28. Gudwani, Mitra, et al., *Indian Healthcare*.
29. Central Square Foundation, http://www.centralsquarefoundation.org.
30. "Scheme for Setting Up of 6,000 Model Schools at Block Level as Benchmark of Excellence," Ministry of Human Resource Development, Government of India.
31. About 1,100 Kendriya Vidyalayas (the name means "central schools") have 1.15 million students. They have an annual budget of about Rs 3,000 crore—or Rs 26,000 per student per year. Most regular (state) government schools are run on much smaller budgets, but the numbers vary widely. The Accountability Initiative (part of the New Delhi–based think tank Centre for Policy Research, works towards improving government accountability, http://accountabilityindia.org) in its paper "How Much Does India Spend on Elementary Education?" has calculated that the figure is usually in the range of Rs 8,000–12,000 per student, but it can be as little

as Rs 4,000 and as much as Rs 20,000. The reputed private schools cost very much more, but small private schools cost a parent as little as Rs 4,000 per child.

32. Figures from Manish Sabharwal, CEO of TeamLease (a leading recruitment and staffing company, http://www.teamlease.com).

CHAPTER 9

1. See details in Chapter 5.
2. Jeffrey Witsoe, *Democracy against Development: Lower-Caste Politics and Politics and Political Modernity in Postcolonial India* (Chicago: University of Chicago Press, 2013), pp. 63–66.
3. David Osborne and Ted Gaebler, *Reinventing Government: How the Entrepreneurial Spirit Is Transforming the Public Sector* (Boston: Addison Wesley, 1992).
4. It is a different matter that, as John Micklethwait and Adrian Wooldridge have shown in *The Fourth Revolution: The Global Race to Reinvent the State* (London: Penguin/Allen Lane, 2014), governments in both countries and in every rich country have continued to bloat. They aver that George W. Bush expanded the US government more than any president since Lyndon Johnson.
5. In the Indian context, the Kendriya Vidyalaya Sangathan (Central Schools Organization) would be an example of such outsourcing to an autonomous body, and one that has worked reasonably well; but there are no performance incentives.
6. Replacing a subsidy on cooking gas cylinders with cash payments unearthed millions of bogus domestic gas connections and, it has been claimed, saved the government thousands of crores of rupees.
7. Payment banks facilitate payments and remittances and are designed to spread banking inclusion. They cannot give loans. There is a Rs 1 lakh cap on deposits, and funds have to be invested in government securities.
8. Daron Acemoglu and James A. Robinson, *Why Nations Fail: The Origins of Power, Prosperity, and Poverty* (New York: Crown, 2012).
9. Sanjoy Chakravorty, *The Price of Land: Acquisition, Conflict, Consequence* (New Delhi: Oxford University Press, 2013).
10. Mancur Olson, *The Logic of Collective Action: Public Goods and the Theory of Groups* (Cambridge, MA: Harvard University Press, 1965).

CHAPTER 10

1. Andimuthu Raja of the DMK and Suresh Kalmadi of the Congress.
2. Lalu Prasad of Bihar, Madhu Koda of Jharkhand, Om Prakash Chautala of Haryana, and B. S. Yeddyurappa of Karnataka.
3. Mulayam Singh Yadav and Mayawati of UP.
4. Tamil Nadu's J. Jayalalithaa.

5. Dayanidhi Maran, Subodh Kant Sahay, Pawan Bansal, and Ashwani Kumar.
6. This account of the entire episode draws substantially from Bhupesh Bhandari's *Spectrum Grab: Inside Story of the 2G Scam* (New Dehli: Business Standard Books, 2012).
7. Laveesh Bhandari and Bibek Debroy, *Corruption in India: The DNA and the RNA* (New Delhi: Konark, 2012).
8. K. N. Wanchoo, *Direct Taxes Enquiry Committee: Final Report*, published by the Ministry of Finance, 1972.
9. *Aspects of the Black Economy in India* (1985); Shankar Acharya and Others; National Institute of Public Finance and Policy.
10. *White Paper on Black Money*, Ministry of Finance, Government of India, May 2012.
11. Dev Kar and Joseph Spanjers, *Illicit Financial Flows from Developing Countries: 2003–2012* (updated report) (Washington, DC: Global Financial Integrity, 16 December 2014).
12. "Indian Money in Swiss Banks Falls by 10.6 Percent: SNB," *Hindu Business Line*, 18 June 2015.
13. "India Will Soon Drag HSBC Geneva to Court," Rediff.com, 16 February 2015.
14. Hamish Boland-Rudder, "HSBC Pays Swiss Authorities Record-Breaking Fine," The International Consortium of Investigative Journalists, ICIJ.org, 4 June 2015.
15. National Securities Depository Ltd website, www.nsdl.co.in.
16. C. Unnikrishnan, "DRI Slaps Rs 2,601 Crore Notice on Essar for Overvaluing Imports," *Times of India*, 2 April 2015.
17. ADR press release, 18 August 2015, http://adrindia.org/content/57-total-income-5-national-parties-during-fy-2013-14-was-sale-coupons-donations-formed-22.
18. Raghuram Rajan, "Why India Slowed," *Mint*, 30 April 2013.
19. *2012 Minerals Yearbook*, US Geological Survey.
20. Telenor's investment in its India business was $3 billion when its joint venture's telecom licenses were canceled. "Telenor's Investment Failure Will Have Political Implications: Norway," *The Hindu*, 12 May 2012; "Etisalat Writes Off $820 Mn against India Operations," *Business Standard*, 9 February 2012; Sistema to Scale Down Its India Exposure," *Business Standard*, 28 November 2012.
21. Ramesh passed on "credit" for the economic slowdown to the "*bhumihar* from Ghazipur," a reference to Vinod Rai, who as the Comptroller and Auditor General highlighted the scams in telecom and coal mine allotment—from Aditi Phadnis, "Lunch with *BS*: Jairam Ramesh," *Business Standard*, 20 September 2013.
22. "Behind Realty Rush in Haryana, a Gilt-Edged Licence Raj," *The Hindu*, 4 February 2013.
23. Quoted in Robert Klitgaard, *Controlling Corruption* (Berkeley: University of California Press, 1988).
24. ADR data on 1,370 reelected MLAs and 200 reelected MPs showed that the average income and assets of India's 100 richest legislators grew by 745 percent

between consecutive elections. Individual legislators saw their assets grow up to twenty-fivefold.

25. Katherine Boo, *Behind the Beautiful Forevers: Life, Death, and Hope in a Mumbai Undercity* (New York: Random House, 2012).
26. Kisangani N. F. Emizet, "Congo (Zaire): Corruption, Disintegration, and State Failure," in E. Wayne Nafziger et al. (eds.), *War, Hunger, and Displacement: The Origins of Humanitarian Emergencies,* Volume 2: *Case Studies* (New York: Oxford University Press, 2000), pp. 261–294.
27. Andrew Wedeman, *Double Paradox: Rapid Growth and Rising Corruption in China* (Ithaca, NY: Cornell University Press, 2002).
28. David Pilling, "Lunch with the *FT*: Jagdish Bhagwati," *Financial Times*, 17 April 2014.
29. Jayant Sinha and Ashutosh Varshney, "It Is Time for India to Rein In Its Robber Barons," *Financial Times*, 6 January 2011.
30. Jürgen Habermas, *The Structural Transformation of the Public Sphere: An Inquiry into a Category of Bourgeois Society*, trans. Thomas Burger (Cambridge, MA: MIT Press, 1989).
31. Perhaps it is in the nature of such phenomena that disillusionment also set in quite quickly.
32. Vivek H. Dehejia, "After the Robber Barons," *New York Times*, 13 April 2011.
33. Abhijit V. Banerjee and Esther Duflo, *Poor Economics: A Radical Rethinking of the Way to Fight Global Poverty* (Noida: Random House India, 2011).
34. S. Y. Quraishi, *An Undocumented Wonder: The Making of the Great Indian Election* (New Delhi: Rupa Publications, 2014).
35. For an extensive account, read Paranjoy Guha Thakurta, *Gas Wars: Crony Capitalism and the Ambanis* (Self-published, 2014).
36. For Rai's account of his period in office, read *Not Just an Accountant: The Diary of the Nation's Conscience Keeper* (New Delhi: Rupa Publications, 2014).
37. The more it changes, the more it's the same thing.

CHAPTER 11

1. Jean Drèze and Reetika Khera, "PDS Leakages: The Plot Thickens," *The Hindu*, 12 August 2011.
2. Reuters report, 25 October 2012.
3. Based on the Lakdawala method of poverty assessment. The subsequent Tendulkar methodology delivered an estimate of 407 million poor in 2004–05, falling to 269.8 million in 2011–12. The later Rangarajan committee estimate for 2011–12 was 363 million. Refer to "Press Note on Poverty Estimates" (2013), and *Report of the Expert Group to Review the Methodology for Measurement of Poverty* (2014), both issued by the Planning Commission, Government of India.

4. "Report of the Expert Group to Review the Methodology for Estimation of Poverty," Planning Commission, Government of India, November 2009.
5. "Report of the Expert Group to Review the Methodology for Measurement of Poverty," Planning Commission, Government of India, June 2014.
6. Prasanta Sahu and Siddhartha P. Saikia, "DBTL Weeds Out 3 Crore Bogus LPG Connections," *Financial Express*, 27 April 2015.
7. TERI University, *Fossil-Fuel Subsidy Reform in India: Cash Transfers for PDS, Kerosene and Domestic LPG*, Research Report, International Institute for Sustainable Development, August 2012, http://www.iisd.org.
8. These estimates have been made by Pranab Bardhan, Himanshu of the Centre for Economic Studies and Planning at Jawaharlal Nehru University, and others.
9. "Recommendations of High Level Committee on Restructuring of FCI," Press Information Bureau, Ministry of Consumer Affairs, Food & Public Distribution, Government of India, 22 January 2015.
10. In all, about 142,000 loaders were used by the FCI in 2014, of which 16,000 were staff loaders. According to the Shanta Kumar Committee, 100,000 contract loaders received Rs 10,000 per month, while 26,000 workers under a "direct payment system" received Rs 26,000.
11. *Economic Survey, 2014–15*, Ministry of Finance, Government of India.
12. Utsa Patnaik, "The Republic of Hunger," Public Lecture, Safdar Hashmi Memorial Trust, New Delhi, 10 April 2004.
13. Angus Deaton and Jean Drèze, "Nutrition in India: Facts and Interpretations," Working Paper 70, Centre for Development Economics, Delhi School of Economics, August 2008, https://ideas.repec.org/p/cde/cdewps/170.html.
14. Angus Deaton, *The Great Escape: Health, Wealth and the Origins of Inequality* (Princeton, NJ: Princeton University Press, 2013).
15. Ashutosh Bhardwaj, "Fake Ration Cards Pile Up in 'Model' PDS State," *The Indian Express*, 1 August 2014.
16. 20.9 percent according to Tendulkar, 21.9 percent according to Rangarajan.
17. Sathish G.T., "Cap on Eligibility for BPL Cards," *The Hindu*, 4 October 2013.
18. Ministry of Rural Development, Government of India, *MGNREGA Sameeksha: An Anthology of Research Studies on the Mahatma Gandhi National Rural Employment Guarantee Act, 2005: 2006–2012* (New Delhi: Orient BlackSwan, 2012).
19. "Poverty in Latin America: New Thinking about an Old Problem," *The Economist*, 15 September 2005.
20. Figures from Celia Lessa Kerstenetzky, "Development and Redistribution: The Case of the Bolsa Familia Program in Brazil," Universidade Federal Fluminense (Federal Fluminense University), June 2008, ISSN 1519–4612.
21. *Key Indicators of Household Consumer Expenditure in India: 2011–12*, National Sample Survey Office, Ministry of Statistics and Implementation, Government of India, 2014.
22. Adjusted for inflation, the monthly income support payout to a family in 2015 would be about Rs 3,200 in rural areas and Rs 4,400 in urban areas. The total

bill would be 2.4 percent of GDP or less. As a reality check on how far the money would go, 35 kilograms of rice for a five-member family would cost about Rs 750; 50 percent subsidy on a cylinder of gas is equivalent to Rs 600; and 50 percent subsidy on 200 units of electricity per month in Delhi would come to Rs 400. The payout to an urban household would leave a residual cushion for subsidizing the cost of buying cooking oil and sugar, thus covering the major household consumption items on which subsidies have been offered at various times.

23. Lewis Carroll, *Through the Looking-Glass, and What Alice Found There* (first published 1871).
24. Pranab Bardhan, "Challenges for a Minimum Social Democracy in India," *Economic and Political Weekly*, 46, no. 10, 5 March 2011.

CHAPTER 12

1. *Global Wealth 2013: Maintaining Momentum in a Complex World* (New York: Boston Consulting Group, 30 May 2013). The report's focus was on assets under management.
2. *Agriculture Census*, 1980–81 and 2010–11, Department of Agriculture and Cooperation, Ministry of Agriculture and Farmers' Welfare, Government of India.
3. These and following figures from *Census of India, 2011*, Ministry of Home Affairs, Government of India.
4. *Fourth Annual Employment and Unemployment Survey, 2013–14*, Labour Bureau, Ministry of Labour and Employment, Government of India.
5. Poverty was defined for this last year, using the Tendulkar Committee methodology, as the monthly consumption level for a five-member household being below Rs 4,080 in rural areas and Rs 5,000 in urban areas. These estimates were superseded by new estimates prepared by the Rangarajan Committee, which, on the basis of higher income cutoffs, put the numbers below the poverty line in 2011–12 at 363 million (or 29.5 percent of the population).
6. *Economic Survey, 2012–13*, Ministry of Finance, Government of India.
7. These numbers find reflection in Ashok Gulati and Shweta Saini's "Taming Food Inflation in India," Discussion Paper No. 4, Commission for Agricultural Costs and Prices, Ministry of Agriculture, Government of India, April 2013: "Nominal wages have been growing at a rate of 9.68 percent in the studied period, i.e., between 1995–96 and 2011–12. However, during 2007–08 to 2011–12, nominal wages increased at a much faster rate, by close to 17.5 percent per annum. . . . If one converts the nominal wage rates to real wages by deflating the nominal wages in each state by that state's CPIAL, then one finds that real farm wages have grown by 3.5 percent in the studied period, while the rate was close to 6.9 percent per annum during the five years between 2007–08 and 2011–12."
8. Data for the following paragraphs from industry sources, Indian Institutes of Management, and so on.

9. Sanjoy Chakravorty, *The Price of Land: Acquisition, Conflict, Consequence* (New Delhi: Oxford University Press, 2013).
10. *Handbook of Statistics on Indian Securities Market, 2014*, Securities and Exchange Board of India.
11. The data are from Reserve Bank of India, Insurance Regulatory and Development Authority of India, Association of Mutual Funds in India, and Central Provident Fund Commissioner. There would be some overlaps because insurance companies and mutual funds put money in the stock market.
12. *Handbook of Statistics on the Indian Economy*, Reserve Bank of India; figures are annual average for 2011–14.
13. World Gold Council.
14. Estimates for the Twelfth Five-Year Plan (2012–17), National Housing Bank, and other sources.
15. Data from industry sources.
16. As a reference point, half of US households had a net worth of more than $81,200 in 2013, according to the US Federal Reserve.
17. Different financial houses put out varying estimates, sometimes using different definitions of wealth. Reference has already been made in note 1 of this chapter to Boston Consulting Group's estimates. Capgemini's 2014 estimate of India's population of high-net-worth individuals was in the same ballpark as Credit Suisse, and the sixteenth-largest country figure.
18. Figures on cost per square foot of real estate in *The Wealth Report 2014* by Knight Frank Research, London; newspaper reports in Mumbai.
19. Figures from *Census of India, 2011*.
20. Data from industry sources.
21. Abhijit Banerjee and Esther Duflo, "What Is Middle Class about the Middle Classes around the World," *Journal of Economic Perspectives* 22, no. 2 (Spring 2008): 3–28.
22. Cited in Christian Meyer and Nancy Birdsall, "New Estimates of India's Middle Class: Technical Note," Center for Global Development, November 2012, www.cgdev.org/doc/2013_MiddleClassIndia_TechnicalNote_CGDNote.pdf.
23. Rakesh Kochhar, "A Global Middle-Class Is More Promise Than Reality: From 2001 to 2011, Nearly 700 Million Step Out of Poverty, but Most Only Barely," Pew Research Center, Washington, DC, 8 July 2015.
24. Surjit S. Bhalla, "Second among Equals: The Middle Class Kingdoms of India and China," unpublished manuscript May 2007,http://www.researchgate.net/.
25. Francisco H.G. Ferreira, Julian Messina, JameleRigolini, et al., *Economic Mobility and the Rise of the Latin American Middle Class*, World Bank Latin American and Caribbean Studies, World Bank, 2012.
26. Homi Kharas, "The Emerging Middle Class in Developing Countries," Working Paper No. 285, OECD, January 2010.
27. Controversially, this figure differed substantially from an earlier conversion number used for the same year, based on a different set of PPP numbers issued in 2005,

and adjusted for later years by calculating the difference in inflation rates in the United States and India. For 2011, this had worked out to Rs 22.40. But the new numbers are reasonably consistent with the PPP numbers in use prior to the 2005 calculation, which therefore is seen by some observers as the outlier.

28. "Private final consumption expenditure" per head in 2014–15 was Rs 59,465—or Rs 4,955 per month. For a five-member family, the monthly consumption expenditure would therefore be Rs 24,777.
29. This is based on surveys of household expenditure patterns (National Sample Survey Office) and after making adjustments for the widely accepted fact that the surveys do not capture all income at higher levels. They should be treated as ballpark numbers, not precise figures.

CHAPTER 13

1. "Battles Half Won: The Political Economy of India's Growth and Economic Policy Since Independence," Working Paper No. 15, Commission on Growth and Development, World Bank, 2008.
2. Santwana Bhattacharya, "Congress to Focus on Middle Class," *New Indian Express*, 21 January 2013.
3. Vandita Mishra, "We Need to Connect to the Middle Class: CPI's Bardhan," *Indian Express*, 18 May 2011.
4. All India Survey on Higher Education, 2012–13, Ministry of Human Resource Development, Government of India.
5. Sharmilla Bhowmick, "Gurgaon Most Prosperous City in India, Chennai Second: Report," *Times of India*, 28 December 2013.
6. Homi Kharas, "The Emerging Middle Class in Developing Countries," Working Paper No. 285, OECD, January 2010.
7. Text of speech delivered on 6 February 2013 at Shri Ram College of Commerce, Delhi University, translated by Dr. Seshadri Kumar, available at http://www.leftbrainwave.com.
8. Speech delivered on 6 February 2013 at Shri Ram College of Commerce, Delhi University.
9. This was, incidentally, not unusual for the time. The peak tax rate in the United Kingdom in 1974 was 83 percent and could go up to 98 percent if there was "unearned" income. In the United States it was 77 percent in 1964 and then 70 percent till 1982.
10. This mirrored a broader marginalization of Muslims, who had tiny representation in the army and the elite civil services (through competitive exams), and sometimes an even smaller percentage in state police forces. Their share of executive jobs in the private sector was unlikely to be very good. Some of this reality reflected bias but was also the result of poor education attainments in a socially conservative and

largely poor cohort, and community leadership that in many cases underplayed the importance of secular education.

11. Stuart, Corbridge, John Harriss, and Craig Jeffrey, *India Today: Economy, Politics and Society* (Cambridge: Polity Press, 2013).
12. Michael Billig, *Banal Nationalism* (London: SAGE, 1995).
13. Fareed Zakaria, *The Future of Freedom: Illiberal Democracy at Home and Abroad* (New York: W.W. Norton, 2003).

CHAPTER 14

1. These events have been reconstructed on the basis of an official source.
2. LASU-LAWS Environmental Blog, www.lasulawsenvironmental.blogspot.in.
3. "Global Metrics for the Environment: 2014 Results," Environment Performance Index, epi.yale.edu.
4. Nitin Sethi, "Only 35 of 793 Coal Blocks Remain Inviolate after Dilution of Policy," *Business Standard*, 14 March 2015.
5. Ramesh later defended his record by compiling his work in the ministry: *Green Signals: Ecology, Growth, and Democracy in India* (New Delhi: Oxford University Press, 2015).
6. "Jayanthi Natarajan Exits Congress; Charges of Stalling, Delaying Projects Get Credence," *Indian Express*, 31 January 2015.
7. "India: Diagnostic Assessment of Select Environmental Challenges: An Analysis of Physical and Monetary Losses of Environmental Health and Natural Resources," World Bank, June 2013.
8. Of this, "outdoor air pollution accounted for Rs. 1.1 trillion followed by the cost of indoor air pollution at Rs. 0.9 trillion, croplands degradation cost at Rs. 0.7 trillion, inadequate water supply and sanitation cost at around Rs. 0.5 trillion, pastures degradation cost Rs. 0.4 trillion, and forest degradation cost Rs. 0.1 trillion." "India: Diagnostic Assessment of Select Environmental Challenges: An Analysis of Physical and Monetary Losses of Environmental Health and Natural Resources," World Bank, June 2013.
9. *Green National Accounts in India: A Framework*, report by expert group convened by National Statistical Organization, Ministry of Statistics and Programme Implementation, Government of India, March 2013.
10. China in the same period, according to these calculations, had a growth rate of 5.63 percent, while for the United States and Brazil the rate was close to zero.
11. Kenneth Arrow, Partha Dasgupta, et al., "Sustainability and the Measurement of Wealth," *Environment and Development Economics* 17 (2012): 317–53.
12. Cited in Jairam Ramesh, "The Two Cultures Revisited: The Environment–Development Debate in India," *Economic and Political Weekly* 45, no. 42 (16 October 2010).
13. See Chapter 8 for details.

14. "Vijaya Paranjpye (1988) estimated that construction of dams had forced the involuntary resettlement of at least 21.6 million people up to that date. According to Taneja and Thakkar (2000), the construction of dams alone displaced between 21 and 40 million people in India. As noted by Mahapatra, development might have displaced 25 million people in India during the second part of the twentieth century (from 1947 to 1997). These figures seem to have been grossly underestimated. According to Nalin Singh Negi and Sujata Ganguly (2011), over 50 million people in India have been displaced over the last fifty years, which is a more accurate statistic if we take project-affected people (PAPs) into account. Dr. Walter Fernandes of the North Eastern Social Research Centre (NESRC) has estimated at 60 million the total number of people displaced and affected by development projects in India. An Indian government statement of 1994 gives the number of over 10 million development-induced displaced people in the country who are still 'awaiting rehabilitation.'" Excerpted from Bogumil Terminski's *Development-Induced Displacement and Resettlement: Theoretical Frameworks and Current Challenges*, Geneva, May 2013, dlc.dlib.indiana.edu/dlc/bitstream/handle/10535/8833/, p. 15.
15. Arundhati Roy, "The Greater Common Good," narmada.org/gcg/gcg.html.
16. *Asian Water Development Outlook 2013: Measuring Water Security in Asia and the Pacific* (Manila: Asian Development Bank, 2013).
17. *Excreta Matters: Seventh State of India's Environment Report*, Vols. I & II (New Delhi: Centre for Science and Environment, 2012).
18. Montek Singh Ahluwalia and Ajay Mathur, "Sustainable Urban Living," in *Urbanisation in India: Challenges, Opportunities and the Way Forward* (New Delhi: SAGE Publications, 2014).
19. Central Electricity Authority, Government of India.

CHAPTER 15

1. Author's conversation with Blackwill.
2. *Tourism Yearbook 2014*, Ministry of Tourism, Republic of Maldives.
3. John W. Garver, *Protracted Contest: Sino-Indian Rivalry in the Twentieth Century* (Seattle: University of Washington Press, 2001).
4. These figures are from China Global Investment Tracker, Heritage Foundation, and American Enterprise Institute, https://www.aei.org/china-global-investment-tracker/.
5. Garver, *Protracted Contest.*
6. Shyam Saran, "The Beijing Paradox," *Business Standard*, 7 July 2015.
7. Zheng Bijian, "A New Path of China's Peaceful Rise and the Future of Asia," Boao Forum for Asia, 2003.
8. Martin Jacques, *When China Rules the World: The End of the Western World and the Birth of a New Global Order* (London: Penguin/Allen Lane, 2009).

9. Graham Allison and Robert Blackwill, *Lee Kuan Yew: The Grand Master's Insights on China, the United States, and the World* (Cambridge, MA: Belfer Center for Science and International Affairs, 2013).
10. Data from a government official in India's Cabinet Secretariat.
11. Arvind Subramanian, *Eclipse: Living in the Shadow of China's Economic Dominance* (Washington, DC: Peterson Institute of International Economics, 2011).
12. Arvind Subramanian and Martin Kessler, "The Renminbi Bloc Is Here: Asia Down, Rest of World to Go?" Working Paper, Peterson Institute of International Economics, Cambridge, MA, 2013.
13. It takes about as long to travel within India, from Kolkata to Kerala's capital of Thiruvananthapuram (nearly 2,500 km).
14. Martin Wolf, "India's Elephant Charges on through the Crisis," *Financial Times*, 2 March 2010.
15. Purchasing power parity (PPP) numbers are derived from dollar conversions of national currencies at market rates by adjusting for differing costs of living in different countries (for instance, a haircut or bus ticket in India would cost less than in the United States).
16. Stockholm International Peace Research Institute, *SIPRI Yearbook 2014: Armament, Disarmament and International Security* (Oxford: Oxford University Press, 2014). In earlier years, India's defense budget was ranked seventh and then eighth largest.
17. "An option that is selected automatically unless an alternative is specified," TheFreeDictionary.com.
18. Text of the speech from Ministry of Foreign Affairs of Japan.
19. *White Paper on Australia in the Asian Century*, October 2012, Government of Australia.
20. Robert D. Kaplan, *The Revenge of Geography: What the Map Tells Us about Coming Conflicts and the Battle against Fate* (New York: Random House, 2012).
21. Created by Fund for Peace, Washington, DC.
22. It is an indicator of India's difficult neighborhood that six of the nine Asian states that figure in the "Alert" and "High Alert" categories of the Fragile States Index are India's neighbors: Afghanistan, Pakistan, Bangladesh, Nepal, Myanmar, and Sri Lanka.
23. Husain Haqqani, "Pakistan's Elusive Quest for Parity," *The Hindu*, 2 February 2015.
24. China Global Investment Tracker, www.aei.org/china-global-investment-tracker/.
25. Luke Patey, *The New Kings of Crude: China, India, and the Global Struggle for Oil in Sudan and South Sudan* (London: C. Hurst, 2014).
26. Data from author's conversation with a senior official in the Ministry of External Affairs who oversees the "development partnership" program.
27. Conal Walsh, "Is China the New Colonial Power in Africa?" *The Guardian*, 28 October 2006.

28. The Brenthurst Foundation and the Australian Strategic Policy Institute, *Fuelling the Dragon: Natural Resources and China's Development*, Special Report, August 2012.
29. Henry Kissinger, *On China* (New York: Penguin Books, 2011).

CHAPTER 16

1. "The Structure of Sea Powers in the Indian Ocean and the Expansion of Chinese Sea Power in the Indian Ocean," *Pacific Journal*, published (in Chinese) by the Beijing Naval Research Centre, 2015.
2. These issues have been captured well by Stephen P. Cohen and Sunil Dasgupta in *Arming without Aiming* (New Delhi: Penguin/Viking, 2010).
3. One reason for the shortfall is a high accident rate. The air force's poor safety record has meant the loss of about a squadron every two years.
4. "Sukhoi's Serviceability to Improve by Year-End: Parrikar," *Business Standard*, 17 March 2015.
5. These are according to the government's budget numbers. The Stockholm International Peace Research Institute (SIPRI) puts the figure for recent years at 2.5 percent of GDP by including budgets for paramilitary forces and space, to the extent that they have military applications.
6. If in doubt, read Anthony Sampson's *The Arms Bazaar: From Lebanon to Lockheed* (London: Penguin/Viking, 1977).
7. Ministry of National Defense, the People's Republic of China, http://eng.mod.gov.cn/Database/WhitePapers/.
8. The air force, meanwhile, has for many years stationed a squadron of combat aircraft at an air base north of Afghanistan, in Tajikistan.

CHAPTER 17

1. Kaustubh Kulkarni and Suchitra Mohanty, "Novartis Loses Landmark India Patent Case on Glivec," Reuters.com, 2 April 2013.
2. The figures here and the paragraphs that follow have been taken or derived from the US Energy Information Administration, the Edgar database created jointly by the European Commission and Netherlands Environmental Assessment Agency, and the World Bank database.
3. *The Final Report of the Expert Group on Low Carbon Strategies for Inclusive Growth*, Planning Commission, Government of India, April 2014.
4. This section has benefited from Amitendu Palit's *The Trans-Pacific Partnership, China and India: Economic and Political Implications* (New York: Routledge, 2014).
5. See V. S. Seshadri, "The Trans Pacific Partnership (TPP)," Discussion Paper # 182, Research and Information Systems for Developing Countries, New Delhi, July 2013.

CHAPTER 18

1. Per capita income, calculated in 1990 Geary–Khamis, or "international," dollars, was as follows for these Olympic host countries: Japan, 1964: $5,670; Mexico, 1968: $4,073; Soviet Union and East Europe, 1980: $6,236; South Korea, 1988: $7,621; China 2008: $6,725. Data from Angus Maddison, *The World Economy* (Academic Foundation, by arrangement with OECD; Indian two-in-one edition, 2007) and the Maddison Project.
2. Nielsen's Global Consumer Confidence Trend Tracker, nielsen.com/consumerconfidence.
3. When the IIM at Bangalore sought to set up a Singapore campus in 2005, it invited ministerial wrath.
4. Gunnar Myrdal, *Asian Drama: An Inquiry into the Poverty of Nations* (New York: Pantheon, 1968).
5. In January 2015, the Central Statistics Office (CSO) raised the growth estimate for 2013–14 to 6.9 percent, from the 4.7 percent of eight months earlier (revised later to 6.6 percent). The change followed the choice of a new base year as well as the use of a more comprehensive corporate database, but it has remained controversial because other data series on industrial production, power generation, the financial results of publicly quoted companies, etc., did not support the thesis of a sharp uptick in growth. On the new basis, the CSO has assessed growth in 2014–15 at 7.2 percent. For 2015–16, the provisional assessment is 7.6 percent; earlier, Finance Minister Arun Jaitley in his February 2015 Budget speech talked of 8–8.5 percent growth and double-digit growth in subsequent years.
6. Central Square Foundation's (New Delhi) calculations for 2013–14, based on data collated by National University of Education Planning and Administration.
7. Meera Mohanty, "Rio Tinto Is Gearing Up to Develop India's Second Diamond Mine in Bundelkhand," *Economic Times*, 18 March 2012.
8. TV ratings for May–June 2015, by the Broadcast Audience Research Council, an industry body, http://www.barcindia.co.in.
9. Letter to Thomas Jefferson regarding proposed Bill of Rights, 17 October 1788, http://www.constitution.org/jm/17881017_bor.htm.

Index